American Mourning

How does the way in which a democratic polity mourns its losses shape its political outcomes? How *might* it shape those outcomes? *American Mourning: Tragedy, Democracy, Resilience* answers these questions with a critical study of American public mourning. Employing mourning as a lens through which to view the shortcomings of American democracy and as a tool for addressing the same, it offers an argument for a tragic, complex, and critical mode of mourning that it contrasts with the nationalist, romantic, and nostalgic responses to loss that currently dominate and damage the polity. Offering new readings of key texts in Ancient and contemporary political thought, as well as in American politics and history, it engages debates central to recent democratic theory concerned with agonism, acknowledgment, hope, humanism, patriotism, and political resilience. The book outlines new ways of thinking about and responding to terrorism, racial conflict, and the problems of democratic military return.

Simon Stow is an associate professor of government at the College of William and Mary, where he teaches classes in the history of and topics in political thought. He is the author of *Republic of Readers? The Literary Turn in Political Thought and Analysis* (2007), a *Choice* Outstanding Academic Title. He coedited *A Political Companion to John Steinbeck* (2013) and has published articles in the *American Political Science Review*, *American Political Thought*, *Perspectives of Politics*, and *Theory & Event*.

American Mourning

Tragedy, Democracy, Resilience

SIMON STOW

The College of William and Mary

CAMBRIDGE
UNIVERSITY PRESS

University Printing House, Cambridge CB2 8BS, United Kingdom

One Liberty Plaza, 20th Floor, New York, NY 10006, USA

477 Williamstown Road, Port Melbourne, VIC 3207, Australia

4843/24, 2nd Floor, Ansari Road, Daryaganj, Delhi – 110002, India

79 Anson Road, #06-04/06, Singapore 079906

Cambridge University Press is part of the University of Cambridge.

It furthers the University's mission by disseminating knowledge in the pursuit of education, learning, and research at the highest international levels of excellence.

www.cambridge.org

Information on this title: www.cambridge.org/9781316610589

DOI: 10.1017/9781316662632

First published 2017

Printed in the United Kingdom by Clays, St Ives plc

A catalogue record for this publication is available from the British Library.

ISBN 978-1-107-15806-1 Hardback
ISBN 978-1-316-61058-9 Paperback

For Caroline and Thea,
and in memory of my brother, Tim Stow (1974–2009).

You may rejoice, I must mourn.
        – Frederick Douglass

Contents

Acknowledgments

Writing this book has taken far longer than I expected, and I have incurred far more debts than I can possibly recall. What follows is, therefore, but an outline of what I owe. To those whom I have forgotten to mention by name, I can but apologize and express the hope that, while obviously insufficient, the evidence of your contribution on the text might serve as some small form of compensation. To those whom I do mention by name, I would like to note that my thanks for your contributions, help, and support is equally inadequate. I am grateful to you all.

My greatest intellectual debt is to Steven Johnston. Much of the book was written in real or imagined dialogue with Steve and his work. Despite he and I disagreeing on so much, he has proven to be my most challenging, engaging, and generous interlocutor. His insights and arguments have consistently forced me to sharpen my ideas, and his knowledge of the field has (mostly) saved me from embarrassing myself with unsustainable claims. My considerable debt to Steve is, however, not solely intellectual. I am also grateful for his ongoing comradeship, unwavering support, fine restaurant choices, and impressive knowledge of *Street Legal*. I am proud to call him a friend.

At the College of William and Mary, I wish to thank Shirley Aceto, John Baltes, Ross Carroll, David Dessler, John Gilmour, Chris Howard, John Lombardini, Paul Manna, John McGlennon, Helen Murphy, Chris Nemacheck, Amy Oakes, Ron Rapoport, Joel Schwartz, Dennis Smith, Rebekah Sterling, and Maurits van der Veen. Indeed, without Shirley, David, Chris, Ron, and Joel, this book might never have been written at all. I owe them a debt I can never repay.

One of the delights of this profession is knowing so many wonderful scholars with whom I have been blessed to engage about my work and theirs and from whom I take continued inspiration. For this and more, I am grateful to Libby Anker, Jane Bennett, Mark Bevir, Kevin Bruyneel, Bill Connolly, Jodi Dean, Joshua Dienstag, Lisa Disch, Peter Euben, Jason Ferrell, Mario Feit, Kennan Ferguson, Michaele Ferguson, Jason Frank, Jill Frank, Michael Gibbons, Cheryl Hall, Danielle Hanley, Alex Hirsch, Bonnie Honig, Jeff Isaac, Deme Kasimis, Joe Lowndes, Robyn Marasco, Dean Matthiowetz, Kirsty McClure, David McIvor, Char Miller, Laurie Naranch, Robert Pirro, Heather Pool, Melvin Rogers, Sara Rushing, Matthew Scherer, Joel Schlosser, John Seery, George Shulman, James Tatum, Chip Turner, Nick Xenos, and Ernie Zirakzadeh. Deme Kasimis and John Lombardini deserve an additional set of thanks for their patience in answering all my questions – no matter how inane – about the Ancient world without ever once correcting my pronunciation unless asked. It is good to have friends who are smarter and better read than you.

In addition to the friends and colleagues listed above, I would also like to thank Hugh and Susan Babinski, David Baumflek, Ben Bowyer, Judy Gallant, Kip Kantelo, Naomi Levy, Ara Osterweil, Jess Paga, Patricia Rapoport, Matthew Rudolph, Dan and Clare Schoenheimer, Kersey Sturdivant, and Jon and Karen Wood for their continued friendship and support. I would not have gotten this far without you.

I was fortunate enough to spend the 2013–2014 academic year at Amherst College as a Copeland Fellow. The year-long colloquium on Catastrophe and the Catastrophic proved to be invaluable to the book, and I am grateful to all of the participants and speakers: Ellen Boucher, Andrés Henao Castro, Catherine Ciepiela, Christopher Dole, Thomas Dumm, Joanna Dyl, Robert Hayashi, Hannah Holleman, David Jones, Kimberly Lowe, Jill Miller, Pooja Rangan, Austin Sarat, and Boris Wolfson. I am also grateful to Jim Schmidt for drawing the fellowship to my attention and for his broader interest in my work. My biggest thanks must go, however, to Andrew Poe. In addition to his relentless and immensely productive interrogation of my work, views, and assumptions, Andy became a great friend and something of a lifestyle guru (who knew that socks don't have to match?). Getting to know him, Liv, and Stelle was the second greatest delight of my time in Massachusetts. My debt to him is enormous, and I only hope I can begin to repay it by repeating in print what I repeatedly told him in person, that he is my most European friend.

I presented a very early version of the "Pericles at Gettysburg and Ground Zero" chapter at the Political Theory Colloquium at the University of Virginia in April 2005. I am grateful to Lawrie Balfour,

Colin Bird, Joshua Dienstag, George Klosko, and the other colloquium participants for their helpful comments on the paper. An earlier version of the chapter on "Homecoming and Reconstitution" was presented at the Political Theory Workshop at the University of North Carolina, Chapel Hill, in October 2011. There I am grateful to Susan Bickford, Michael Lienesch, Hollie Mann, Jeff Spinner-Halev, and the graduate students who attended the talk for their excellent feedback. A much-revised version of the same chapter was presented at the conference Performing Memory in the Ancient World: A Dialogue Between Past and Present at the New York University Center for Ancient Studies in December 2011. I am grateful to Peter Meineck both for the invitation and for his advice and helpful remarks and to Paul Woodruff for an inspiring conversation about the themes of the conference. Finally, I presented an overview of the book at the 2016 ASPECT Conference at Virginia Tech. My thanks go to François Debrix for the invitation and to the attendees for their generous comments.

As part of my research for the chapter on military homecoming, I attended a staged reading of Greek tragedy that was part of Bryan Doerries's Theater of War/The Philoctetes Project at the Uniformed Services University of the Health Sciences in Bethesda, Maryland, in April 2009. It was a remarkable experience, and I greatly benefitted from it, both as a scholar and as someone who had recently experienced the sudden loss of a loved one. I am grateful to Bryan Doerries, Colonel Chuck Engel, and Major Joyce Kilgore for allowing me to attend and to Steven Johnston for accompanying me. Given their generosity and the sensitivity of some aspects of my argument, this would, perhaps, be the best place to make clear that all of the views expressed in the book and, indeed, any and all mistakes are my own.

Earlier versions of the first and second chapters were previously published as "Pericles at Gettysburg and Ground Zero: Tragedy, Patriotism, and Public Mourning," *American Political Science Review*, 101(2), 2007, 195–208, and "Agonistic Homegoing: Frederick Douglass, Joseph Lowery, and the Democratic Value of African American Public Mourning," *American Political Science Review*, 104(4), 2008, 681–697.

At Cambridge University Press, I am grateful to Robert Dreesen for his patient support and to the three anonymous reviewers whose generous readings and insightful comments greatly enhanced the final product.

As ever, I owe much to my extended family. My parents, Graham and Christine Stow, were typically generous with their time, love, and resources throughout the entire writing process, and I am grateful for all of their support. My in-laws, John and Sandra Hanley, were equally generous and always willing to help with whatever was asked of them, be it hospice care for a dying dog or a place to stay at very short notice. I also owe thanks to my brother Andrew, my sister-in-law Charlotte, my niece Jessie, and my nephew Marty.

I owe still more to my immediate family, which has expanded since I began writing. Caroline Hanley has been my partner for sixteen years, and it is no coincidence that they have been the happiest of my life. She continues to make me and my life better, and I have so much to thank her for that whatever I write here will, by necessity, be hopelessly inadequate. As my neighbor once observed, I married above myself. It is, then, seemingly impossible but nevertheless true that this happiness should have been exponentially expanded by the birth of our daughter, Theodora Stow, in June 2014. To try to describe the joy that she has brought to my life would be to run up against the limits of language. Such, perhaps, is the miracle of natality.

And yet, death shall have its dominion. It is a sad irony that on February 7, 2009, during the long period that I was writing this book on mourning, my brother Tim took his own life at the age of thirty-four. This book is also dedicated to him as a marker of his having been in the world, an acknowledgment of his passing, and a lament for the life that he might have led. I miss him.

Introduction

> [P]olitical theory might explore public forms of grieving, allowing "we the people" to confront, integrate, but also move on from loss.
> – J. Peter Euben, *Platonic Noise*

The dead are alive in the American polity. This is a book about their political participation. Although this participation takes many forms – from the Founding Fathers' embrace of the Roman Republic to the rituals of Memorial Day and the political Right's veneration of Ronald Reagan – the focus here is on the role of the dead in the years since the planes.[1] The aim is not to replicate the now voluminous research on the ways in which the sudden deaths of nearly 3,000 people shaped the politics of the period – although it will inevitably offer some such analysis – but rather to use these years as a starting point for thinking critically about the relationship between death, democracy, and public mourning. As such, the book might be seen as yet another contribution to the already considerable cross- and multidisciplinary literature on memory, mourning, and politics, much of it written in what Art Spiegelman memorably called "the shadow of no towers."[2] While the book draws on and is indebted to much

---

[1] The "the planes" formulation is adapted from Don DeLillo's novel *Falling Man* (New York: Scribner, 2007).

[2] Art Spiegelman, *In the Shadow of No Towers* (New York: Pantheon, 2004). For recent work on memory, mourning, and politics, see: Judith Butler, *Precarious Life: The Powers of Mourning and Violence* (New York: Verso, 2006); Jenny Edkins, *Trauma and the Memory of Politics* (Cambridge: Cambridge University Press, 2003); Bonnie Honig, *Antigone, Interrupted* (Cambridge: Cambridge University Press, 2013); and Marita Sturken, *Tourists of History: Memory, Kitsch, and Consumerism from Oklahoma City to Ground Zero*, (Durham, NC: Duke University Press, 2007).

of this previous literature, what separates it is the attempt to deploy public mourning both as an analytical lens through which to view the shortcomings of American democracy and as a tool for addressing the same. For although some have argued that the recent turn to mourning is evidence of a deflationary tendency or a defeatist tone in political thought – that the politics of mourning all too quickly becomes the mourning of politics[3] – this work is both diagnostic and ambitiously prescriptive. It belongs to a tradition of political theory identified by Hanna Pitkin concerned with those "features of our lives which might be different if we chose to change them."[4] Offering some rereadings of a number of overworked texts, it aims to be a book both *of* and *about* political theory – one that draws on a particular set of literatures to think critically about the contemporary polity. Its only justification is the plausibility of its arguments. While acknowledging that mourning often constitutes a problematic form of political activity that can undermine democracy, the book nevertheless argues that it can also serve as an important mode of critical-theoretical reflection and a rich resource for democratic innovation, education, and resilience. Even if, it argues, the politics of mourning inevitably becomes the mourning of politics, the consequences of this transformation depend crucially on the *form* these lamentations take.

The central diagnostic claim of the book is that the stories a polity tells about the dead help shape political outcomes of the living. Its central prescriptive claim is that the democratic polity should tell the mourning stories most conducive to its political well-being. Toward establishing these claims, the book offers a typology of public mourning drawn largely from Athenian but also from American – and pre-American – history that it employs as a lens through which to examine a number of recent moments of public loss. It seeks to show not only how our public mourning practices currently shape politics and the political but also the ways in which it might be employed to shape our future outcomes. This understanding of "politics" and "the political" is drawn from the work of Chantal Mouffe. "[B]y 'the political,'" she writes, "I mean the dimension of antagonism which I take to be constitutive of human societies,

[3] Bonnie Honig, "The Politics of Public Things: Neoliberalism and the Routine of Privatization," *No Foundations: An Interdisciplinary Journal of Law and Justice*, 10, 2013: 59–76. See also Honig, *Antigone, Interrupted*, 56. For the deflationary tendency in contemporary political theory, see J. Peter Euben, *Platonic Noise* (Princeton, NJ: Princeton University Press, 2003).

[4] Hanna Pitkin, *Wittgenstein and Justice: On the Significance of Ludwig Wittgenstein for Social and Political Thought* (Berkeley: University of California Press, 1973), 299.

while by 'politics' I mean the set of practices and institutions through which an order is created, organizing human coexistence in the context of conflictuality provided by the political."[5] Thus, the book is concerned with how – in Josiah Ober's words – we might "go on together" as a democratic polity in the face of loss.[6]

Democracy is not, of course, the only system in which the dead remain politically active.[7] Nevertheless, the long-standing relationship between democracy and public mourning and the role the latter played in the founding of the former suggest that paying close attention to America's rituals of loss might offer a valuable source of insight into the problems of the contemporary polity and a potentially fecund resource for democratic revitalization.

MOURNING, GRIEF, AND DEMOCRACY

Nicole Loraux's observation that the funeral oration invented Athens as much as Athens invented the funeral oration suggests the considerable importance that rituals of public loss played in the founding of democracy.[8] In the most famous example of the genre – Pericles' funeral oration to the Athenians – the speaker pays little attention to the dead, focusing instead on the virtues of the city. As Thucydides recounts in his *History of the Peloponnesian War*, the ceremonies for those killed in the first year of the war with Sparta were necessarily public. After two days set aside for private offerings, the dead became the property of the city. A funeral procession with ten wooden coffins – one for each tribe of Athens – and an empty bier for the missing led to the public burial place, "in the most beautiful quarter outside the city walls."[9] There, speaking from a high platform, the orator addressed the crowd. In his speech, Pericles praises Athens for placing political power "in the hands not of a minority but of the whole people," proudly noting "that everyone is equal before the law" and that "in positions of public responsibility, what counts is not membership of a particular class, but the actual ability which the man

[5] Chantal Mouffe, *On the Political* (New York: Routledge, 2005), 9.

[6] Josiah Ober, *Athenian Legacies: Essays in the Politics of Going On Together* (Princeton, NJ: Princeton University Press, 2007).

[7] See Katherine Verdery, *The Political Lives of Dead Bodies: Reburial and Postsocialist Change* (New York: Columbia University Press, 2000).

[8] Nicole Loraux, *The Invention of Athens: The Funeral Oration in the Classical City* translated by Alan Sheridan (Cambridge, MA: Harvard University Press, 1986).

[9] Thucydides, *History of the Peloponnesian War* translated by Rex Warner (New York: Penguin books, 1972), 143.

possesses."[10] Additionally he points to the city's openness to foreigners, its practice of deliberating before action, its commitment to upholding laws, its military prowess, and its friendly relations with other city-states. "Taking everything together," Pericles boasts, "... I declare that our city is an education to Greece."[11] As such, the oration was less a lament for the fallen than an occasion for the speaker to offer an idealized vision of the city – a storehouse of myths – that sought to bind the polity together in the face of mass death. In this, the Ancient oration was predicated on an understanding of mourning that differs quite considerably from that underpinning the work of many of the more recent theorists of loss.

Ever since the publication of the essay "Mourning and Melancholia" in 1917, Western understandings of loss have largely been shaped by the work of Sigmund Freud. For Freud, mourning was a mental process of working through grief in order to relinquish attachment to the lost love-object. Only when this working through had been completed and the patient had been able to invest her attachment elsewhere could she be said to have returned to psychic health.[12] Subsequent work on mourning – public and personal – has wrestled with Freud's legacy, embracing it, adapting it, or seeking alternative psychoanalytic accounts that nevertheless define themselves in opposition to his approach. Such theories have profitably been employed in political thought and analysis by a diverse array of thinkers.[13] Here, however, the work of Freud and the other psychoanalytic theorists is bracketed in favor of a – potentially more illuminating – account of public mourning suggested by the Greeks. This is not to dismiss the psychoanalytic or its insights – not least because the approach outlined here might be fruitfully employed as a complement to it – but simply to recover an older set of public responses to loss that might be thought to provide a similarly or even more useful way of understanding the politics of mourning. It is a tradition that relies less on claims about private motivations and/or mental states writ large than it does on the observable actions of public political actors.[14] Given the enormity

[10] Ibid., 145.
[11] Ibid., 147.
[12] Sigmund Freud, *Murder, Mourning and Melancholia* (New York: Penguin Books, 2005).
[13] For example, both Judith Butler and Bonnie Honig make considerable use of the work of Freud, Melanie Klein, and Donald Winnicott in their work on mourning and politics. See also David McIvor, "Bringing Ourselves to Grief: Judith Butler and the Politics of Mourning," *Political Theory*, 40(4), 2012: 409–436.
[14] Even its claims about the necessity of cultivating a particular ethos of mourning are claims about an ethos that is expressed in action.

of the literature on psychoanalysis and loss, it is a methodological
choice best justified by the value of the insights that follow.

Public mourning is here defined as the attempt to employ grief for
political ends, where grief is understood as the expression of "deep emotional anguish, usually about death and loss."[15] As such, the analysis
does not rest on a distinction between rationality and emotion but rather
on a distinction between democratically productive and unproductive
mobilizations of grief. It is a distinction that goes back to the Ancients.
For the Greeks, concerns about the relationship between grief and politics were concerns about the potentially negative impact of the former
on the latter. In *The Republic*, Socrates identifies the problems posed
to the *polis* by laments for the dead, arguing that witnessing the grief
of others corrupts the judgment of the good citizen.[16] Likewise, in *The
Laws*, Plato forbids both dirges and public displays of grief, permitting
only private mourning and nighttime processions lest these displays
of emotion damage the city.[17] Nevertheless, for the Greeks it was not
grief per se that was the problem but rather the *manner* in which it was
expressed. Indeed, the Greek concern with undue public expressions of
grief was part of a larger concern with hubris, or excess, and with their
broader commitment to moderation.[18] Democracy was considered to
be especially susceptible to such hubris because it requires a particular
mode of engagement – one promoting productive discussion, good judgment, and careful deliberation among its citizens[19] – that is threatened
by powerful emotions.

In the Greek world, the excessive expression of grief in mourning was
inevitably associated with women, and the city's rituals of public loss were
developed precisely to limit the danger that such emotion was thought to
pose to the polity. In the city of Ceos, for example, the women who laid out
and prepared the body for burial were considered contaminated and kept
apart from those who attended at the graveside. The latter were expected
to depart before the men lest the unbridled emotions of their laments

[15] Erika Doss, *Memorial Mania: Public Feeling in America* (Chicago: University of Chicago
   Press, 2012), 80.
[16] Plato, *The Republic*, 387e–388a, 606a–606b.
[17] Plato, *The Laws*, 959e–960b.
[18] For hubris as excess, see Walter Kaufmann, *Tragedy and Philosophy* (Princeton, NJ:
   Princeton University Press, 1964), 68. See also James Davidson, *Courtesans and
   Fishcakes: The Consuming Passions of Classical Athens* (New York: Harper Perennial,
   1999).
[19] See, for example, William E. Connolly, *Pluralism* (Minneapolis: University of Minnesota
   Press, 2005); Mouffe, *On the Political*.

were permitted to have the last word over the ceremonies.[20] As Loraux observes, *oikeîon pénthos* – the private mourning of the household – was subordinated to the public mourning of the formal procession. "This is," she argues, "... the civic way of assigning limits to the loss of self ... The reasoning is that the *oikeîon pénthos* must not contaminate the city, just as more generally, funeral rites should not intrude on the political institutions' operations. When this happens ... it is a sure sign of problems for the city."[21] The danger is, she writes, that the emotions provoked by loss can all too easily become *álaston pénthos* – mourning without end – or "unforgettable grief."[22] When grief cannot be forgotten, she continues, it becomes an indelible anger, "the ultimate justification for revenge, for the spirit of vendetta, for all the horrors of retaliation against earlier horrors," or what the Greeks called *mênis*.[23] Eroding all considerations of reciprocity, justice, and even self-interest in favor of its own singular perspective, the grief-wrath of *mênis* is, Loraux observes, the "worst enemy of [democratic] politics."[24] Although such *mênis* was inextricably associated with women, the association was itself part of the city's broader ideological construction of gender and a further way in which public manifestations of private grief were regulated in the *polis*. The suggestion that a man was acting like a female in the face of loss was a common insult, and Greek drama is replete with negative parallels between male and female grief.[25] The failure of – the albeit predemocratic – Achilles to moderate his despair over the death of Patroclus was, moreover, seen to be the immediate cause of his downfall and a lesson to Greek men about the dangers of failing to regulate their own responses to loss. As such, men too were understood to be susceptible to hubris in mourning.[26] Indeed, many scholars see the reforms of mourning practices

[20] Nicole Loraux, *Mothers in Mourning: With the Essay of Amnesty and Its Opposite* translated by Corinne Pache (Ithaca, NY: Cornell University Press, 1998), 22.
[21] Ibid., 26.
[22] The translation is from Athena Athanasiou and Elena Tzlepis, "Mourning (as) Woman: Event, Catachresis, and 'That Other Face of Discourse'" in *Rewriting Difference: Luce Irigaray and 'the Greeks'* edited by Elena Tzlepis (Albany: State University of New York Press, 2010), 110. Corinne Pache translates the term from Loraux's French as "mourning that cannot forget." Loraux, *Mothers in Mourning*, 54.
[23] Loraux, *Mother in Mourning*, xii.
[24] Ibid., 98.
[25] Although she denies that tears are necessarily evidence feminization in Greek tragedy, Ann Suter provides a nice list of male characters who understand their own tears in this way. Ann Suter, "Tragic Tears and Gender" in *Tears in the Graeco-Roman World*, edited by Thorsten Fögen, (New York: Walter de Gruyter, 71).
[26] Although predemocratic, Leonard Muellner, *The Anger of Achilles: Mênis in Greek Epic* (Ithaca, NY: Cornell University Press, 2004).

enacted by Solon the Lawgiver in the sixth century BCE aimed at reining in such excesses – among both men and women – as a necessary precursor to the emergence of the democratic city.

Olga Taxidou, for example, argues that Solon's legislative innovations – aimed at curbing aristocratic excess – ritualized responses to loss, helping diminish the power of the aristocracy by reducing their opportunities for lavish displays of wealth.[27] Similarly, Gail Holst-Warhaft notes that Solon's rituals served to undermine the cycles of vengeance – emerging from clan strife – for which funerals were often a locus.[28] Drawing a distinction between Homeric and democratic modes of mourning, Bonnie Honig argues that Solon's reforms helped turn the former into the latter.[29] Whereas Homeric mourning focused on the uniqueness of the individual and was marked by breast beating, face clawing, and loud lamentation – by both men *and* women – democratic mourning sought to restrain such displays, turning the focus of the dirges away from the loss of the individual and toward the collective good of the city. The overall impact of these reforms was to reduce the power of the aristocracy in a way that helped precipitate popular rule.[30] Thus, public mourning was not only a cornerstone of democracy's founding but also a central part of its ongoing practice.

BEARING GIFTS, OR THE PAST IMPERFECT

It would, of course, be fallacious to suggest that just because rituals of mourning were of great importance to the founding and functioning of early democracy, they are necessarily imbued with the same significance in the contemporary polity: that categories drawn from an Ancient participatory democracy might be applied unproblematically to our present system of government. For this reason, it is necessary to say a word or two about method. The approach here will be to eschew what Honig calls classicism – a method predicated on the assumption that the classical captures the universal and is thus applicable to diverse audiences across space and time – and to embrace what she labels classicization: an

---

[27] Olga Taxidou, *Tragedy, Modernity and Mourning* (Edinburgh: Edinburgh University Press, 2004), 176. See also Robert Garland, *The Greek Way of Death* (London: Duckworth, 1985).

[28] Gail Holst-Warhaft, *Dangerous Voices: Women's Laments and Greek Literature* (New York: Routledge, 1992), 114.

[29] Bonnie Honig, "Antigone's Laments, Creon's Griefs. Mourning, Membership, and the Politics of Exception," *Political Theory* 37(1), 2009: 5–43.

[30] Honig, *Antigone, Interrupted*, 100.

engagement with the present that turns to previous circumstances, texts, and images for "analogies that might illuminate our condition or even mirror our circumstances."[31] The proof of the methodological pudding is, of course, in the analytical eating, and as the conclusions of the book cannot be shown in advance, it might be useful to point to two instances of our recent responses to loss that suggest the continued relevance of the Ancients as both an analytical framework and a prescriptive foundation for considering contemporary democratic politics. In the first instance, Greek concern about the dangers of grief in politics is employed as a lens to show how contemporary democratic deliberation can be undermined by rhetorical strategies that consciously or unconsciously employ loss for specific political ends. In the second, the potential for public mourning to be employed as a tool for addressing the shortcomings of contemporary democratic practice is suggested by a consideration of the parallels between American rituals of loss and those central to the Greek theatrical festival, the Great Dionysia.

On June 6, 2006, the conservative commentator Ann Coulter appeared on NBC's *The Today Show* to promote her book *Godless: The Church of Liberalism*. In it she argued that a group of widows – nicknamed the Jersey Girls after the Tom Waits song popularized by Bruce Springsteen – who campaigned for a national commission to investigate the 2001 terrorist attacks that killed their husbands had illegitimately inserted grief into the democratic process. "They were using their grief to make a political point while preventing anyone from responding ... Because then if we respond," Coulter observed on the show, "... [we] are questioning their authenticity."[32] As Loraux points out, the Greeks believed democratic politics was threatened by the excessive "pleasure of tears," that which "the afflicted can find in weeping for himself or a loved one."[33] Unaware, perhaps, of the historical pedigree of her claims, Coulter declared, "These broads are ... lionized on TV and in articles about them, reveling in their status as celebrities and stalked by grief-arazzis. I've never seen people enjoying their husbands'

---

[31] Ibid., 32. See also Bernard Williams, *The Sense of the Past: Essays in the History of Philosophy* (Princeton, NJ: Princeton University Press, 2006), 259.

[32] "Ann Coulter on Today Show," www.youtube.com/watch?v=4xvo5FK69KU. Accessed Nov. 18, 2013.

[33] Nicole Loraux, *The Mourning Voice: An Essay on Greek Tragedy* translated by Elizabeth Trapnell Rawlings (Ithaca, NY: Cornell University Press, 2002), 47. For a discussion of "the pleasure of tears" in the contemporary polity, see Simon Stow, "*Portraits 9/11/ 01: The New York Times* and the Pornography of Grief" in *Literature After 9/11* edited by Jeanne Follansbee Quinn and Ann Keniston (New York: Routledge, 2008), 224–241.

deaths so much."[34] The swift and bipartisan backlash to Coulter's remarks suggested that she had indeed identified something important about the way in which grief can undermine democratic deliberation. "Perhaps her book should have been called *Heartless*," observed Hillary Clinton. "As someone who considers herself right of center," *Boston Globe* columnist Cathy Young declared, "it makes me ashamed to be on the same side."[35] In almost every instance, Coulter's critics responded with moralizing, ad hominem attacks best evidenced by an editorial in *The Philadelphia Inquirer* entitled "Ann Coulter Rips the 'Jersey Girls'; Consider the Source."[36] That little to no attempt was made to engage with the *substance* of Coulter's critique – no real discussion of her claim that injecting grief into public discussion was an illegitimate form of political engagement – suggests, perhaps, the problems that grief continues to pose for democratic politics.[37]

In the first instance, the sententious response to Coulter points to the way in which those who experience grief in the contemporary polity are often granted a moral authority that appears to trump politics even as it serves political ends. Coulter's comments were, of course, deliberately provocative, but they merely revealed rather than precipitated the grief-induced descent of politics into morality. Indeed, the Coulter controversy was not the only instance in which grief appeared to trump democratic politics in the years following the planes. Writing in 2005 about the failed attempts of the so-called peace mom Cindy Sheehan – whose son Casey had been killed in Iraq – to speak to President Bush at his ranch in Crawford, Texas, *New York Times* columnist Maureen Dowd declared that the Commander-in-Chief failed to "understand that the moral authority of parents who bury children killed in Iraq is

---

[34] Ann Coulter, *Godless: The Church of Liberalism* (New York: Crown Forum, 2006), 103. Coulter was not, however, the first to launch such an attack on the women; see Dorothy Rabinowitz, "The 9/11 Widows," *The Wall Street Journal*, 4/14/06, A14.

[35] "Sen. Clinton: Coulter's 9/11 remarks 'vicious, mean-spirited,'" *USA Today*, 06/07/06. usatoday30.usatoday.com/life/people/2006-06-07-clinton-coulter_x.htm. Accessed Nov. 22, 2013. Cathy Young, "Coulter's Crudeness," *The Boston Globe*, 06/19/06. www.cathyyoung.net/bgcolumns/2006/coulterscrudeness.html. Accessed Nov. 22, 2013.

[36] Editorial: "Ann Coulter Rips the 'Jersey Girls'"; Consider the source," *The Philadelphia Inquirer*, 06/11/06. articles.philly.com/2006-06-11/news/25403252_1_widows-iraq-war-jersey-girls. Accessed Nov. 23, 2013.

[37] Although John Tierney of *The New York Times* did acknowledge that Coulter had raised a genuine issue of concern, his was a minority voice. John Tierney, "Mourning in America," *The New York Times*, 06/10/06. Coulter's history of controversial claims no doubt mediated the extent to which her claims were given a fair hearing; nevertheless, the general point stands. www.nytimes.com/2006/06/10/opinion/10tierney.html?_r=0. Accessed Nov. 25, 2013.

absolute."[38] A mother in mourning, Sheehan was hailed as a latter-day Antigone, her worldview apparently legitimated by her son's death, even as her "absolute moral authority" may have led some of her supporters to overlook the more troubling aspects of her political views.[39] Similarly, even the very modest attempts to place the 2001 attacks in a historical context at the National Memorial in New York City – with a proposed museum that situated them within a decidedly Hegelian narrative about the unfolding of American freedom – were abandoned on the grounds that they "might include exhibits critical of America that would pain families."[40] In each instance, the insertion of grief into democratic politics appeared to elevate certain people and issues above the political fray. Paradoxically, however, these same people and issues continued to be subjects of a political debate, but one refracted through a prism of disavowal. For although some of Coulter's comments about the Jersey Girls were focused on the *manner* in which they made their claims, her broader concerns were clearly substantial and partisan.

"These self-obsessed women" observed Coulter, "... acted as if the terrorist attacks happened only to them. The whole nation was wounded, all of our lives reduced. But they believed the entire country was required to marinate in their exquisite personal agony. Apparently, denouncing [President] Bush was an important part of their closure process."[41] As she further noted, some of the widows had been highly critical of the Bush administration, and one – Kristen Breitweiser – appeared in a

---

[38] Maureen Dowd, "Why No Tea and Sympathy?" *The New York Times*, 8/10/2005. www .nytimes.com/2005/08/10/opinion/10dowd.html?_r=0. Accessed Nov. 11, 2013.

[39] For an account of Sheehan as Antigone, see Donald E. Pease, *The New American Exceptionalism* (Minneapolis: The University of Minnesota Press, 2009), 192–204. Some of Sheehan's comments seemed to align her with former Louisiana congressman and Klan Grand Wizard David Duke. Although there is some controversy over the exact nature of her remarks, Duke enthusiastically approved of Sheehan's views on Israel. See Christopher Hitchens, "Cindy Sheehan's Sinister Piffle. What's wrong with her Crawford protest," *Slate*, August 15, 2005. www.slate.com/articles/news_and_politics/fighting_ words/2005/08/cindy_sheehans_sinister_piffle.html?nav=fo. Accessed Dec. 9, 2013. *Anderson Cooper 360 Degrees*, 08/15/2005. transcripts.cnn.com/TRANSCRIPTS/0508/ 15/acd.01.html. Accessed Dec. 9, 2013. David Duke, "Why Cindy Sheehan is Right," DavidDuke.com, 08/14/2005. davidduke.com/why-cindy-sheehan-is-right/. Accessed Dec. 9, 2013.

[40] William Murphy, "Keeping focus on memorial; NY Representatives say Congress will act if Ground Zero project will include exhibits not related to 9/11," *Newsday*, 7/2/2005. www.newsday.com/news/keeping-focus-on-memorial-1.623948. Accessed Feb. 15, 2012. See also Simon Stow, "From Upper Canal to Lower Manhattan: Memorialization and the Politics of Loss," *Perspectives on Politics*, 10(3), 2012: 687-700.

[41] Coulter, *Godless*, 103.

2004 presidential campaign ad for the Democratic nominee, John Kerry. Nevertheless, Coulter offered no such criticism of the similarly bereaved family members who expressed support for the Bush administration by speaking at the 2004 Republican Convention in New York City, a venue that was chosen specifically to capitalize on the president's much-admired initial response to the attacks.[42] She was similarly silent on the president's brandishing of a deceased Port Authority officer's badge – given to him by the man's mother – in his address to a joint session of Congress on September 20, 2001.[43] Even as Coulter employed grief for political ends, she criticized others for doing the same. Thus, she mirrored those family members who organized to ensure that "[p]olitical discussions" would "have no place at the World Trade Center ... Memorial,"[44] even as, perhaps, Coulter was more conscious of the possible – and possibly cynical – contradictions in her position.[45]

Analytically then, the Greek concern with the dangers of grief to democratic politics serves as a useful lens for revealing the ways in which the contemporary polity is susceptible to the same. Grief is seen to collapse politics into morality in a way that undermines democratic discourse: first, by appearing to insulate arguments by and about certain people and issues from critical evaluation; and second, by filtering the actual debates about those issues and people through a disavowal that frequently obfuscates the intentions and structure of political arguments. This is not, of course, to suggest that grief distorts what would otherwise be a Habermasian "ideal-speech" situation.[46] It is simply to note the ways in which the political embrace of grief after 2001 made some things impossible to say, prevented some people from speaking, and thus damaged American democracy. It is also to identify the manner in which mass grief can engender the state of exception identified by Carl Schmitt and Giorgio Agamben: that which suspends previously existing

---

[42] Peter Baker, *Days of Fire: Bush and Cheney in the White House* (New York: Doubleday, 2013).

[43] For an obvious, though apocryphal, parallel, see Stephen Budiansky, *The Bloody Shirt: Terror after Appomattox* (New York: Viking, 2008).

[44] Doss, *Memorial Mania*, 171.

[45] Even if Coulter was unaware of the contradictions of her position, it is interesting to note the ways in which she appropriated the democratic and Homeric modes of mourning identified by Hong for her own ends. Initially she castigated the women with the democratic mode and then celebrated the Homeric when it better served her purposes.

[46] Jürgen Habermas, *Theory of Communicative Action Volume One: Reason and the Rationalization of Society* (Boston: Beacon Press, 1985), 25–26, 42. I am grateful to David McIvor for suggesting this clarification.

political processes in favor of emergency-driven actions.[47] The Coulter controversy, moreover, further suggests the ways in which, as Elaine Scarry observes, grief can lead to the suspension of the thought processes – both individual and social – that necessarily underpin a healthy democratic politics.[48]

The second, prescriptive possibility – that rituals of public mourning might be employed as a tool for addressing the shortcomings of American democracy – is suggested by a reflection on another set of Athenian rituals of loss: those embedded in their annual springtime theatrical festival, the Great Dionysia. One of the few occasions on which the city came together as a whole, the theater and the festival of which it was a part were celebratory and interrogative institutions that many scholars identify as the primary source of political education in Athens.[49] The theater, wrote Peter Burian, "gave Athens a powerful instrument for the celebration, criticism, and redefining of its institutions and ideals, for examining the tensions between heroic legend and democratic ideology, and for discussing political and moral questions."[50] Indeed, the theater's fundamental importance to the Greeks is suggested by the *theoric* fund established by the city to support those who would otherwise be too poor to attend. Labeled "the glue of democracy" by Demades, the fund was considered sacrosanct and protected from other uses, even in times of war.[51] The Dionysia itself constituted a city within a city, and just as the funeral oration was considered central to the Athenian founding, many scholars have pointed to the importance of the rituals of mourning to the creation and functioning of the festival's *polis*.[52] Among other rituals of loss, the ceremonies included

[47] Carl Schmitt, *Political Theology: Four Chapters on the Concept of Sovereignty* translated by George Schwab (Chicago: University of Chicago Press, 2005); and Giorgio Agamben, *State of Exception* translated by Kevin Attell (Chicago: University of Chicago Press, 2005).

[48] Elaine Scarry, *Thinking in an Emergency* (New York: W.W. Norton & Company, 2009). Once again, however, this is not to suggest that such thought processes are devoid of emotion. See Martha Nussbaum, *Upheavals of Thought: The Intelligence of Emotions* (Cambridge: Cambridge University Press, 2003).

[49] See, for example, J. Peter Euben, *Corrupting Youth. Political Education, Democratic Culture, and Political Theory* (Princeton, NJ: Princeton University Press, 1997).

[50] Peter Burian, "Myth into *Muthos*: The Shaping of Tragic Plot," in P. E. Easterling, *The Cambridge Companion to Greek Tragedy* (Cambridge: Cambridge University Press, 1997), 206.

[51] Peter Hunt, *War, Peace, and Alliance in Demosthenes' Athens* (Cambridge: Cambridge University Press, 2010), 49. In this the theater served as a means of what Elaine Scarry would call "thinking in an emergency." Scarry, *Thinking in an Emergency*.

[52] Simon Goldhill, *Love, Sex and Tragedy: How the Ancient World Shapes Our Lives* (Chicago: The Chicago University Press, 2004), 224.

a parade of the war orphans and a declaration of their commitment to die, like their fathers, for the good of the city.[53] For moderns, what is, perhaps, most surprising about these ceremonies is that they were immediately followed by plays – both tragic and comic – that problematized the very values for which the fallen were said to have given their lives. In stark contrast to America's contemporary rituals of loss, Greek theater embraced the opportunity to subject the city's highest ideals to critical scrutiny.

Among the many scholars who believe that the Dionysia was central to the cultivation of democratic values, Simon Goldhill argues that even the physical layout of the Theater of Dionysus – arranged by tribe and by rank, marking out citizens according to their sociopolitical status – represented the city to itself in a manner conducive to democratic reflection.[54] For the Greeks, these ritualized moments of togetherness were considered essential to the health and well-being of the polity. In the absence of a contemporary equivalent to the Dionysia, modern democracy appears to have very few such opportunities for ritualized togetherness, even as those moments provide an opportunity for the polity to tell the stories that shape its communal understanding and create what Benedict Anderson called the "imagined community" of nation.[55] Although some have suggested that the Super Bowl with its nationalistic rituals, militaristic displays, and imperialistic overtones – including the crowning of the "World Champions" of an entirely American sport – is the event that most closely resembles the Dionysia, the occasion is entirely devoid of critical content.[56] The festivities surrounding the Super Bowl could not possibly

---

[53] J. J. Winkler, "The Ephebes' Song: Tragoidia and Polis," *Representations*, 11 (Summer), 1985, 32–33.

[54] Goldhill, *Love, Sex and Tragedy*, 224.

[55] Benedict Anderson, *Imagined Communities: Reflections on the Origins and Spread of Nationalism* (London: Verso, 1991). For a typically imaginative suggestion of what such a festival might look like in the contemporary polity, see, however, Steven Johnston, "American Dionysia," *Contemporary Political Theory*, 8, 2009: 255–275.

[56] See, for example, David Konstan, "Introduction" in *Euripides Cyclops* translated by Heather McHugh (Oxford: Oxford University Press, 2001), 6. Indeed, ever since Whitney Houston's famous rendition of *The Star Spangled Banner* during Super Bowl XXV – at the height of the first Gulf War – unquestioning jingoism has become a hallmark of American sporting events both major and minor. I am grateful to Tom Dumm for this point. See Andrew J. Bacevich, *Breach of Trust: How Americans Failed Their Soldiers and Their Country* (New York: Metropolitan Books, 2013), 1–5. In 2016, however, Beyoncé Knowles appeared to buck this trend. Appearing as a "special guest" during the halftime show, she performed a new song, "Formation," that had only been released the day before. The video for the song contained both aural and visual references to Hurricane Katrina and expressions of black pride. Although these specific political references were absent from her Super Bowl performance, Beyoncé, her dancers, and

constitute a tool for addressing the nation's shortcomings because they are predicated precisely on their absence. Edward Linenthal's book on the 1995 Oklahoma City bombing nevertheless points to an alternative moment of ritualized national togetherness – in the sense of shared focus rather than of national consensus – that possesses considerably more interrogative potential.

"Perhaps one of the greatest attractions of a nationwide bereaved community," writes Linenthal, "is that it is one of the only ways Americans can imagine themselves as one; being 'together' with millions of others through expressions of mourning bypasses or transcends the many ways in which people are divided – by religion, by ideology, by class, by region, by race, by gender."[57] In this, Linenthal echoes the work of William Seston and John Dewey. Focusing on the *iustitium*, the Roman law which suspended legal functioning as a mark of mourning and emergency, Seston writes, "Framing the funerary rites within a sort of general mobilization, with all civil affairs stopped and normal political life suspended, the proclamation of the *iustitium* tended to transform … death … into a national catastrophe, a drama in which each person was involved, willingly or not."[58] Likewise, in *The Public and Its Problems*, Dewey argued that publics were formed by the emergence of problems that revealed shared associations and public connectivity.[59] Unlike Dewey, Linenthal is far from naïve about the claims to national unity that inevitably follow such events: his book offers a nuanced account of the tensions between the rhetoric of togetherness expressed both by the local community and by the nation at large and of the internecine conflicts between interest groups seeking to exploit the event for their own perceived interests.

the musicians surrounding her were dressed in in a way that was widely seen to be an homage to the Black Panthers. Predictably, the political right took deep offense. See, for example, Maeve McDermott, "Rudy Giuliani Calls Beyoncé's Super Bowl Performance an Attack on Cops," *USA Today*, February 9, 2016. www.usatoday.com/story/life/people/2016/02/08/rudy-giuliani-criticizes-beyonce-super-bowl-formation-attack-on-cops/80018490/. Accessed Feb. 9, 2016.

[57] Edward T. Linenthal, *Unfinished Bombing: Oklahoma City in American Memory* (New York: Oxford University Press, 2001), 111. Similarly, James E. Young argues, "Public monuments, national days of commemoration, shared calendars thus all work to create common loci around which seemingly common national identity is formed. The aims of a state's national memorial mandates, in other words, are twofold: to commemorate particular events and to create a unifying sense of shared history." James E. Young, "Mandating the National Memory of Catastrophe," in *Law and Catastrophe* edited by Austin Sarat, Lawrence Douglas, and Martha Merrill Umphrey (Stanford: Stanford University Press, 2007), 132.

[58] Seston is quoted in Agamben, *State of Exception*, Kindle Locations, 912–914.

[59] John Dewey, *The Public and Its Problems* (University Park, PA: Penn State Press, 2012).

Written before the September 2001 terrorist attacks but published shortly thereafter, Linenthal's book proved to be remarkably prescient about the domestic politics of their aftermath. In both instances, any attempt to disrupt – or to suggest the existence of anything other than – a national consensus on the meaning of the violence in the days, months, and even years following the attacks was greeted with deeply moralized outrage.[60] In such circumstances, any effort to employ the rituals of one of the few moments of shared national focus as a tool for diagnosing and/or addressing and the problems of the polity would seem to be quixotic at best. Nevertheless, there are, this book will argue, a handful of moments in American history in which such public mourning has indeed been employed to both interrogative and prescriptive ends.

Just as Nicole Loraux observed that the funeral oration invented Athens as much as Athens invented the funeral oration, the historian Garry Wills argued that the Gettysburg Address created the Second American Republic.[61] Lincoln, it might be noted, had made the argument set out in the Address – that the Declaration of Independence, with its commitment to equality, was the founding document of the nation – on a number of occasions prior to November 19, 1863.[62] Part of what made the Address so successful at Gettysburg, it will be suggested, is the time and place of its delivery: at the dedication of the national cemetery for those Union troops fallen in one of the bloodiest battles of the Civil War. Bucking the dominant trend in the discourse of public mourning – that which tells an idealized story about the polity and its values – Lincoln offered an interrogative speech that functioned as a means of both revealing and addressing the nation's shortcomings. At Gettysburg, it will be argued, Lincoln demonstrated the possibility of public mourning as a

[60] In the days after the attacks, Susan Sontag and Bill Maher offered similar critiques of President Bush's description of the terrorists as "cowardly." Both were vilified for their remarks. Susan Sontag, "The Talk of the Town," *The New Yorker*, September 24, 2001. www.newyorker.com/archive/2001/09/24/010924ta_talk_wtc. Accessed Dec. 10, 2013. Bill Maher, "This is the comment Bill Maher was fired for – Politically Incorrect." www.youtube.com/watch?v=brI6b77x19A. Accessed Dec. 10, 2013. See also the negative response to William Langewiesche's *American Ground: Unbuilding the World Trade Center* (New York: North Point Press, 2002) in which he points to possible looting by New York City firefighters during the September 2001 rescue operations.
[61] Garry Wills, *Lincoln at Gettysburg: The Words that Remade America* (New York: Simon & Schuster, 1992).
[62] On July 4, 1863, celebrating the Union victories at Gettysburg and Vicksburg, Lincoln had foreshadowed the Address. "How long is it?" he asked, "eighty-odd years – since the Fourth of July for the first time in the history of the world a nation by its representative assembled and declared as a self-evident truth that 'all men are created equal.'" Abraham Lincoln, *Speeches and Writings 1859–1865* (New York: Library of America, 1989), 475.

source of critical-theoretical reflection, democratic pedagogy, and political innovation. Moments such as these, it will be suggested, point to the interrogative and prescriptive possibilities of our own public responses to loss.

DEATH AND THE POLITICS OF THEORY

That death should offer an opportunity for critical thought should be no surprise. When those close to us die, our lives almost always change, and there exists a period of grieving and reflection. Indeed, Peter Euben argues that Plato invented philosophy as an act of mourning.[63] In the case of mass death – the event which most often precipitates *public* mourning – there exists a parallel opportunity for the political community to engage in a similar process of critical reflection. "Just as, during periods of anomie and crisis," writes Agamben, "normal social structures can collapse and social functions and roles break down to the point where culturally condition behaviors and customs are completely overturned, so are periods of mourning usually characterized by suspension and alteration of all social relations."[64] It is no coincidence that political theory often emerges from such moments of crisis or catastrophe, moments in which the polity's old explanations no longer work, when – borrowing from Wittgenstein – both philosophical *and* political problems are of the form "I don't know my way about."[65] While the overwhelming majority of mourning rituals in the contemporary polity are marked less by a commitment to rigorous interrogation of the nation's values than by an unquestioning celebration of the same, such ritualized moments of shared national focus nevertheless embody considerable democratic potential that has, on occasion, been employed as a source of critical reflection on and as a corrective to the problematic aspects of our democratic life and politics. In its prescriptive register, this book attempts to isolate and

---

[63] Euben, *Platonic Noise*, 15. For a thoughtful account of the relationship between death and political theory, see John Seery, *Political Theory for Mortals: Shades of Justice, Images of Death* (Ithaca, NY: Cornel University Press, 1996).

[64] Agamben, *State of Exception*, Kindle Locations 888–893.

[65] Ludwig Wittgenstein, *Philosophical Investigations* translated by P.M.S. Hacker (Oxford: Wiley-Blackwell, 2009), cxxxiii. See also Marshall Berman, *All That Is Solid Melts into Air: The Experience of Modernity* (New York: Penguin Books, 1988); James Boyd White, *When Words Lose Their Meaning: Constitutions and Reconstitutions of Language, Character, and Community* (Chicago: University of Chicago Press, 1985), 59–92; and Sheldon Wolin, *Hobbes and the Epic Tradition of Political Theory* (Los Angeles: William Andrews Clark Memorial Library, 1970).

recover a number of such moments, seeking to offer an account of a critical response to loss that might – properly cultivated – reinvigorate and/or reshape American democracy through its rituals and practices of public mourning. In so doing, it also aims to contribute to recent debates in democratic theory, especially those concerned with agonism and emergency politics.[66] Given the relative paucity of critique in our contemporary mourning practices, it is an attempt that might seem somewhat misplaced as an untimely advocacy for a utopian ideal in a period of crisis. Nevertheless, as Sara Monoson observes, "A good political theory requires no emendation on account of practicality issues."[67]

The suggestion that what is true in theory might not be true in practice has long been a stick with which critics of political theory have chosen to beat its practitioners.[68] "As for the philosophers," wrote Francis Bacon in 1605, "they make imaginary laws for imaginary commonwealths; and their discourses are as the stars, which give little light because they are so high."[69] In Plato's *Republic*, frustrated by Socrates' increasingly outlandish proposals for the Ideal City – the quintessential 'imaginary commonwealth' – Glaucon demands: "The more you say such things, the less we'll let you off from telling how it is possible for this regime to come into being. So speak, and don't waste time."[70] While Socrates' answer, "We were not seeking them for the sake of proving that it's possible for these things to come into being,"[71] is unlikely to mollify theory's critics – little wonder that he was put to death – it nevertheless points to an important aspect of theory's practice.[72] While some might regard suggesting the ways in which our current rituals of mourning could be reconfigured for democratic purposes – even when that reconfiguration is shown to be a return to an older tradition or a revivification of an

---

[66] See Bonnie Honig, *Emergency Politics: Paradox, Law, Democracy* (Princeton, NJ: Princeton University Press, 2009).

[67] Sara Monoson, *Plato's Democratic Entanglements: Athenian Politics and the Practice of Philosophy* (Princeton, NJ: Princeton University Press, 2008), 131.

[68] And one recognized by those same practitioners. See Immanuel Kant's 1793 essay "Theory and Practice."

[69] Wolin, *Hobbes*, 13.

[70] Plato, *The Republic of Plato* translated by Allan Bloom (New York: Basic Books, 1991), 152, 472b.

[71] Ibid., 152, 472d.

[72] The Athenians were not alone in their frustration. "Reading the Socratic dialogues," observed Wittgenstein, "one has the feeling; what a frightful waste of time! What's the point of these arguments that prove nothing and clarify nothing?" Ludwig Wittgenstein, *Culture and Value* translated by Peter Winch (Chicago: University of Chicago Press, 1980), 14e.

actually existing practice – as the sort of exercise in futility identified by
Bacon, the positing of even outlandish proposals can serve as a practical political intervention into an existing polity.[73] Writes Peter Euben, "A
theory, or at least a political theory, does not merely describe the world
but carries prescriptive force in the sense of creating an imaginary future
that either invites or discourages theoretical and political agency."[74] The
prescriptive aspects of this project should be seen as just such an invitation. Its goal is suggested by Joshua Dienstag's observation that "[t]o plot
in the manner of political theory means to take up the challenge of alter-
ing the connection between past and future, thereby taking responsibility
for both."[75]

In keeping with this theoretical approach, there is, at the heart of this
book, a no-doubt-distasteful suggestion that it will seek to make more
palatable by the time of its conclusion: that Americans should mourn the
death of Osama bin Laden. Although the suggestion appears outlandish or hyperbolic – a prime example of the slender grasp of reality that
Francis Bacon ascribes to the practitioners of political thought – it is
nevertheless offered with a straight face: a way of seeking to change those
things that might be different if we chose to change them, even if the
credibility of the "might be" seems stretched, almost to breaking point,
by the nature of the proposal. It is, nevertheless, no more implausible or
outlandish than the suggestion, made by Israeli historian and Auschwitz
survivor Yehudah Elkana, that Israel should forget the Holocaust because
the urge to remember was no longer about mourning the lost but rather
about justifying violence against its enemies, real and imagined. "Relying
on the lessons of the past in order to build the future," he wrote, "exploit-
ing past suffering as a political argument – these mean involving the
dead in the political life of the living."[76] The parallel is instructive. For
Elkana, remembering the Holocaust had become a way of employing
grief towards political ends, what is here being termed "public mourning." It is a practice that he believed to be problematic for a political

[73] See, for example, Danielle Allen's discussion of precisely this approach. Danielle Allen,
Why Plato Wrote (Oxford: Wiley-Blackwell, 2010). Similarly, as Arendt reminds us,
words are themselves a form of action. Hannah Arendt, *The Human Condition* (Chicago:
University of Chicago Press, 1998).

[74] Euben, *Platonic Noise*, 100.

[75] Joshua Dienstag, *"Dancing in Chains": Narrative and Memory in Political Theory* (Palo
Alto, CA: Stanford University Press, 1997), 207.

[76] Yehuda Elkana, "The Need to Forget," *Haaretz*, March 2, 1988. The English translation
from which these extracts are taken is available at: www.scribd.com/doc/108590800/
The-Need-to-Forget-by-Yehuda-Elkana. Accessed Dec. 17, 2013.

system predicated on majority rule. "The very existence of democracy is," he declared, "endangered when the memory of the dead participates actively in the democratic process."[77] For this reason, the proposition that Americans should mourn Osama bin Laden may be more grounded than that made by Elkana, for it recognizes that the dead will *always* participate in democratic politics.[78] What is crucial for democracy, this book suggests, is *how* they do so. The claim that Americans should mourn their greatest enemy is, nevertheless, such that it may be necessary to offer an important clarification of its claims.

In 2005, the University of Colorado professor Ward Churchill became the *bête noir* of the conservative media when he suggested that the victims of the 2001 World Trade Center attacks – whom, he said, constituted "a technocratic corps at the very heart of America's global financial empire" – were guilty of the type of unthinking evasion of moral responsibility that Hannah Arendt ascribed to Adolf Eichmann.[79] In a world in which political theory was read by anyone beyond the confines of academia, the claims of this book might raise a similar furor. Making an important distinction between his argument and that being presented here might, nevertheless, save it from the self-righteous condemnation – itself a significant mobilization of grief toward political ends – that may ultimately have cost Churchill his job, and, indeed, serve to clarify the nature of the claims being made here.[80] Churchill's condemnation of the workers killed in the towers – workers whom, it should be noted, in a way that he did not, included janitors, service workers, secretaries, administrators, rescue workers, and federal employees, as well as the financial service workers who seemed to be the real focus of his ire – was a claim about the *dead*. This is a book about the *living*. It is only through the living that the dead can participate in politics: either by being made to speak – in a process that the Greeks called *prosopopeia* – or by being invoked as an example of sacrifice and suffering. The book, then, seeks to overcome the fetishism of the dead in democratic politics – the danger of which was

---

[77] Ibid.
[78] As has already been suggested, however, realism or practicality should not necessarily be the criteria by which we judge the value of political thought. Moreover, political theory with its attempts to employ the works of long-deceased thinkers to contemporary ends might itself be considered just such a form of post-mortem participation.
[79] Ward Churchill, "Some People Push Back: On the Justice of Roosting Chickens." www.kersplebedeb.com/mystuff/s11/churchill.html. Accessed Jan. 7, 2014.
[80] Dan Frosch, "Professor's Dismissal Upheld by Colorado Supreme Court, *The New York Times*, September 10, 2012. www.nytimes.com/2012/09/11/us/court-upholds-colorado-professor-ward-churchills-firing.html?ref=wardlchurchill. Accessed Jan. 24, 2014.

identified by no lesser an American than Thomas Jefferson[81] – returning power to the living in a way that allows citizens to do consciously what they have hitherto done unconsciously: to employ grief for political ends. The argument presented here aims to do so in a way that invigorates rather than undermines the democratic polity. As such, despite its normative intent, it is an argument without partisan content.

AMERICAN MOURNING

The book begins with an account of the public memorial on the first anniversary of the 2001 terror attacks on New York City. Noting that the organizers of the event chose the Gettysburg Address as a eulogy for the fallen, this chapter situates the Address in its Ancient Greek and American historical contexts to suggest the ways in which the 2002 reading corresponded to Socrates' critique of the funeral oration tradition in Plato's *Menexenus*: one that suggested eulogies were necessarily platitudinous, anachronistic, and banal. Drawing on Thucydides' presentation of Pericles' Funeral Oration in his *History of the Peloponnesian War* – a text which many consider to be something of a funeral oration for Athens – the chapter shows how both Thucydides, and later Lincoln, were able to subvert the funeral oration tradition criticized by Plato. In so doing, it suggests, they offered productive critiques of their respective democracies, employing a critical perspective – predicated on a worldview borrowed from Greek tragedy and imbued with complexity, contradiction, and conflict – that sought to address their respective polities' most pressing problems. The chapter seeks, within the broader framework of the book, to establish both the problems posed to democracy by a nationalist mode of mourning committed to imperialism, bellicosity, and exceptionalism, and the contrasting promise of a tragic mourning that, it argues, offers the possibility of a democratically productive and critical patriotism.

Framing its argument around a discussion of the 2006 funeral for civil rights icon Coretta Scott King, the following chapter seeks to identify and recover an indigenous tradition of tragically oriented public mourning that was central to the fight against racial oppression even before the founding of the nation. Tracing the history of this politically

---

[81] Committing the polity to an unchanging constitution, wrote Jefferson admonishingly, was equivalent to the notion "that the earth belongs to the dead, and not to the living." Louis Menand, *The Metaphysical Club: A Story of Ideas in America* (New York: Farrar, Strauss, & Giroux, 2002), Kindle Locations 4094–4095.

motivated response to loss through the history of slavery, opposition to post-Reconstruction violence, and the struggle for civil rights, it connects Frederick Douglass's eulogies for Abraham Lincoln to Reverend Joseph Lowery's deeply political eulogy for King. It argues that the political controversy generated among both blacks and whites by Lowery's speech is indicative of the ways in which this political mourning tradition has declined among an increasingly economically stratified and unchurched African American population. Suggesting, nevertheless, that this tradition continues to offer the possibility of a tragic alternative to the romantic mode of mourning whose commitment to unity and consensus obscures democratically productive, and thus important tensions within the polity, the chapter closes with a discussion of the ways in which this tradition has been somewhat revived – albeit in a mutated form – by the Black Lives Matter movement.

Following this largely historical analysis, the following three chapters pivot toward the prescriptive, considering the ways in which a tragic mode of mourning might help the polity to address the problems posed to American democracy by the politics of the postplanes era. Suggesting, in a typically tragic fashion, that the moment of the polity's seemingly greatest triumph, the assassination of Osama bin Laden, might also be the moment of its greatest defeat – the point at which the damaging excesses that followed the 2001 attacks on America seemed to be vindicated rather than exposed as a danger to democracy – the first chapter in this section draws on Aeschylus' *The Persians* to consider what it might mean for a polity to mourn its enemies. It suggests that doing so might provide an opportunity for the polity to consider that enemy in all of its complexity rather than simply as a hypertrophied evil. Resisting the temptation to reduce politics to morality, the argument suggests that a certain kind of public mourning might function as a mode of critique and construction for democratic politics. The consequences of this approach, it argues, would not be confined solely to the domestic. By tempering the *mênis* that has driven American foreign policy in the years since bin Laden's attacks, mourning for the enemy promises a more considered realist response to the actions of the nation's foes, encouraging a critical perspective more akin to that of tragedy's audience than that of its protagonists and, with it, a less self-defeating engagement with those who would do America harm. For this reason, it will be argued, Aeschylus demonstrates that Bonnie Honig's rejection of mourning predicated on shared humanity is misplaced and that such responses to loss offer a far more productive form of politics – emergency or otherwise – than she suggests.

The penultimate chapter focuses on a further human cost of the planes, one both generated and exacerbated by a nostalgic mode of mourning – committed to an often-imaginary past – whose influence has long been felt in the American polity. Identifying the threat to the American polity posed by the returning warrior – a danger recognized by democracy's founders – this section of the book engages with attempts by contemporary psychologists, theater activists, and the military itself to revive Greek tragedy as a way of helping the veterans of America's post-2001 military campaigns return to the polity of which they were once a part. Building on an argument made in the previous chapters – that the modes of mourning embraced by the polity in the aftermath of the 2001 attacks helped cultivate the grief wrath of *mênis* that led the nation into a series of ill-advised and poorly planned wars – this chapter points not only to the ways in which the American response to those losses generated yet more death but also to the ways in which it continues to undermine democracy in complex ways. Situating returning soldiers within the same nostalgic narrative of heroism and sacrifice that America employs with its returning dead – a narrative that Socrates believed was endemic to democratic mourning – the polity, it will be argued, effectively mourns its living returnees in a way that denies their experiences, excludes their actions, and silences their voices on key issues that constitute significant threats to democratic politics. Engaging with the recent attempts to employ tragic theater as a tool for social and political reintegration of returning veterans, this chapter identifies the nostalgic commitment to restoration and the politics of recognition that underpins even this veteran-centric approach. By way of contrast, it outlines a more complex response predicated on a tragic understanding of loss, one that offers an understanding of return as an ongoing process of reconstitution rather than a simple matter of restoration. Tragic mourning, it argues, embodied as both ritual and memorial, offers a politics of acknowledgment and democratic futurity that might be embraced by the polity as a whole.

A concern with democratic futurity also underpins the final chapter of the book. It notes that in the face of perceived threats to human existence such as terrorist attacks or natural disasters, economists, urban planners, and other social theorists have turned to a focus on resilience – itself a commitment to "going on together" – rather than prevention. Predicated on an acceptance of the inevitability of potentially catastrophic events, practices of resilience seek to maintain core system functions in the face of disasters that might threaten them. Although the literature on resilience has proliferated in other fields, little to no attention has been paid to the concept in political theory.[82] Certain theories of resilience, it is argued, are predicated on an unacknowledged tragic worldview whose self-conscious cultivation – not least through a tragic mode of mourning – would better achieve its goals by serving as a source of democratic pedagogy in the face of loss. Presenting Thucydides' *History of the Peloponnesian War* as just such a form of tragic mourning for Athens, the book concludes with an account of the ways in which, as a form of *textual* mourning, the *History* offers an example of a nonritualized response to loss that might best serve an age of democratic atomism and political estrangement.

The book, then, offers much by way of critique of our contemporary practices of mourning. Sharing Marx's reticence about "prescribing recipes for the cook shops of the future," it nevertheless only gestures towards the rituals and practices that might embody what, it argues, are more democratically productive responses to loss. Its focus is, rather, on showing why such practices should be embraced, identifying the *ethos* that they should express, and locating resources within the polity that might be reconstituted – or revived – to engender and enact it. In so doing, the text embraces its own democratic commitments: returning the responsibility for cultivating these practices and values to its readers understood as democratic citizens.

---

[82] Although American political institutions evince a concern with maintaining a chain of command in the face of a catastrophic event, it is a *military* not a *political* priority. As far as political theory is concerned, see, however, Irena Rosenthal, "Aggression and Play in the Face of Adversity: A Psychoanalytic Reading of Democratic Resilience," *Political Theory*, August 14, 2004: 1–26. Such an approach is, however, at odds with the deliberately nonpsychoanalytical method employed here.

I

Pericles at Gettysburg and Ground Zero: Tragedy, Patriotism, and Public Mourning

As is so often the case in democratic politics, how we tell the story matters a great deal. It also matters what stories we tell.

– Bonnie Honig, Emergency Politics

The first anniversary of the planes was marked in New York City by a reading of the Gettysburg Address. It was, as many commentators noted, an unusual choice of eulogy, comparing the unwitting victims of a foreign terrorist attack to the willing participants in a bloody civil war.[1] The history of the funeral oration suggests, however, that the eliding of such distinctions is endemic to the tradition. Indeed, much of the contemporary criticism simply echoed Socrates' complaints in the *Menexenus* that public eulogies are necessarily ill fitting, anachronistic, and banal. There, Socrates satirizes what he perceives to be the emptiness of democratic responses to loss by offering his own eulogy marked by anachronism, cliché, and platitude. That his speech was repeated in Antiquity by those who failed to get the joke seems to confirm that he was right about what democracy demands from public mourning: that the Athenians be praised in Athens.[2] Underpinning the more recent criticism was, however,

---

[1] Michiko Kakutani, "Vigilance and Memory: Critic's Notebook; Rituals, Improvised or Traditional," *New York Times*, September 12, 2002; and John McWhorter, *Doing Our Own Thing: The Degradation of Language and Music and Why We Should, Like Care* (New York: Gotham Books, 2003).

[2] Plato, "Menexenus," in *The Dialogues of Plato, Volume One* translated by R. E. Allen (New Haven, CT: Yale University Press, 1984), 317–344, 235d. In this context, little turns on this distinction between Plato, the Socrates who appears in the Platonic dialogues, and Socrates the historical figure.

a suggestion that something was missing from the 2002 reading of the Address that was present in 1863: that Lincoln had transcended the genre in a way that is now lost to us.[3] Attempts to identify the source of this transcendence have largely relied for their explanatory leverage on the rhetorical genius of Abraham Lincoln.[4] It is an explanation without import for the contemporary polity. This chapter identifies the difference between the 1863 and 2002 readings of the Address by employing a distinction between nationalistic and tragic modes of mourning. Using Plato's critique of the funeral oration tradition to identify the problems of the nationalist approach to loss and contrasting it with the tragic mode of mourning embedded in the Great Dionysia, the chapter argues that what was missing from the September 2002 commemoration that was present in 1863 was a tragic perspective whose complexity was marked by a capacity for simultaneous national celebration and critique: what is here being called a *Dionysian* or tragic patriotism. It is an absence with significant consequences for the practice of American democracy.

Although the turn to the Greeks in this chapter is part of the book's broader method of classicization – that which suggests that "it is ... possible ... that the far-off history of Athenian democracy constitutes valuable experimental terrain for helping us to think this present full of uncertainties"[5] – in this case there may be further reason for embracing the Ancients: the possibility of Greek influence on Lincoln's speech. Those familiar with both Pericles' Funeral Oration and the Gettysburg Address cannot help, perhaps, but be struck by their rhetorical, thematic, and stylistic similarities.[6] Following Garry Wills and Florence Jeanne Goodman, it will here be suggested that Lincoln was deeply influenced by Thucydides' presentation of Pericles' speech.[7] Regardless of whether Lincoln's connection to

---

[3] Susan Sontag, "Real Battles and Empty Metaphors," *The New York Times*, September 10, 2002.

[4] See, for example, Ronald C. White Jr., *The Eloquent President. A Portrait of Lincoln Through His Words* (New York: Random House, 2005); Garry Wills, *Lincoln at Gettysburg: The Words That Remade America* (New York: Simon & Schuster, 1992).

[5] Nicole Loraux, *The Divided City: On Memory and Forgetting in Ancient Athens* (New York: Zones Books, 2002), 245.

[6] As Anne Norton recounts: "When I was at Chicago, there were two speeches read by virtually all students in the Common Core: Pericles' Funeral Oration and Lincoln's Gettysburg Address. One of our classmates famously confused the two and – more famously – appealed the rather bad grade he got in consequence on the grounds that, after all, they were very much the same." Anne Norton, *Leo Strauss and the Politics of American Empire* (New Haven, CT: Yale University Press, 2004), 134–135.

[7] Wills, *Lincoln at Gettysburg*; Florence Jeanne Goodman, "Pericles at Gettysburg," *The Mid-West Quarterly*, 6 (Spring), 1965: 311–336.

Thucydides is genealogical or – as some have suggested – merely heuristic, it will be argued that the parallel with Pericles' speech sheds considerable analytical light on both the problems of nationalist mourning and the promise of tragic responses to loss for democratic life and politics.[8]

The chapter begins by establishing its typology with a history of Greek mourning practices. Setting out the tropes of the funeral oration, it details Plato's critique of the tradition and shows how the rituals of mourning associated with the Great Dionysia transcended it. Demonstrating the ways in which Thucydides incorporates aspects of the rituals of mourning associated with the Festival into his presentation of Pericles' Oration, it identifies the possibility of a mode of democratic mourning that is tragic – or Dionysian – in structure and effect. It argues that Thucydides effectively offers his readers *two* Pericles: the *nationalistic* Pericles, a figure whose one-sided perspective is that of tragedy's protagonists; and the *tragic* Pericles, a figure whose more complex perspective is that of tragedy's audience. Using these Pericles as a heuristic for analyzing two moments of public mourning genealogically linked by a reading of the

---

[8] Although – drawing on Wills and Goodman – I have previously argued that Lincoln was influenced by Thucydides, recent work by Jennifer Roberts has called that claim into question. Noting that Goodman attempts to put Pericles' speech in Lincoln's hands by listing books that reference the Oration that he is known to have read, Roberts tracks down these references and shows that they are less compelling than Goodman suggests. Certainly none of the works identified by Goodman contain the text of Pericles' speech. Roberts acknowledges, nevertheless, that although "the flaws in Goodman's case undermine her argument, they do not in any way argue against Lincoln's having known the Periclean *epitaphios*" (148). As Lincoln was only a reader and not a collector of books, attempts such as Goodman's to put the *History* directly in his hands are probably overly ambitious. There are, however, still good reasons – even beyond the striking similarities between the two speeches – for believing that Lincoln's Address may have been influenced by Thucydides, not least among which is that as a notorious autodidact who went so far as to read *Neilson's Exercises in Greek* in order that he might understand Greek oratory in the original, Lincoln is, perhaps, unlikely to have missed the opportunity to read a speech by a figure whom at least two of the texts he is known to have read identify as Athens' greatest orator. Goodman argues that Lincoln read Hugh Blair's *Lectures on Rhetoric and Belles Lettres*, Plutarch's *Lives*, and Charles Rollin's *Ancient History*. Although these texts do not quite do all the work that Goodman suggests, they nevertheless point to Pericles' skill and importance as an orator. See Simon Stow, "Pericles at Gettysburg and Ground Zero: Tragedy, Patriotism, and Public Mourning," *American Political Science Review*, 101 (2), 2007: 195–208; and Jennifer Roberts, "Mourning and Democracy" in *Thucydides and the Modern World. Reception, Reinterpretation and Influence from the Renaissance to the Present* edited by Katherine Harloe and Neville Morley (Cambridge: Cambridge University Press, 2012): 140–156. Hugh Blair, *Lectures on Rhetoric and Belles Lettres* (New York: G. & C. & H. Carvill, 1829), 267; Charles Rollin, *Ancient History of the Egyptians, Carthaginians, Assyrians, Babylonians, Medes and Persians, Macedonians, and Grecians Volume III* (London: James, John, and Paul Knapton, 1735), 350.

Gettysburg Address, it considers which Pericles was present – and, thus, what kind of mourning was enacted – at both Gettysburg and Ground Zero. Arguing that the tragic Pericles provided the model for the initial reading of the Address and the nationalistic Pericles for the 2002 delivery, the chapter concludes by showing how these modes of mourning served to shape democratic outcomes during two key moments of crisis in the American polity.

THE ATHENIAN ORATION

For the Greeks, the annual wintertime funeral and oration for the war dead was an inextricably political affair. "[T]he orator's aims," wrote Nicole Loraux, "belong to the sphere of practical politics: at the end of the year of war, on the eve of new battles, the oration must attest to the cohesion of the community and to help strengthen it."[9] As such, it was necessarily public and traditional. Chosen "for his intellectual gifts and his general reputation," the speaker was expected to follow community conventions that were already "ancient" when Thucydides described them. Indeed, in the *History*, Pericles acknowledges "the institution of this speech at the close of our ceremony."[10] Two such conventions were *epainesis* and *parainesis*: praise for the fallen and advice for the living. Pericles praises the dead for "their gallant conduct against the enemy in defense of their native land," noting that "they thought it more honorable to stand their ground and suffer death than to give in and save their lives."[11] Such *epainesis* is, of course, an indirect form of *parainesis*: as with all public mourning, the real focus of the rituals is the living not the dead. Of the fallen, Pericles tells the Athenians: "It is for you to try to be like them." The living must, he says, "resolve to keep up the same daring spirit against the foe."[12] Tellingly, there are no individuals here, only Athenians of noble conduct – Pericles refers only to "these men," "the dead," and "they" – making the city, not the dead, the subject of his speech. As Loraux points out, the funeral oration was "an institution of speech in which the symbolic constantly encroached on the functional, since in each oration the codified praise of the dead spilled over into

---

[9] Nicole Loraux, *The Invention of Athens: The Funeral Oration in the Classical City* translated by Alan Sheridan (Cambridge, MA: Harvard University Press, 1986), 123.
[10] Thucydides, *History of the Peloponnesian War* translated by Rex Warner (London: Penguin Books, 1972), 143–144.
[11] Ibid., 148, 149.
[12] Ibid., 149.

generalized praise of Athens."[13] Adopting the conventions of the genre to
structure his speech and setting his "praise for the dead … in the bright
light of evidence," Pericles offers Athens an idealized vision of the city
and her values.[14]

The great majority of Pericles' Funeral Oration is spent praising Athens
and her customs: her openness to others; her democratic practices; her
measured use of wealth; her generosity; her freedom; and her toleration.
It is for all these reasons that Pericles famously declares Athens "an education to Greece."[15] He makes no attempt to hide his motives. "What
I would prefer," he declares, "is that you should fix your eyes every day
on the greatness of Athens as she really is, and should fall in love with
her."[16] Indeed, he suggests that such love of *polis* finds its fullest expression in the fallen: men whose lives had value precisely because they were
given in defense of Athenian ideals. It was, he asserts, a fate that ennobled
those who suffered it. "Some of them," he observes, "no doubt had their
faults; but what we ought to remember is their gallant conduct against
the enemy in defense of their native land. They have blotted out evil with
good, and done more service to the commonwealth than they ever did
harm in their private lives."[17] Like Greek politics itself, the focus of the
oration was decidedly masculine. Standing in opposition to the private
laments of women mourners, the oration was meant to gird the soldier-
citizens for battle. Indeed, Pericles declares that "the consummation
which has overtaken these men shows us the meaning of manliness" and
famously relegates the role of women to childbirth and to being "least
talked about by men."[18] The oration was, furthermore, something of an
imperialistic paradox: claiming hegemony over others – "an education to
Greece" – while being addressed primarily to Athenians.[19] Pericles claims,
nevertheless, that "Our city is open to the world,"[20] and contemporary
sources, including the *Menexenus*, confirm that foreign observers would
have been present.[21] The masculine and imperialistic aspects of the oration culminate in the final convention identified by Loraux: the claim that
only they, the imperial power, could cause their own downfall. Losses, she

---

[13] Loraux, *The Invention of Athens*, 2.
[14] Thucydides, *History*, 148.
[15] Ibid., 147.
[16] Ibid., 149.
[17] Ibid., 148.
[18] Ibid., 148, 150–151.
[19] Loraux, *The Invention of Athens*, 87–88.
[20] Thucydides, *History*, 146.
[21] Plato, *Menexenus*, 235b.

writes, were to be attributed only to mistakes of the city: to its internal divides, not to the skill of the enemy.[22]

The Athenian funeral oration was then an occasion for the glorification of the city that sought to cultivate unity and consensus through a manipulation of grief. It was a nationalistic form of mourning predicated on an understanding of Athenian exceptionalism that sought to reaffirm social ties, community values, and an established political identity. Although some might balk at the use of the term "nationalist" in this context, there are sufficient family resemblances between the values espoused in the oration and those encompassed by the term to make the category analytically useful and temporally appropriate.[23] Certainly, Benedict Anderson's famous formulation of a nation as an "imagined community" suggests the way in which the term captures an idealized sense of unity between a people otherwise divided by class, region, age, and clan.[24] "Nationalism" is, moreover, a term employed by a number of classicists and historians to refer to the Athenian self-understanding, one inculcated by rituals and practices echoed by those seeking similar effects in the modern era, most obviously the uncritical form of devotion embodied by the mantra "my country – or my *polis* – right or wrong."[25] Such was the nature of the funeral oration. It was not, despite Pericles' assertion in the *History* that he "wanted to make it clear that for us there is more at stake than there is for others who lack our advantages,"[26] an occasion for a detailed discussion of the problems that had led to the war, the mistakes made in its execution, nor a time to wonder whether the

[22] Loraux, *The Invention of Athens*, 138–139.
[23] It is, perhaps, no more or less anachronistic than the use of the term "city state" to refer to the *polis*. I am grateful to John Lombardini for this point.
[24] Benedict Anderson, *Imagined Communities: Reflections on the Origin and the Spread of Nationalism* (London: Verso, 1983). For a compelling account on the notion of autochthony and its importance to the Athenian notion of themselves as separate from and superior to the rest of the Greek world, see Demetra Kasimis, "The Tragedy of Blood-based Membership: Secrecy and the Politics of Immigration in Euripides' *Ion*," *Political Theory*, 41:2, 2013: 231–256.
[25] "While there is inevitably some difference," writes Greg Anderson, "in the techniques and media used in the ancient and modern world to encourage a sense of belonging to those imagined political communities, even some of these are strikingly similar: the invention of new traditions, the creation of symbolic spaces for the commemoration of national heroes and achievements, the organization of the calendar around annual celebrations of national unity and fellowship." Greg Anderson, *The Athenian Experiment: Building an Imagined Political Community in Ancient Attica 508–490 B.C.* (Ann Arbor: University of Michigan Press, 2003), 215. See also Susan Lape, *Race and Citizen. Identity in the Classical Athenian Democracy* (Cambridge: Cambridge University Press, 2010).
[26] Thucydides, *History*, 148.

casualties inflicted were worth the gains accrued nor, indeed, the losses inflicted. It was the unquestioning, uncritical, and all-consuming nature of this nationalist worldview that drew Plato's ire and Socrates' scorn in the *Menexenus*.

PRAISING THE ATHENIANS IN ATHENS

Although death is a perennial theme of the Platonic dialogues, the *Menexenus* is particularly useful here because it deals explicitly with the funeral oration. It is a rhetorical tradition that Socrates holds in low regard. With habitual irony, he declares,

... in many ways it's a fine thing to die in battle. A man gets a magnificent funeral even if he dies poor, and people praise him even if he was worthless. Wise men lavish praise on him, not at random but in speeches prepared long in advance, and the praise is so beautiful that although they speak things both true and untrue of each man, the extreme beauty and diversity of their words bewitches our souls.[27]

It is this "bewitchment of our souls" and the glossing over of important distinctions that is of particular concern for Socrates. It occurs because the speakers focus on the general – the city – rather than the specifics of the dead:

For in every way, they eulogize the city and those who died in battle and all our forebears, and even us who are still alive, until finally, Menexenus, I feel myself ennobled by them. I every time stand and listen, charmed, believing I have become bigger, better born, and better looking on the spot.[28]

Far from reminding the citizenry of their roles and responsibilities, he suggests, the speech merely distracts its listeners. "I almost suppose I'm dwelling in the Isles of the Blessed," Socrates declares. "So skillful are our orators."[29] Its effect is, he believes, solely to bind the citizens to an idealized vision of a unified city in a way that dulls their critical faculties. That it does so regardless of the values of that city is, furthermore, a problem both perpetuated and evidenced by the anachronism inherent in the orations themselves.

More than once Socrates notes that funeral orations are "prepared long in advance."[30] Indeed, the eulogy that Socrates ascribes to Aspasia – Pericles' mistress – is said to be "pieced together from leftovers from"

[27] Plato, *Menexenus*, 234c.
[28] Ibid., 235a–b.
[29] Ibid., 235c.
[30] Ibid., 234c, 235d.

Pericles' Oration.[31] As such, he suggests, the conventions of the funeral oration are mere commonplaces or platitudes: the simple repetition of old ideas on which everyone can agree. For Socrates, the problem with such platitudes is that they are purely comforting: they console in their generality and deliver the listener from critical reflection. By contrast, the sort of critical dialectic prized by Socrates requires specificity: it is precise, delicate, and hard to pull off.[32] Moreover, a number of scholars have noted that the timing of the *Menexenus* seems decidedly out of joint: the speech tells the story of Athens down to the end of the Corinthian War and the King's Peace of 387 BC, but Socrates died in 399; Aspasia, who delivered the speech, almost certainly died before Socrates; and Pericles, who had died in 429 BC, is spoken of as if he is still alive.[33] This vagueness, which has long puzzled scholars, may be an authorial comment on the platitudinous nature of the funeral oration. It does not matter when it is delivered, Plato seems to suggest, because it is not concerned with the specificity of truth but rather with the generalizations of nationalism.

Unsurprisingly given his concern with specificity, Plato appears to have a particular target in mind. The funeral oration in the *Menexenus* explicitly recalls Thucydides' claim that Athens was an "aristocracy with the approval of the multitude,"[34] and Socrates speaks disparagingly of someone who learned his rhetoric from Antiphon of Rhamnusia, a teacher under whom Thucydides is said to have studied.[35] Likewise, Socrates employs the term "Peloponnesians" to refer to the Athenians, a term that is employed only by the author of the *History*.[36] Thus, declares R. E. Allen, the "*Menexenus* is primarily a criticism of Thucydides, not Pericles."[37] So, although Socrates appears to be addressing the Funeral Oration of Pericles, it might be the whole of Thucydides' *History* that is the subject of his scorn, not least when he declares, "If one had to speak well of Athenians to Peloponnesians, or of Peloponnesians to Athenians, he would have to be a good orator indeed to be persuasive. But when one performs before the very people he is praising, it is perhaps no great

[31] Ibid., 236b.
[32] See Stanley Fish, *Self-Consuming Artifacts: The Experience of Seventeenth-Century Literature* (Berkeley: University of California Press, 1972), 1.
[33] Plato, *Menexenus*, 235e.
[34] Ibid., 238c.
[35] Ibid., 236a.
[36] Monoson, *Plato's Democratic Entanglements*, 186.
[37] R. E. Allen, "*The Menexenus* Comment" in *The Dialogues of Plato, Volume One* translated by R. E. Allen (New Haven, CT: Yale University Press, 1984), 325. See also Loraux, *The Invention of Athens*, 189.

thing to appear to speak well."[38] In praising the Athenians in Athens, Socrates suggests, Pericles, and by extension Thucydides in his *History*, have taken on the easiest of tasks: the rhetorical speech that flatters to deceive and serves only the basest interests of men and the city, generating a sentimental connection to an idealized – nationalist – view of the city. It is a criticism Plato makes not only of the funeral oration but also of Thucydides as a whole, a text that, in its structure and form, might be regarded as something of a funeral oration for the once-great city.[39]

It may be, however, that Plato's criticism of Pericles' Funeral Oration, and by metonymic extension the *History*, is misplaced. For Thucydides also presents a more sophisticated account of these rituals of public mourning, one that moves beyond the simple flattery and unquestioning nationalism of the funeral oration and offers his readers the possibility of the kind of dialectic prized by Socrates. He does so by mimicking the structure of another set of rituals of Athenian public mourning: those surrounding the Festival of Dionysia. Setting out these conventions allows us to identify them in Thucydides' work, demonstrating the ways in which he was able to transcend Socrates' criticism of the genre and offer a truly tragic oration that sought a democratically productive dialectical effect.

THE GREAT DIONYSIA

In his work on the Great Dionysia, the Athenian springtime festival of theatrical competition, Simon Goldhill identifies what he calls "the fundamentally questioning or agonistic nature of Greek tragedy."[40] He suggests that the hero of such tragedy "does not simply *reverse* the norms of what it means to fit into society but makes a *problem* of such integration."[41] This much is well known: the theater offered the Greeks a way of casting critical light on their core values. Goldhill goes on to argue, however, that

---

[38] Plato, *Menexenus*, 235d.

[39] That the *History* contains both *epainesis* and *parainesis* is militaristic in nature and seems to suggest that Athens was responsible for its own downfall. I am not alone in suggesting this connection between the Oration and the work as a whole, and although Loraux asserts that "once the funeral oration is over, the historian loses interest in the ceremony" (16), she does note that others have observed "the homological relationship that has... been observed between the *epitaphios* and the work as a whole" (289). Loraux, *The Invention of Athens*. If it is indeed an oration for Athens, the *History* is, fittingly, a tragic one.

[40] Simon Goldhill, "The Great Dionysia and Civic Ideology" in *Nothing to Do with Dionysos? Athenian Drama in Its Social Context* edited by John J. Winkler and Froma I. Zeitlin (Princeton, NJ: Princeton University Press, 1990), 98.

[41] Ibid., 116.

the Festival contributed to this questioning by providing a context for the presentation of socially transgressive theater that was itself a reminder of the civic values that were being problematized. Central to this aspect of the Festival were the ceremonies that preceded the plays. "The space of theatrical performance was politicized by these rituals and this frame changed how the plays communicated with their audience."[42] Tellingly, these important civic ceremonies not only echoed those of the funeral oration but also included their own rituals of public mourning.

As with the funeral ceremonies and oration for the fallen, the rituals of the Dionysia were concerned with death, militarism, masculinity, city, and empire. Just as the oration demanded a notable figure for its speaker, the Festival formally began with sacrifices and libations poured by the city's most prominent citizens, the ten generals. The announcement of the city's benefactors that followed was, as Demosthenes and Aeschines noted, a way for the city to encourage all her citizens to make similar civic sacrifices. "Such rhetoric," writes Goldhill, "encapsulates a standard democratic ideal: that every man should act to benefit the collective of the state, and a citizen's actions are evaluated according to how they contribute to the city."[43] The ceremonies were not, however, simply concerned with promoting the city to a domestic audience; indeed, the nationalist and imperialistic aspects of the oration find their parallel in the ceremonial display of tribute sent by the Empire. The most obvious parallel between the rituals of the Dionysia and those of the funeral and oration for the fallen was, however, the on-stage parade, in full military uniform, of the war orphans educated by the state who had grown to manhood. Each was announced by a herald who identified the orphan's father, gave a speech praising the deceased's exploits on behalf of the

---

[42] Simon Goldhill, *Love, Sex & Tragedy: How the Ancient World Shapes Our Lives* (Chicago: University of Chicago Press, 2004), 224. See also Charles Segal, *Dionysiac Poetics and Euripides' Bacchae* (Princeton, NJ: Princeton University Press, 1982), 14. "The tragic performance itself exists in a kind of contradiction.... As part of the civic ritual of Athens, the performances in the theater of Dionysus affirm the social order at a state-sponsored occasion in a public and holy place. Tragedy also endorses that order through its lofty poetic language, traditional and dignified, through the elaborateness of the state-financed costumes and the discipline of the dancers, and through the choral odes, which often celebrate the city or the moral and heroic values of the city or comment on the action from the point of view of ordinary citizens. Yet the narrative material of the myths that tragedy dramatizes shockingly violates this order with the most feared and abominated pollutions: matricide, incest, patricide, fratricide, madness. The actual content of these works denies what their ritual context affirms."

[43] Ibid., 225.

city, and declared that the son would do the same. It was only after the orphans had taken an oath to this effect that the plays could begin.

The prominent tribute to the war dead and, indeed, the significant role granted to the sons of the fallen, both suggest the ways in which the rituals of public mourning were an integral part of the Great Dionysia. Indeed, John J. Winkler notes the appearance in Euripides' *Suppliant Women* of a chorus of the sons of the fallen who mourn their fathers and look forward to the day when they too can take up arms for the city. It suggests, he argues, the centrality of these rituals of mourning and militarism to the Festival, not least because there were significant restrictions on direct representation of Athenian life in tragic theater.[44] Given the importance of these rituals of public mourning to the Festival and of the Festival to the city – an importance suggested by the *theoric* fund, which paid the entrance fee for citizens otherwise too poor to attend – it is, perhaps, somewhat shocking for moderns to consider that these rituals extolling the city and the sacrifices of her war dead were immediately followed by theater that served to question the very values for which the soldiers were said to have given their lives. This tension between celebration and critique was, however, but one of the binary oppositions through which the Greeks made sense of the world. Greek prose was noted for the prevalence of binary opposites, and such juxtapositions, it has been argued, were central to the dialectical experience: a way of permitting the Greeks to reflect on the extremes of human existence in the hope – if not necessarily expectation – that both might be avoided.[45]

Inscribed at Delphi was a statement that has been translated as both "Remember your mortality" and "Nothing in excess."[46] The apparently close connection between these two concepts suggests the way in which,

---

[44] J. J. Winkler, "The Ephebes' Song: Tragoidia and Polis," *Representations* 11 (Summer), 1985, 33. See also Nicole Loraux, *Mothers in Mourning: With the Essay of Amnesty and Its Opposite* translated by Corinne Pache (Ithaca, NY: Cornell University Press, 1998). Such restrictions were aimed at limiting excess, even in the more directed mourning embodied by the Greek theater. Herodotus recounts the politically problematic response to Phrynichus's play *The Capture of Miletus*, which depicted the Persian sacking of a city dear to Athens. So powerful was the production that it moved its audience to tears, and "the author was fined a thousand drachmas for reminding them of their own evils, and they forbade anybody ever to put the play on the stage again." Herodotus, *The Histories*, translated by Aubrey de Sélincourt (New York: Penguin Books, 1994), 6.21.

[45] See, for example, Helene P. Foley, *Female Acts in Greek Tragedy* (Princeton, NJ: Princeton University Press, 2001), 8–9; and Nancy Sorkin Rabinowitz, *Greek Tragedy* (Chichester, UK: John Wiley & Sons, 2008). This is perhaps what Wittgenstein meant when he said that language games are connected to a form of life. Ludwig Wittgenstein, *Philosophical Investigations* (Oxford: Basil Blackwell, 2001).

[46] J. Peter Euben, *Platonic Noise* (Princeton, NJ: Princeton University Press, 2002), 17.

for the Greeks, excess was associated with death. The juxtaposition of opposites was meant to be a way of avoiding such excess and to achieve balance through the agonism of conflicting perspectives: negotiating between them so as not only to live, in Aristotle's phrase, but also to live well.[47] Excess was inextricably associated with a lack of vision: a one-sidedness that prevented the afflicted from seeing the partiality of his or her own perspective. Such lack of vision is evident in the protagonists of Athenian tragedy. Walter Kaufmann argues that hubris – the quality most often associated with tragic heroes – is best translated by contrasting it with "established usage, order, and right" and "moderation, temperance, [and] (self-) control."[48] In tragedy, such lack of self-control and disregard for the social order is inevitably associated with blindness: either literal, as in *Oedipus the King*, or figurative, as in *Antigone*. Such blindness is, furthermore, associated with a rigidity of mind. In the *Bacchae*, Pentheus' commitment to the polarities of his culture – expressed in platitudes – rather than to negotiating between them, leads to his demise. That his death arises from a rejection of the god Dionysos is suggestive of the consequences of the failure to embrace the perspective of both the Festival and its plays. It is here, perhaps, that the pedagogical and civic functions of the Great Dionysia are most clearly presented.

Simon Goldhill's suggestion that tragedy is "fundamentally questioning" captures the genre's moral complexity. Characters are not simply good or bad, but figures whose downfall often emerges from a failure to control what is best in them: figures caught in double binds with conflicting needs and desires. Tragedies are not simple morality plays requiring mimetic fidelity on the part of the citizenry. Rather, they demand that the audience engage in interpretation and contemplation. *Theōreō*, the origin of the modern word "theory," meant both to be a member of an audience and to engage in judging or comparison.[49] It is an activity essential to democracy, a political system whose very structure demands ongoing agonistic

---

[47] Aristotle, *Politics* translated by Carnes Lord (Chicago: University of Chicago Press, 1985). For the Greek concern with excess, see James Davidson, *Courtesans and Fishcakes: The Consuming Passions of Classical Athens* (New York: Harper Collins, 1997).

[48] Walter Kaufmann, *Tragedy and Philosophy* (Princeton, NJ: Princeton University Press, 1968).

[49] There are, of course, limits on what can plausibly be claimed here, and Simon Goldhill sensibly notes that he is "not suggesting that every member of an audience left the theater deeply perplexed and reflecting on the nature of civic ideology – but the picture of an audience uniformly and solely interested in 'pleasure,' 'entertainment,' is equally banal. What I hope to describe here is a tension between the Festival of drama as a civic institution and a reading of the texts of that institution." Goldhill, "The Great Dionysia and Civic Ideology," 115.

negotiation between conflicting viewpoints. Indeed, Sara Monoson suggests that such theatrical negotiation was more than merely training for the Assembly and Agora, but "a vigorous civic practice closely identified with the exercise of democratic citizenship."[50] For theater's audience, to fail to engage in the judgment demanded by the plays – to fail to embrace the theoretical perspective – was to risk emulating tragedy's protagonists. Indeed, one of tragedy's great ironies is that its protagonists are incapable of achieving the perspective that the plays seek to engender in their audiences. In contrast to Greek comedy, a genre marked by self-referential meta-theatricality, tragedy's protagonists were unable to see that they are characters in a play and were thus prevented from adopting the theoretical perspective that might otherwise have saved them from their fates. Goldhill's work suggests the ways in which the rituals surrounding the plays facilitated this tragic pedagogy. "The ceremonials before the play," he writes, "can bring the generals on the stage, and tragedy will then reveal the misplaced arrogance, disastrous overconfidence and failure of control of those in authority. The ceremonials before the plays may assert the military values of the state – yet drama after drama, set in a time of war, undermines all jingoism and certainty of purpose."[51] In this, the mourning rituals of Greek theater helped to cultivate the tragic perspective – or "bicameral orientation"[52] – of the Dionysia, an outlook that was considered central to democratic thought and practice.

The Great Dionysia offers then a second model of Athenian public mourning, one that Socrates – his own comments on the theater notwithstanding – would be hard pressed to dismiss. The juxtaposition of celebration and critique offered the possibility of agonism and dialectic and, with it, the further possibility of a complex love of the city – or tragic patriotism – one that sought to improve the polis even as it recognized the inevitability of its flaws. It is the possibility of an oration, tragic in structure and transfiguring in effect, that Thucydides demonstrates in his *History*.

THUCYDIDES' TRAGIC ORATION

From the outset of his *History of the Peloponnesian War*, Thucydides is keen to distinguish his work from that of his predecessors. Most obviously

---

[50] Monoson, *Plato's Democratic Entanglements*, 88.
[51] Goldhill, *Love, Sex & Tragedy*, 231.
[52] William Connolly, *Pluralism* (Durham, NC: Duke University Press, 2005), 4.

he identifies the ways in which his work differs from the poets "who exaggerate the importance of their themes" and the "prose chroniclers" who "are less interested in telling the truth than catching the attention of the public."[53] Nevertheless, he also signals that his work demands interpretation and judgment on the part of the reader. His proposal "to give an account of the causes of complaint" that the two sides had against each other, followed by his assertion that "the real reason for the war is, in my opinion most likely to be disguised by such an argument," suggests that his readers have to do more than simply pass their eyes over the text.[54] It demands that they construct the significance of these events for themselves. Nor is his narrative that of a disinterested observer. Thucydides' hope that his words will be "judged useful by those who wish to understand clearly the events which happened in the past and which (human nature being what it is) will, at some time or other and in much the same ways, be repeated in the future," suggests a definite pedagogical end.[55] That end seems to be making his readers move beyond their own partial perspectives: that of which Athens itself seemed incapable. Athens' focus on its own interests at the expense of all other values had, as James Boyd White points out, self-defeating consequences: like a tragic protagonist, it failed to recognize the limitations of its own perspective.[56] Indeed, the *History* echoes the institution of Greek tragedy in at least two other ways: first, by identifying community values and displaying the dangers of failing to balance them appropriately and second, by offering

[53] Thucydides, *History*, 47.
[54] Ibid., 49.
[55] Ibid., 48. It is particularly telling that during the "Civil War in Corcyra," when Thucydides famously declares that to "fit in with the change of events, words too had to change their usual meanings" (242), his narrative device breaks down and he is forced to break the fourth wall, telling his readers directly what they had hitherto been left to deduce for themselves. His method of seldom speaking in his own voice – much of the *History* is in the mimetic form criticized by Plato in the *Republic* or in the form of reportage – demands that the readers construct the significance of the events for themselves. Traditionally "mimetic" has been taken to mean exactly the sort of speech in which the *Republic* itself is presented – reported dialogues. Kaufmann argues, however, that "imitation" is but one of two senses of the word, the other being "pretending" or "make believe," suggesting that even the mimetic speech of the *History* should be regarded as more literary than historical. As such, the focus here – as in tragic theater – should be on the rhetorical effects of Thucydides' work rather than its historical accuracy. Kaufmann, *Tragedy and Philosophy*, 37–38.
[56] James Boyd White, *When Words Lose Their Meaning: Constitutions and Reconstitutions of Language, Character and Community* (Chicago: University of Chicago Press, 1984), 59–92.

its readers a potential corrective: the opportunity to negotiate between the two visions of Athens set forth in the Funeral Oration and the Plague.

While it is certainly true that the picture of Athens presented in Pericles' Funeral Oration is an exaggeratedly ideal one – where the city is just, the men are men, and the women are silent – it is not the only account of the city that Thucydides provides in Book Two of the *History*. He also gives an account – the "Plague of Athens" describing the actions of her citizens during a time of natural disaster – in which almost every virtue elaborated by Pericles is juxtaposed to and undercut by its opposite. It is particularly telling that he does so *directly* after the Oration. For, while it could be argued that the juxtaposition is motivated by simple historical chronology, Thucydides' stated aims in writing the text suggest that he chose to highlight certain aspects of the historical events and to play down others. In condensing his account of the events that occurred between the Funeral Oration and the Plague, Thucydides alerts his readers to the suggestion that there is more going on here than mere historical chronology. Indeed, his Dionysian juxtaposition of the two visions of Athens offers us a version of the tragic double perspective identified by Goldhill. It is one in which the virtues of Athens are thrown into sharp relief and problematized by the context in which they are presented. From one perspective, the audience hears Pericles' account of Athens' greatness; from the other, they can see how the very virtues of which he boasts are undercut by the actions of her citizens in a time of crisis. In so doing, Thucydides employs an oratorical device – the juxtaposition of binary opposites – from the Oration itself.[57]

In the Funeral Oration, there are several such juxtapositions: the one and the many; Athenians and others; male and female; past and present; and life and death. There is another such an opposition in the juxtaposition of the accounts of the Plague and the Funeral Oration, and indeed, in the *details* of these accounts. Most obviously, there is the opposition between the elaborate funeral rites accorded to the war dead and the *ad hoc* approach adopted during the Plague; Pericles' boast about Athens' law-abiding nature and the lawlessness brought about by epidemic; the opposition between honor, value, and tradition in the Oration, and "the pleasure of the moment, and everything that might conceivably contribute to that pleasure" of the plague period.[58] Additionally, there is the

---

[57] I am not the first to notice this juxtaposition. Typically, Peter Euben has been there before me. See J. Peter Euben, *The Tragedy of Political Theory: The Road Not Taken* (Princeton, NJ: Princeton University Press, 1990), 177.

[58] Thucydides, *History*, 155.

contrast between the care of the widows and orphans and the neglect of the sick; between citizens coming together for the Oration and staying in their houses during the illness; between the masculinity of the Oration and the impotence caused by the Plague; and between the historical memory of Athens recounted and constituted by the Oration and the loss of memory suffered by the sick, a loss that left them, unlike the Athens of the Oration, "unable to recognize their friends."[59] In setting up this juxtaposition of the two Athens, Thucydides offers his readers the opportunity for critical reflection: the chance to experience dialectic. They move between two worlds, recognizing that neither presents Athens in its entirety but that each is a partial perspective from which they should seek to construct a more-complex picture of the city and its actions. Thucydides offers a tragic, complex perspective and, with it, the opportunity to think critically about the events that he is presenting. He seeks not to sway his readers with uncritical nationalism in the way that Socrates suggests but instead offers them the possibility of a tragic and critical mourning: one in which the celebration makes the criticism palatable, and the criticism tempers the celebration, cultivating a complexity of perspective akin to that cultivated in the audience at the Great Dionysia. Thucydides' sophistication is such that he presents both models of public mourning simultaneously – one nationalistic, the other tragic – offering in effect, two Pericles and two orations.

The first Pericles is the Pericles of the Oration alone: the nationalistic Pericles. This Pericles embodies the partial perspective of tragedy's protagonists. His funeral oration offers an idealized view of Athens and demands little of its audience. Lacking a critical perspective sufficient to counterbalance its jingoistic militarism, the speech simply serves to perpetuate the basest instincts of the Athenian people, diminishing their capacity for critical reflection and hastening them down the road to ruin. It is a further measure of the sophistication of Thucydides' work that the pathos of this Pericles is intensified by his apparent struggle to understand his status as a character in a historical drama. There are several occasions on which this Pericles, like Oedipus, comes close – but not close *enough* – to understanding his fate. Two such moments occur when he attempts to inject some restraint into the Oration but is ultimately overwhelmed by the weight of its conventions. Pericles says of his oratorical predecessors,

It seemed to them a mark of honor to our soldiers who have fallen in the war that a speech should be made over them. I do not agree. These men have shown

[59] Ibid.

themselves valiant in action, and it would be enough, I think for their glories to be proclaimed in action, as you have done as this funeral organized by the state.⁶⁰

What might be intended as a note of caution becomes, in the context of the oration and its surrounding ceremonies, a kind of *occupatio*: a way of multiplying the efficacy of words by denying their value. Consequently, when this Pericles later claims that the Athenians "do not think there is an incompatibility between words and deeds,"⁶¹ even as he has undermined this claim at the outset of his speech, the interpretive demand that this claim makes on its audience is restricted to suggesting a purpose of the Oration greater than eulogizing the dead: the glorification of Athens. Any notes of caution struck by the speaker are distorted by the kind of nationalism engendered by the Oration absent an awareness of the tragic context provided by the Great Dionysia. As with any tragic protagonist, the words of the nationalistic Pericles have unintended consequences: they do so because he lacks the perspective offered by the tragic Pericles.

The tragic Pericles is the Pericles of the context established by Thucydides' presentation of the oration juxtaposed with the plague in a way that mimics the structure of the Dionysia. This Pericles embodies the theoretical perspective of tragedy's audience. If the role of the first Pericles is to teach the audience of the dangers of the kind of nationalism engendered by the Funeral Oration absent any critical perspective, the role of the tragic Pericles is to show Thucydides' audience how the perspective of the nationalistic Pericles might be avoided. The difference between the two Pericles is, then, the difference between the perspective of tragedy's protagonists and tragedy's audience: between a one-sided perspective and a theoretical one. In this sense, then, Socrates is right about the funeral oration tradition but wrong about Thucydides. Indeed, Thucydides seems not only to be aware of the problems inherent in the oration tradition but also to have preempted Socrates' critique. The dramatic irony arising from Thucydides' presentation of the tragic Pericles seeks to affect his readers in the same way that Oedipus' attempts to escape his fate sought to affect Sophocles' audience: drawing them into an interpretive and agonistic exercise conducive to developing a more critical perspective than those depicted in the text.

The historical Athens, of course, adopted the perspective of the nationalistic Pericles. Despite this Pericles' best efforts, the Athenians saw in the Oration only what they wished to see. It was a disastrous mode

⁶⁰ Ibid., 144.
⁶¹ Ibid., 147.

of – nontheoretical – reading further evidenced by their response to the Dorian myth at the end of the Plague section:

At a time of distress people naturally recalled old oracles, and among them was a verse which the old men claimed had been delivered in the past and which said:
War with the Dorians comes, and a death will come at the same time.
There had been a controversy as to whether the word in this ancient verse was "dearth" rather than "death"; but in the present state of affairs the view that the word was "death" naturally prevailed; it was a case of people adapting their memories to suit their sufferings.[62]

In reading into the myth precisely that which they wished to see, the Athenians demonstrated the one-sidedness of thought and vision endemic to both nationalism and the protagonists of tragedy. They abandoned the kind of critical thinking and evaluation that had been at the heart of their democratic practices in favor of a fear-motivated embrace of historical platitude. When viewed through the perspective established by the second Pericles, however, the suffering that resulted from Athens' embrace of nationalist platitudes becomes a lesson for the readers of the text. In drawing attention to the way in which the Athenians adopted a single perspective on the ancient myth, Thucydides alerts his readers to the dangers of failing to engage in critical reflection: the failure, that is, to engage in the proper practices of democratic citizenship. The consequences of this lack of critical reflection are depicted in the tragic structure of the *History* as a whole, where Athens, the most powerful nation in the Greek world, is humiliated, her fleet and democracy destroyed by hubris. In this, the nationalistic Pericles becomes an "education to Greece" in a way that he simply could not know. With dramatic irony, the author appeals over the head of his character to his readers, teaching them a lesson that this Pericles could never learn.

Thucydides offers us then two models of public mourning, each corresponding to a particular Pericles and a particular perspective. He suggests that each model has definite consequences for the polity that chooses it. One corresponds to the nationalistic Pericles who gave an oration that was a manifestation of the kind of blindness and one-sidedness of thought endemic to the protagonists of tragedy. As such, it was what Socrates suggests that democratic orations must necessarily be: banal, anachronistic, unquestioning in its patriotism, and committed to unity and consensus. It is a model of public mourning that may simply perpetuate the need for funeral ceremonies by precipitating further deaths. The other corresponds

---

[62] Ibid., 156.

to the tragic Pericles, a figure from whom the reader derives the theoretical capacity for a more complex perspective on Athens and its actions. The context of his funeral oration – juxtaposed with Thucydides' account of the Plague – echoes that of the Great Dionysia and makes its tragically patriotic perspective anything but banal and unquestioning. It offers the opportunity for critical reflection on the values that are presented and, with it, the potential for a more complex, less hubristic perspective.

Together, these models constitute a lens through which to view the two moments of American mourning linked by the reading of the Gettysburg Address. Such an analysis suggests that while the 1863 reading offered its listeners the opportunity to consider its values and embrace a new political identity, the 2002 reading offered little more than the nationalistic commitments satirized by Socrates in the *Menexenus*.

PERICLES AT GETTYSBURG

The Gettysburg Address was delivered publicly by Abraham Lincoln on November 19, 1863, at the dedication of the cemetery for the nearly ten thousand men who fell during the battle fought in the first three days of July of that year. Lincoln was not, of course, the main speaker at the commemoration. That honor fell to the orator and classics scholar Edward Everett. His speech lasted more than two hours, Lincoln's not much more than two minutes. Both, however, demonstrated the influence of a nineteenth-century revival in Greek thought: what Rome had been to the Founding Fathers, Greece was to Lincoln's generation.[63] As might be expected of a noted classicist, Everett identified the Greek pedigree for both the commemoration and his oration, invoking and quoting Pericles in his closing remarks. Lincoln made no such mention of the Greeks. Nevertheless, as befits one whose wife conducted séances in the White House and members of whose cabinet engaged in the popular craze of "spirit-rapping," Lincoln simply seemed to channel Athens' most prominent citizen.[64]

The considerable similarities between Pericles' Funeral Oration and the Gettysburg Address suggest the strong possibility that the former influenced the latter. Just as Pericles failed to identify a single Athenian by name, Lincoln is equally circumspect, referring only to "a great battle-field," "the brave men," "these honored dead," and "this nation."[65] Lincoln

---

[63] Wills, *Lincoln at Gettysburg*, 43.

[64] Thomas Keneally, *Abraham Lincoln* (New York: Penguin Books, 2003), 118–119.

[65] All references to the Gettysburg Address come from Abraham Lincoln, *Speeches and Writings 1859–1865* (New York: Library of America, 1989), 536.

similarly identifies the community conventions that make the speech an appropriate one. "It is," he declared, "altogether fitting and proper that we should do this." Pericles' possibly inadvertent *occupatio* finds its parallel in Lincoln's more deliberate use of the device in the Address. "But in a larger sense," he asserted, "we cannot dedicate – we cannot consecrate – we cannot hallow – this ground. The brave men, living and dead, who struggled here, have consecrated it, far above our power to add or detract." Indeed, the irony of Lincoln's claim that the "World will little note, nor long remember what we say here," even as he was keeping at least one eye on posterity, suggests that he was seeking to emulate Pericles' ultimately failed attempt at an interrogative oration: inviting the audience into an interpretive exercise, one that suggested a purpose of the speech greater than that of merely eulogizing the dead. Like Pericles' speech, Lincoln's Address also followed the conventions of the oration, invoking both *epainesis* and *parainesis*. Lincoln extols "those who here gave their lives that the nation might live" and asserts that: "It is rather for us to be here dedicated to the great task remaining before us – that from these honored dead we take increased devotion to that cause for which they gave the last full measure of devotion." Indeed, Lincoln's speech is almost all *parainesis*, and it is clear that like that of Pericles, its focus is the living not the dead.

The similarities between the two speeches extend from their content to their contexts. Both were delivered in wartime by – at least nominally – military men: a general and a Commander-in-Chief. Both were concerned, in part, with the immediate concerns of the conflict in which they were engaged. As a wartime president, Lincoln faced a number of pressing political problems: forthcoming elections in several states including Maine, Massachusetts, Pennsylvania, and Ohio threatened his own prospects for reelection; and paradoxically, perhaps, Union victories at Vicksburg and Gettysburg had strengthened the belief that the Confederacy was on its last legs and increased the pressure on the president to make peace and restore the Union "as was."[66] As such, a number of prominent figures including Horace Greeley and John Murray Forbes had urged Lincoln to make a speech identifying the causes of the war and the conditions for peace, and the funeral oration at Gettysburg provided him an opportunity to do just that. Less obviously, the imperialist aspects of Pericles' Funeral Oration are, perhaps, paralleled in Lincoln's desire to impose his vision of the war on both the North and the South. Lincoln,

---

[66] David Herbert Donald, *Lincoln* (New York: Simon & Schuster, 1995), 455.

who refused to countenance the war as anything other than at most a *civil* war – despite the obvious Southern claims to the contrary – was nevertheless keen to make his conception of the conflict clear to the watching world, especially to those who might have been tempted to recognize the Confederacy and further complicate the conflict or a potential peace.

If, as the similarities between the speeches might suggest, Pericles' Funeral Oration was indeed the inspiration for the Gettysburg Address, or even just a useful heuristic, in the context of the established typology, it raises the questions: which Pericles, and which oration? Having delivered two previous funeral orations – those of Zachary Taylor and Henry Clay – Lincoln was well aware of the potential for misrepresentation inherent in the eulogy. In 1858, at the funeral of a famously vain politician, Lincoln is said to have observed that if the deceased had "known how big a funeral he would have, he would have died years ago."[67] Likewise, his oft-told anecdote about the man who, when asked what he meant by his claim "I feel patriotic," responded "I feel like either killing somebody or stealing something," suggests a similar awareness of the potential problems posed by a certain kind of patriotism.[68] It is then no surprise to find that Lincoln – with his well-known love of theater, and tragedy in particular[69] – offered a funeral oration that mimicked the complexity of the Great Dionysia in its structure and potentially transfiguring effect: one that celebrated a nation with a government of, by, and for the people but that also sought to shift its self-understanding by offering a critique both of its actions and of the Constitution on which it was based. It is an oration that suggests that his was the tragic Pericles.

The boldest claims about the nature and origin of the transfiguring qualities of the Gettysburg Address have been made by Garry Wills. The 1863 mourners, he declares, "walked off, from those curving graves on the hillside; under a changed sky, into a different America. Lincoln had revolutionized the Revolution, giving people a new past to live with that would change their future indefinitely."[70] The Address, he argues, had the significant effect of making the United States a singular noun, thereby shoring up the intellectual claims of the Union. The sources of this transfiguration were, he suggests, two movements between "the ideal and the real": one

---

[67] Merrill D. Peterson, *Lincoln in American Memory* (New York: Oxford University, 1994), 102.

[68] Allen, "*The Menexenus* Comment," 324–325.

[69] Doris Kearns Goodwin, *Team of Rivals: The Political Genius of Abraham Lincoln* (New York: Simon & Schuster, 2005), 723.

[70] Wills, *Lincoln at Gettysburg*, 38.

physical, the other intellectual.[71] The first claim is, nevertheless, somewhat problematic. Noting the importance of the rural cemetery movement in nineteenth-century America, Wills suggests that the mourners' *physical* movement between the burial space where the Address was delivered and the America outside the cemetery was a source of transfiguring contrast. While it is always possible that such a movement had a transfiguring effect on *some* citizens, the Greek experience suggests that this is not a particularly convincing explanation of any such change. For the Athenians, there would have been a similar physical movement between the *ceramicos* – the burial space outside the city walls where Pericles spoke – and the city of Athens. It is, however, clear that this movement was insufficient to transfigure the outlook of Athens' mourners; indeed, it is precisely the absence of this transfiguration that Thucydides seems to be lamenting in his *History*. As such, Wills seems to be on much stronger ground when he discusses the way in which the Address brought the Declaration of Independence into dialogue with the Constitution.

The math involved in the famous opening sentence of the Address, math that, perhaps, forces the listener in to an interpretive exercise similar to that demanded by the tragic Pericles, connects the Address not to the Constitution but to the Declaration of Independence. It asserts that a *nation* – not a confederation of states – was founded in 1776, one "dedicated to the proposition that all men are created equal." In arguing that the Declaration was the real founding document of the nation, Lincoln called into question both the Constitution and the 1857 Dred Scott decision in which the Supreme Court had held that African Americans were excluded from the rights of citizenship enshrined in it. That the radicalism of Lincoln's claim is now all but lost to a contemporary audience is a measure of his success at Gettysburg: so much is the current polity a part of the "new birth of freedom" that he helped to create. For, in 1863, the view that African Americans were guaranteed the freedoms granted by the Constitution as a direct result of the claims made in the Declaration was a view most commonly associated with radicals and abolitionists. Indeed, David Blight argues that Frederick Douglass was "the intellectual godfather of the Gettysburg Address."[72] As early as 1800, the slave

---

[71] Ibid., 103.

[72] David W. Blight, *Race and Reunion: The Civil War in American Memory* (Cambridge, MA: Harvard University Press, 2001), 15. In a previously published version of this chapter, I wrongly discounted this suggestion in favor of the classical thesis. The issue is, however, much less clear-cut than I initially suggested. Certainly the work of Douglass and other abolitionists made Lincoln's transfiguring moment possible. Part of Lincoln's

Gabriel Prosser cited the Declaration as justification for his plan to attack Richmond, Virginia, as did Denmark Vesey for his planned attack on Charleston, South Carolina, in 1822. That Lincoln himself had made the claim on at least one previous occasion suggests that part of what made Gettysburg so notable was the *context* of his claim.[73] On an occasion when most were expecting the platitudes of the funeral oration, Lincoln offered a speech that, while celebrating the nation and its founding and lamenting the war dead, was also highly critical of its current practices. It was a tragic oration – Dionysian in structure and effect – in which the celebration of the nation was offset by a critique whose impact was to shift America's understanding of both itself and its key documents.

It is a paradox of Lincoln's transcendence of the platitudes of the funeral oration that his achievement was to establish another such platitude: his controversial claim about the Declaration of Independence becoming part of the bedrock understanding of the Constitution. Just as Thomas Paine had earlier helped precipitate the Declaration by presenting his views in such a way that they became the "Common Sense" of his title, Lincoln's political poetry at Gettysburg helped make his view "that all men are created equal" extended to African Americans all but unchallengeable and ultimately as "self-evident" as it was initially claimed.[74] Whether one agrees with McPherson's claim that Lincoln won the war with metaphors, it is clear that Lincoln's language helped – initially at least –win the peace.[75] For although the Civil War Amendments that formally ended slavery, established equal protection under the law, and granted voting rights

success emerged, no doubt, from who he was and where and when he was speaking. Lincoln did not conjure his argument about the Declaration out of thin air. Claims about Douglass's influence are, however, not incompatible with the suggestion that Lincoln was influenced by the Greeks. If Douglass provided the political and intellectual impetus and context for the Address, the Greeks may have helped provide its rhetorical form. See Simon Stow, "Agonistic Homegoing: Frederick Douglass, Joseph Lowery, and the Democratic Value of African American Public Mourning," *American Political Science Review*, 104(14), 2010: 687, *n.* 10.

[73] Celebrating the Union victories at Gettysburg and Vicksburg, Lincoln foreshadowed the Address on July 4, 1863. "How long is it?" he asked. "Eighty-odd years – since on the Fourth of July for the first time in the history of the world a nation by its representatives assembled and declared as a self-evident truth that 'all men are created equal.'" Lincoln, *Speeches and Writings*, 475.

[74] See Jacques Derrida, "Declarations of Independence," *New Political Science*, 15, 1986: 7–15; and Bonnie Honig, "Declarations of Independence: Arendt and Derrida on the Problem of Founding a Republic," *American Political Science Review* 85(1) 1991: 97–113.

[75] James M. McPherson, *Abraham Lincoln and the Second American Revolution* (New York: Oxford University Press, 1991), 93–112.

to African Americans, were all passed after Lincoln's death, his success in making the language of the Declaration part of our understanding of the Constitution was, as Eric Foner's work illustrates, central both to these achievements and to later African-American political mobilization.[76] The impact of the Address can also be measured in at least three other ways. First, in the number of times that the president was asked to provide autographed copies of the speech: there are at least five copies in Lincoln's own hand, more than for any other document he ever wrote.[77] Second, in the contrast between the reverence with which the actual physical document of the Declaration is treated today – carefully displayed and protected at the National Archives Rotunda – and the way in which it was all but neglected, in stark contrast to the Constitution itself, during the early Republic. Indeed, on November 19, 1863, the already battered and faded document was hanging opposite a large window in the Government Patent Office in Washington, DC.[78] Finally, in the strong responses that Lincoln's words at Gettysburg drew from the press. Their reaction suggested that his funeral oration transcended the simple flattery that Socrates believed was inherent in the genre. Although the *Chicago Tribune* asserted that, "The dedicatory remarks of President Lincoln will live among the annals of the war,"[79] the *Chicago Times* railed that

It was to uphold this constitution, and the Union created by it that our officers and soldiers gave their lives at Gettysburg. How dare he, then, standing on their graves, misstate the cause for which they died, and libel the statesmen who founded the government? They were men possessing too much self-respect to declare that Negroes were their equals, or where entitled to equal privileges.[80]

By consciously or unconsciously taking the tragic Pericles as his model, Lincoln was able to offer an oration that mimicked the Dionysia – in

---

[76] Eric Foner, *A Shorter History of Reconstruction* (New York: Harper Collins, 1990). The continuing importance of the Address to the American struggle for racial equality is evidenced by its role in another moment in American history in which a speech mimicked the Great Dionysia: the 1963 March on Washington. Both John Lewis and Martin Luther King invoked the promise of the Declaration in their speeches at the Lincoln Memorial, with King in particular seeking to write a "sort of Gettysburg Address" that began with the phrase "Five score years ago" and that called on America to fulfill the promise of Jefferson's document. Drew D. Hansen, *The Dream: Martin Luther King, Jr., and the Speech that Inspired a Nation* (New York: Harper Collins, 2003), 47, 65, 69.

[77] Donald, *Lincoln*, 465.

[78] See Pauline Maier, *American Scripture: Making the Declaration of Independence* (New York: Vintage Books, 1997).

[79] R. C. White, *The Eloquent President: A Portrait of Lincoln Through His Words* (New York: Random House, 2005), 256.

[80] Wills, *Lincoln at Gettysburg*, 38–39.

its juxtaposition of celebration of the nation's founding and its critique of her current practices – to seek a transfiguring effect. "His outwardly smooth sentences," wrote Carl Sandburg, "were inside of them gnarled and tough with the enigmas of the American experiment."[81]

Identifying Thucydides' importance to the Gettysburg Address is not, of course, to diminish Lincoln's oratorical and political skill; it is, rather, to add to the understanding of the richness of the speech. It is, however, also to move away from a reliance on that skill to explain Lincoln's success at Gettysburg and to identify the possibility of a tragic public mourning whose impact is to help alleviate – rather than exacerbate – the tensions that made such mourning necessary; one that might be revived in Lincoln's absence. By adopting the theoretical perspective of the tragic Pericles rather than the partial perspective of the nationalist one, Lincoln's oration was able to help America achieve a complex and critical perspective on its own values and thereby to adopt a new political identity and embrace new political solutions in the face of mass death. In 2002, however, the re-reading of the Address seemed to have the opposite effect.

PERICLES AT GROUND ZERO

For many critics, the most puzzling aspect of the September 2002 commemoration of the New York City dead was the decision by the event organizers to eschew any original oratory in favor not only of the Gettysburg Address but also readings from the Declaration of Independence and Roosevelt's Four Freedoms. One of the most commonly cited justifications for the decision was "politics," or, more precisely, the desire to avoid anything that smacked of partisanship. State Assembly Speaker Sheldon Silver noted that there was "a desire not to make it a political event,"[82] while New York City Mayor Michael Bloomberg asserted, "One of the things I've tried very hard to do in the ceremonies for 9/11 is to keep politics out of it."[83] The tension in such claims is, however, suggested by Bloomberg's further claim about the readings. "[E]verybody's flying the American flag,"

---

[81] Carl Sandburg, *Abraham Lincoln: The War Years 1861–1865* (New York: Tess Press, 2005), 316.

[82] Joel Stashenko, "Pataki will read cherished speech on Sept. 11," *Associated Press State & Local Wire*, September 8, 2002.

[83] Randal C. Archibold, "Political Ad and 9/11 Speech May Be an Unwelcome Mix," *New York Times*, August 15, 2002. www.nytimes.com/2002/08/15/nyregion/political-ad-and-9-11-speech-may-be-an-unwelcome-mix.html. Accessed Jan. 22, 2014.

he observed, "– what's wrong with a little patriotism?"[84] In the context of the history of the funeral oration, the claim that such a public eulogy is "nonpolitical" is obviously somewhat problematic. The bigger issue, however, appears to be the partiality of perspective suggested by the claim that patriotism and seeking to inculcate such patriotism are not in themselves political acts, not least, perhaps, because – absent any critical outlook – "nationalism" might be a better word for the perspective they sought to achieve. The implicit assumption of consensus, that American values are – in some sense – neutral seems to suggest the figurative blindness of tragedy's protagonists: the inability to see the contingency of their own perspectives. It is a justification that suggests that the Pericles at Ground Zero was the nationalist Pericles, a suggestion that seems to be borne out by the pertinence of Socrates' critique to the 2002 commemoration.

Socrates' complaint that such orations are "prepared long in advance" and mindlessly repeated in perpetuity obviously hits its target in the 2002 commemoration, not least because this was not the first occasion on which the Address had been used as a eulogy or a rallying cry. As early as 1868, Edward Stanton, campaigning for Ulysses S. Grant in Pennsylvania, delivered the Address and declared: "This is the voice of God speaking through the lips of Abraham Lincoln! ... You hear the voice of Father Abraham tonight. Did he die in vain?"[85] Similarly, Allen Sandburg's famous "Remember Dec. 7th!" poster issued by the Office of War Information in response to the attack on Pearl Harbor featured the words "... we here highly resolve that these dead shall not have died in vain ..." over a tattered American flag flying at half-staff before a billowing cloud of smoke.[86] As such, Socrates' complaint that the oration was filled with little more than commonplaces finds its target twice over. First, by making its equality claim a platitude, Lincoln's Address became something of a self-consuming artifact, one whose initial effect on its audience destroyed the possibility of it ever being heard in the same way again: so powerful was its effect that by the time of its subsequent readings, the

[84] Michael R. Bloomberg, "Threats and Responses: Perspectives/Mayor Michael R. Bloomberg; 'We Owe It to Those We Lost to Expand Our Quest,'" *New York Times*, September 11, 2002. www.nytimes.com/2002/09/11/us/threats-responses-perspectives-mayor-michael-r-bloomberg-we-owe-it-those-that-we.html?pagewanted=all&src=pm. Accessed Jan. 22, 2014.
[85] David Herbert Donald, *Lincoln Reconsidered: Essays on the Civil War Era* Third Edition, Revised and Updated (New York: Vintage Books, 2001), 6.
[86] Emily Rosenberg, *A Date Which Will Live: Pearl Harbor in American Memory* (Durham, NC: Duke University Press, 2002).

Address could only ever be a reminder of something already believed to be true.[87] Second, the multiple subsequent uses of the Address made it the sort of commonplace against which Socrates railed. Indeed, the speech has become so much a part of the American national consciousness that its only capacity to shock or to transfigure lies in, perhaps, just how much of a commonplace it has become: a billboard for a shopping mall outside the town of Gettysburg once declared it, "*The* Gettysburg Address for Shopping."[88] As one commentator observed, "The Gettysburg Address is more than a eulogy. It's a soybean, a versatile little problem solver that can be processed into seemingly infinite, ingenious products."[89]

Socrates' complaint about the anachronistic qualities of the funeral oration was similarly pertinent in 2002. Most obviously this was signaled when New York Governor George Pataki read the line, "Four score and seven years ago our fathers brought forth on this continent, a new nation," a claim that was off by some nearly seven-score years. More than this, however, the Address – in its anonymity – contrasted sharply with the modern tendency toward personalization of the dead. In the "Guiding Principles" of the *World Trade Center Memorial Competition Guidelines,* first among the design requirements was that a memorial "Recognize each individual who was a victim of the attacks."[90] Indeed, the winning design, "Reflecting Absence" by Michael Arad and Peter Walker, incorporates a ribbon listing the names of the 2,983 victims of the 1993 and 2001 attacks, with police officers, firefighters, and rescue workers designated with their departmental affiliations.[91] The memorial commemorating the 184 people killed at the Pentagon on September 11, 2001, is similarly rich in individual detail. Each victim is memorialized by an individual marker: 59 facing toward the Pentagon, commemorating those killed in the building; 125 facing outward, commemorating those killed on American Airlines Flight 77.[92] This tendency toward greater individual commemoration extends then to drawing attention to the

---

[87] Fish, *Self-Consuming Artifacts,* 40.
[88] Sarah Vowell, *The Partly Cloudy Patriot* (New York: Simon and Schuster, 2002), 1. The modern-day parallel would, of course, be something like "Ground Zero for Savings."
[89] Ibid., 5.
[90] Lower Manhattan Development Corporation, *World Trade Center Memorial Competition Guidelines* (New York: Lower Manhattan Development Corporation, 2003), 19.
[91] www.911memorial.org. Accessed Jan. 22, 2014. See also Simon Stow, "From Upper Canal to Lower Manhattan: Memorialization and the Politics of Loss," *Perspectives on Politics,* 10 (3), 2012: 687–700.
[92] pentagonmemorial.org. Accessed Jan. 22, 2014.

details of the victims' deaths, suggesting that it is only by breaking down such events into their constitutive parts that many in the contemporary polity can seek to comprehend it.[93] It also serves to obscure still further the political aspects of such loss, drawing attention away from the tensions and policies that produced it. To compensate for the unfashionable lack of specificity of the Gettysburg Address in 2002, a list of the names of the 2,801 people then believed to have been killed in the Towers and planes was read out by a parade of dignitaries and celebrities. The reading paused twice – at 9:04 AM to mark the moment when United Airlines Flight 175 hit the South Tower and at 10:29 AM when the second tower collapsed – drawing attention, once again, to the details of the victims' deaths.[94]

The Socratic criticism that the funeral oration is necessarily ill fitting also played out in the claims about nationalistic or patriotic sacrifice implicit in the Address. For while Donald Rumsfeld's invocation of the speech at the Pentagon ceremony on the same day *might* be considered appropriate for the victims of that attack – for the Pentagon workers, if not the passengers and crew on Flight 77 – it is unlikely that any of the World Trade Center victims saw their quotidian activities of work and travel as being in any sense part of a commitment to nation.[95] Indeed, even though these were clearly attacks on America, the number of non-Americans killed – including many undocumented

---

[93] The memorial to the Oklahoma City Bombing consists, in part, of 168 bronze chairs, one for every person who was killed there. Nineteen of those chairs are half size to memorialize the children who were killed in the Murrah Building's day-care center. Maya Lin's Vietnam War Memorial in Washington, DC, which lists the names of the 58,158 Americans killed in that conflict is an earlier example. Among the rejected designs for the World Trade Center Memorial was one with sculptures of two planes, with each passenger and crew member's name inscribed in their seat and another that featured figures in business attire falling from the sky. www.wtcsitememorial.org. Accessed Feb. 23, 2014. Moreover, *The New York Times* series "Portraits in Grief," later published in book form, which gave mini-biographies of those killed in the attacks. For a discussion of the problems posed to democracy by this kind of Homeric individuation of the dead, see Simon Stow, "*Portraits 9/11/01: The New York Times* and the Pornography of Grief" in *Literature After 9/11* edited by Jeanne Follansbee Quinn and Ann Keniston (New York: Routledge, 2008), 224–241.

[94] Dan Barry, "Vigilance and Memory: Ceremonies. A Day of Tributes and the Litany of the Lost," *The New York Times*, September 12, 2002. www.nytimes.com/2002/09/12/us/vigilance-memory-ceremonies-day-tributes-tears-litany-lost.html?pagewanted=all&src=pm. Accessed Jan. 22, 2014.

[95] See John Tierney, "Vigilance and Memory: The Pentagon Ceremony. Honoring Those Lost and Celebrating a New Symbol of Resilience," *The New York Times*, September 12, 2002. www.nytimes.com/2002/09/12/us/vigilance-memory-pentagon-ceremony-honoring-those-lost-celebrating-new-symbol.html. Accessed Jan. 22, 2014.

foreign workers – should necessarily complicate any attempt to invoke a nationalistic narrative.[96] That it does not suggests that Socrates was right about the all-consuming nature of the nationalism engendered by this kind of funeral oration. Much the same might be said about the nation's willingness to invoke this trope of nationalistic sacrifice seemingly irrespective of the circumstances. Speaking at the dedication of the memorial to those killed by domestic terrorists in the Alfred P. Murrah Building in Oklahoma City on Patriot's Day, 1995, President Clinton declared, "there are places in our national landscape so scarred by freedom's sacrifice that they shape forever the soul of America – Valley Forge, Gettysburg, Selma. This place is sacred ground." As with the World Trade Center victims, however, it is hard to see how federal workers going about their business – and, indeed, the nineteen children killed in the Murrah Building's day care center – could be regarded as freedom fighters. "These people's lives," observed Linenthal, "were not given in an act of conscious sacrifice for their nation; they were taken in an act of mass murder. The landscape to which Oklahoma City is connected is not Valley Forge, Gettysburg, and Selma but sites of political terrorism and mass murder: the Sixteenth Street Baptist Church in Birmingham, Alabama, the McDonald's in San Diego, and Columbine High School."[97] Ground Zero is another such location, but as Socrates noted, a key feature of the kind of worldview engendered by the nationalistic funeral oration is its capacity to elide important distinctions. Indeed, the kind of mourning embodied in the choice of the Gettysburg Address as a eulogy in September 2002 not only serves to obscure specificity and truth, it also seems to undermine the quest for it.

If the mode of mourning employed at Gettysburg provided a language useful for negotiating the tensions that had led to mass death, the mode of mourning at Ground Zero seems to have produced a nationalistic language useful only for exacerbating them. This is seen most obviously in the use of such language to evade critical inquiry into the attacks. One example stands for many. Among those killed in the World Trade Center were an estimated 200 firefighters believed to have been inside the North Tower when it collapsed, this despite a general evacuation order having

---

[96] Lawrence Wright, *The Looming Tower: Al-Qaeda and the Road to 9/11* (New York: Alfred A. Knopf, 2006), 368. Erika Doss notes that the victims of the September 2001 attacks came from 92 countries. Erika Doss, *Memorial Mania: Public Feeling in America* (Chicago: University of Chicago Press, 2010), 120.

[97] Edward T. Linenthal, *Unfinished Bombing:Oklahoma City in American Memory* (New York: Oxford University Press, 2001), 234.

been issued following the collapse of the first Tower. Due to a series of communication problems, including a lack of working interagency radios and territorial disputes between the services, many of those in the North Tower did not receive the order: of the fifty-eight firefighters who escaped, only four said that they had known that the South Tower had fallen. Nevertheless, in 2004, at the official inquiry into the emergency response, former New York City Mayor Rudolph Giuliani asserted that those in the North Tower received the evacuation order but elected to stay to help civilians. "Rather than giving us a story of men, uniformed men fleeing while civilians were left behind," he observed, unconsciously echoing the nationalist Pericles, "which would have been devastating to the morale of this country ... they gave us an example of very, very brave men and women in uniform who stand their ground to protect civilians ... Instead of that we got a story of heroism and we got a story of pride and we got a story of support that helped get us through."[98] When the Commission of inquiry into the attacks raised questions about these deaths and their relationship to the Fire Department's shortcomings, New York City Officials – including both Giuliani and Mayor Bloomberg – responded with outrage, demanding to know how anyone could challenge the bravery, sacrifices, or heroism of the firefighters.[99]

A crisis, wrote Hannah Arendt, only becomes a disaster "when we respond to it with preformed judgments."[100] That much of America responded to the September 2001 attacks with little more than preformed judgments is suggested by the familiarity of the responses to this supposedly "unique" event. The claims of "lost innocence" that accompanied the attacks were far from original: industrialization, the Mexican-American War, Pearl Harbor, and Watergate were all moments when America had previously claimed to have lost her virtue.[101] Even the alleged novelty of the "Bush Doctrine" of preemption is compromised by its reliance on the long-standing trope of American innocence in a world of sin, one in which a dehistoricized evil attacked a morally righteous nation. This partiality of perspective and uncritical use of the past is manifested in and perpetuated by the adoption of a mode of mourning that simply echoed

[98] Jim Dwyer and Kevin Flynn, *102 Minutes: The Untold Story of the Fight to Survive Inside the Twin Towers* (New York: Times Books, 2005), 251–252. cf. "In the fighting, they thought it more honorable to stand their ground and suffer death than to give in and save their lives." Thucydides, *History*, 149.

[99] Dwyer and Flynn, *102 Minutes*, 251–252.

[100] Hannah Arendt, *Between Past and Future* (New York: Penguin Books, 1989), 174–175.

[101] Linenthal, *Unfinished Bombing*, 17.

the nationalist Pericles, one that celebrated – but failed to acknowledge the limits of – American virtue. Whereas Lincoln's turn to the past was self-conscious and critical, producing an oration that exhibited similar qualities, the contemporary turn was, like the oration it produced, largely unreflective and uncritical. It is a difference that suggests that the contemporary American polity has lost a certain capacity for critical self-analysis, what is here being termed a tragic or Dionysian perspective. "To say something worthwhile," observed Hendrik Henderson of the 2002 commemoration, "you'd probably have to say something that everyone would agree with."[102] In the choice of the Gettysburg Address – the voices of a few critics not withstanding – America seemed to achieve exactly that. That this bland consensus should be considered "worthwhile" is, perhaps, evidence of the almost complete absence of a self-critical perspective from the mourning rituals of the contemporary polity. It is an absence that produces a nationalist mourning demanding little more than a recommitment to an idealized understanding of the *status quo* rather than a tragic approach seeking a critical perspective on the nation's actions and values. Grief, in this context, marks out dissent as deviance and shores up state power at the expense of the citizenry.

RECALLING OLD ORACLES

Death, as John Seery argued in *Political Theory for Mortals*, can be a moment to engender great critical reflection.[103] A polity's capacity for such critical reflection might be both measured – and, indeed, expanded – by its willingness to adopt a critical mode of mourning akin to that of the Festival of Dionysia, one that avoids the simple comforts of the traditional oration in favor of a more complex and agonistic perspective. Although it might be asked what is wrong with a rhetorical address at a time of crisis – denying the bereaved any modicum of comfort seems churlish to say the least – there is, nevertheless, an important distinction to be drawn between private grief and the rituals of public mourning. Public ceremonies and the stories told there help shape policy. The idealized view of Athens presented by the nationalistic Pericles produced a policy of arrogance and insensitivity that culminated in the slaughter at Melos and ended in Athens' eventual defeat and humiliation. The story told by Lincoln at Gettysburg paved the way for a more just and equitable

[102] McWhorter, *Doing Our Own Thing*, xxii.
[103] John Seery, *Political Theory for Mortals Shades of Justice, Images of Death* (Ithaca, NY: Cornell University Press, 1996).

America. In the first instance, the nationalistic oration lacked any critical perspective, and Athens continued on her path to self-destruction. In the second, the self-analysis to which Lincoln's Address subjected America produced quite a different nation. In both instances, the public stories told about the dead affected the policies of the living.

It is, of course, hard to say what *should* have been said in New York City on the first anniversary of the 2001 attacks. The aim of this chapter is simply to identify the apparent absence from the contemporary polity of a tragic or Dionysian perspective that might produce or have produced a more critical mode of public mourning. Nevertheless, it might be argued that a polity with a more well-developed tragic perspective – one able to read both the Declaration of Independence *and* Frederick Douglass's "What to a Slave is the Fourth of July?" as part of its national celebrations – would certainly have been one capable of a more nuanced and complex response to the events of September 2001. As Sandra M. Gilbert notes, the term "Ground Zero" referred originally to the point of impact of a nuclear strike. As such, it should perhaps evoke not only the violence that was done to America but also the violence America has done to others.[104] Although such a suggestion neither identifies a moral equivalence nor suggests any kind of justification for either act – simply offering a perspective from which to begin thinking about the relationship between American modes of mourning and the democratic consequences of its possible responses – it is, nevertheless, one that is unlikely to be welcomed in our current discourse on death and politics. The controversy generated by *Nightline* anchor Ted Koppel's decision on April 30, 2004, to read the names of the then 737 Americans killed in Iraq as part of the "War on Terror" suggests that the simple-minded public response to death and its failure to engender critical reflection is endemic to American society.[105] Indeed, the outcry over and eventual shelving of plans to locate

[104] Sandra M. Gilbert, *Death's Door: Modern Dying and the Ways We Grieve, a Cultural Study* (New York: W. W. Norton & Company, 2006).
[105] The Sinclair Broadcast Group, which owns a number of ABC franchises, preempted the broadcast, arguing that "'Nightline' is not reporting news; it is doing nothing more than making a political statement." It was a decision that drew a number of angry responses from, among others, Senator John McCain. Koppel's own editorial following the reading of the names suggests, however, that there may be sources of critical reflection still within the polity. "The reading of those 721 names was," said Koppel, "neither intended to provoke opposition to the war, nor was it meant as an endorsement. Some of you doubt that. You are convinced that I am opposed to the war. I'm not. But that's beside the point. I am opposed to sustaining the illusion that war can be waged by the sacrifice of a few without burdening the rest of us in any way. I oppose the notion that to be at war is to forfeit the right to question, criticize, or debate our leaders' policies or for that

a permanent exhibit at the Ground Zero site that placed the events of 2001 within a broader, decidedly pro-American narrative about struggles for freedom – including the treatment of American Indians and Jim Crow segregation – suggests that there might be little hope for emergence of an appropriately complex account of the attacks.[106]

In the face of a changed world and the absence of a tragic perspective in the public culture, much of America has stuck stubbornly and unconsciously to the nationalist explanations and values of the past. In a time of political distress, it – like the Athenians – abandoned the critical thinking that, Elaine Scarry suggests, such emergencies require, naturally recalling "old oracles" such as the Gettysburg Address.[107] Thucydides' work suggests, however, that the specter of Athens looms large over the polity unless it can learn to place such oracles in a tragic context and, in the words of Thucydides, avoid "adapting our memories to suit our sufferings."

The possibility that the contemporary polity might yet adopt such a tragic mode of public mourning, one that invigorates democracy by giving power to the citizenry not the state, might be thought to depend, in part, on the existence of a viable model for this kind of response to loss. While the contemporary ignorance about the scope of Lincoln's achievement at Gettysburg – suggested by the notion that it was a "nonpolitical" oration appropriate for eulogizing the victims of a terrorist attack – may indicate the absence of any such example, especially one derived from a classical model, a 2006 row over the funeral of Coretta Scott King suggests the possibility of an alternative model of tragic mourning might be drawn from an indigenous American tradition. It is one that offers the possibility of a critical agonism and, with it, a more democratically productive future.

---

matter the policies of those who would become our leaders." American Broadcasting Company. 2004. *Nightline,* April 30.

[106] William Murphy, "Keeping focus on memorial; NY Representatives say Congress will act if Ground Zero project will include exhibits not related to 9/11," *Newsday,* 7/2/2005. www.newsday.com/news/keeping-focus-on-memorial-1.623948. Accessed Feb. 15, 2012. See also Stow, "From Upper Canal."

[107] Elaine Scarry, *Thinking in an Emergency* (New York: W. W. Norton & Company, 2012).

2

A Homegoing for Mrs. King: On the Democratic Value of African American Responses to Loss

> Poets, prophets, and reformers are all picture-makers, and this ability is the
> secret of their power and achievements, they see what ought to be by the
> reflection of what is, and endeavor to remove the contradiction.
>
> – *Frederick Douglass, "Pictures and Progress"*

In February 2006, the alleged politicization of the funeral of civil
rights icon Coretta Scott King generated a media furor. Remarks by
the Reverend Joseph Lowery and former President Jimmy Carter critical of the Bush administration drew particular fire. Despite the presence
of President Bush, three former presidents, and numerous members of
Congress, it was widely suggested – in a response that cut across racial
and party lines – that a funeral was neither the time nor the place for politics.[1] Advocating an approach to mourning that echoed that embodied by
the 2002 commemoration at Ground Zero, critics of Lowery and Carter
condemned their comments as a breach not only of decency and decorum
but also of an alleged national consensus on issues of race. Responding
to the furor, Lowery declared that those "who are criticizing me don't
understand the tradition of a black funeral."[2] Employing an analytical binary of tragic and romantic mourning, this chapter situates Mrs.
King's funeral within an African American tradition of tragic and self-
consciously political responses to loss, one that was central to the fight
against slavery and post-Reconstruction violence, and to the struggle

---

[1] Then-Senator Barack Obama was also present.

[2] Hamil R. Harris, "Lowery Defends His Criticism of Bush at Coretta King Funeral," *The
Washington Post*, February 22, 2006. www.washingtonpost.com/wp-dyn/content/article/
2006/02/21/AR2006022101611.html. Accessed Jan. 27, 2014.

for civil rights. Identifying the relationship between these two modes of mourning and their concomitant understandings of democracy – democracy as consensus and democracy as agonism – the argument suggests that this black tradition might serve as a framework for a reconstituted approach to public mourning, one that revitalizes democracy by embracing tragedy as a response to the polity's tragic condition.

Even as, however, the chapter notes the democratic value of this black tragic response to loss, it also identifies the ways in which the very success of this tradition has undermined the conditions for its survival. It nevertheless concludes by discussing the emergence, with the Black Lives Matter movement, of a new, similarly political mode of African American public mourning. While somewhat different in outlook and ethos from historical forebears, it is argued that this approach to loss embraces the oppositional stance and humanist commitments of its predecessor, even as it too faces the challenges posed by polity's ongoing commitment to consensus. In its reliance on a form of mortalist humanism as a basis for political action, it is further suggested, the Black Lives Matter movement gestures toward the political importance of such humanism to democratic politics, a claim that stands in opposition to a number of political-theoretical claims to the contrary. As such, this account provides a segue to the discussion of mortalist humanism, tragedy, and public mourning in the following chapter. The aim here, of course, is not to instrumentalize black suffering for the benefit of democracy, precisely that to which, perhaps, the tragic black mourning tradition has been a response. It is, rather, to identify the existence of an indigenous response or set of responses to loss that might suggest that the hegemonic power of nationalist and/or romantic responses to loss might yet be resisted in the American polity.

The chapter begins by drawing a distinction between two different kinds of mourning, the romantic and the tragic, and by tracing their relationship to two different understandings of democracy. It then identifies a tradition – understood as a core set of ideas or practices with clear historical evidence of influence and shared understandings across time[3] – of self-consciously political black mourning. This tradition, it argues, is best understood as a tragic response to a tragic condition. It is one that seeks to cultivate an agonistic politics capable of disrupting an American consensus on issues of race, a consensus that is exclusionary in both design and effect. Using Frederick Douglass's Decoration Day speeches and

---

[3] See Mark Bevir, *The Logic of the History of Ideas* (Cambridge: Cambridge University Press, 1999).

eulogies for Abraham Lincoln as its exemplars, the chapter shows how this mourning tradition offers a democratic pedagogy that seeks to generate and reinforce the ambivalent "double consciousness" of black life in its audience as a means of fighting the social conditions that produced it: girding African Americans for their struggle and seeking to undermine white complacency about issues of race. By identifying Douglass's inability to establish this tragic sense in his white audience and contrasting it with Lincoln's success at Gettysburg, this section also provides a historical precedent for considering the impact of the decline of tragic mourning on the contemporary polity. Establishing the tradition's continuity by identifying its importance to post-Reconstruction resistance and the struggle for civil rights, the penultimate section places Mrs. King's funeral at a generational intersection of conflicting demands for romantic and tragic responses to loss, locating many of the causes of this generational shift in the history of the tragic tradition's successes. The chapter concludes by situating the emergence of a new mode of politically motivated African American public mourning – precipitated by the violent deaths of Trayvon Martin, Michael Brown, Eric Garner, Sandra Bland, and many others – in relation to its tragic antecedent, identifying both its continuity and divergence from this earlier tradition and suggesting its potential value to democratic politics.

MODES OF MOURNING AND DEMOCRATIC UNDERSTANDINGS

In the face of death, romantic public mourning demands little of its audience except a recommitment to the polity's idealized vision of itself. Employed in the sense suggested by the historians David Blight, Eric Foner, and Gary Laderman, the term "romantic" here identifies a narrative that draws on and shares much with the Romantic movement of the eighteenth and nineteenth centuries.[4] There is, nevertheless, a considerable debate about what the term "romantic" might mean in this context. As early as the 1920s, the philosopher and historian Arthur Lovejoy suggested that the word was so nebulous as to have no meaning at all.[5]

---

[4] David W. Blight, *Race and Reunion: The Civil War in American Memory* (Cambridge, MA: Belknap Press, 2001); Eric Foner, *Forever Free. The Story of Emancipation and Reconstruction* (New York: Random House, 2005); and Gary Laderman, *The Scared Remains: American Attitudes toward Death, 1799–1883* (New Haven, CT: Yale University Press, 21996).

[5] See, for example, A. O. Lovejoy, "On the Discriminations of Romanticism" in *Essays in the History of Ideas* (Baltimore, MD: Johns Hopkins University Press, 1948).

Nevertheless, as M. H. Abrams observes, "romantic" "is one of those terms that historians can neither make do with nor make do without."[6] As such, following Seamus Perry, the focus here will be on what the word "romantic" has been made to do, rather than on what it "means."[7] At the heart of this understanding of the romantic is a commitment to art, the imagination, and sentiment and an obsession with death, largely understood as an aesthetic and spiritual experience. In the nineteenth century, romantic mourning found its fullest expression in the idea of the "Good Death." In white antebellum America, individuals were expected to expire at home, surrounded by their families, preferably after having offered some memorable final words. In this, Washington, Adams, and Jefferson provided a model for the larger American public.[8] For whites, death was to be welcomed, not as an escape to a better place but as part of a natural spiritual progression toward the afterlife.[9] It was an aestheticized, maudlin, and deeply sentimental understanding of mortality that evinced a commitment to unity over conflict, even as that conflict was frequently suppressed rather than resolved.[10] Indeed, Lovejoy suggests that while the romantic expressed a commitment to the individual over the collective, for many, such "individuality" referred not only to persons but also to groups, races, and nations.[11] For this reason, he argued, the romantic tradition generated a paradoxical tendency toward a homogeneity of perspective, "a particularistic uniformitarianism, a tendency to seek to universalize things originally valued because they were not universal," one that occurs "in the policies of great states and the enthusiasms of their populations."[12] As such, romantic mourning is predicated on and cultivates an understanding of democracy as consensus.

[6] M. H. Abrams, "Rationality and the Imagination in Cultural History" in *Doing Things With Texts: Essays in Criticism and Critical Theory* ed. Michael Fischer (New York: Norton, 1991), 117.

[7] Seamus Perry, "Romanticism: A Brief History of a Concept" in *A Companion to Romanticism* ed. Duncan Wu (Oxford: Blackwell, 1998), 4. Nevertheless, following Wittgenstein, what a word "means" and how it is used are, for this author at least, synonymous.

[8] Gerald E. Kahler, *The Long Farewell: American Mourns the Death of George Washington* (Charlottesville: University of Virginia Press, 2008), 4; Schantz, *Awaiting the Heavenly Country*, 23–24.

[9] Gary Laderman, *The Sacred Remains: American Attitudes Toward Death, 1799–1883* (New Haven, CT: Yale University Press, 1996), 130. See also Cavitch, *American Elegy*.

[10] Carl Schmitt, *Political Romanticism* translated by Gary Oakes (Cambridge, MA: MIT Press), 149.

[11] Arthur Lovejoy, *The Great Chain of Being: A Study of the History of an Idea* (Cambridge, MA: Harvard University Press, 1936), 310.

[12] Ibid., 313.

Embodying a *telos* of reconciliation and agreement that – consciously or unconsciously – eschews politics, democracy as consensus finds expression not only in the Greek obsession with political unity and fear of *stasis* but also in the more recent attempts of John Rawls and Jürgen Habermas to identify a position of thicker political accord beyond that offered by mere liberal neutrality.[13] Arguing that this commitment to consensus serves as an "ideology for the divided city," one that "denies the very possibility of thinking about real divisions," Nicole Loraux notes that it can exist in tandem with – and sometimes even exacerbate – the very sectional conflict that it seeks to suppress.[14] That the ideology of consensus is frequently a rhetorical commitment rather than a political reality does not diminish its capacity to shape democratic outcomes. Indeed, for critics of this understanding of democracy, the overriding concern with consensus often excludes minority voices in a way that diminishes democracy, with the drive toward "normalization" and agreement marking out disagreement as "deviant" or "other."[15] Thus not only are minority views often excluded from public discourse, they are frequently demonized, with democratic politics becoming marked by shrill antagonisms rather than reasoned debate. As such, even as romantic mourning eschews and disavows politics, it has political effects. In this, it stands in opposition to the complex and conflicting worldview of tragic mourning, that which embraces its political aims and impact. It is an approach predicted on and that cultivates an agonistic understanding of democracy.

Tragic public mourning – understood as a *response* not as a *condition* – is predicated on a worldview that is pluralistic in outlook, critical, and self-consciously political. The key distinction between tragedy as condition and tragedy as response is suggested by James Finlayson's work on Hegel:

[A] theory of the tragic tells us something about human experience, human actions and the ethical-life of a community in which the actions are played out. The tragic arises from the way in which our institutions, customs, and practices within which we become what we are, shape our actions on the one hand, and

[13] John Rawls, *Political Liberalism* (New York: Columbia University Press, 1993); Jürgen Habermas, "Ideologies and Society in the Postwar World" in *Habermas: Autonomy and Solidarity: Interviews with Jürgen Habermas* edited by Peter Dews (London: Verso, 1992), 43–62.
[14] Loraux, *Divided City*, 30. The accusation that another party is failing to seek consensus can be a rhetorical stick with which to beat that party, even as the party making the accusation is frequently engaged in the same practice.
[15] See William Connolly, *Pluralism* (Minneapolis: University of Minnesota Press, 2005); and Mouffe, *On the Political*.

take shape through our actions on the other. Hence the question of the tragic enjoys a certain priority over the question of tragedy. The works of theater we call tragedies exist because of the tragic, not vice versa.[16]

Tragedy as condition is constituted by an understanding of the world as one of suffering, irreconcilable conflicts, paradoxical demands, and frustrated human agency, a world in which "humans, in their pursuit of knowledge, their attempts to change things, their hope to escape from the narratives in which they find themselves enmeshed, are relentlessly and with grim irony drawn back into disaster at every turn."[17] Tragedy as response shares the worldview of tragedy as condition and serves not to overcome that condition but rather as a coping strategy for human beings who must face it. It is, in the words of Paul Gilroy, "suffering made productive, made useful but not redemptive."[18]

Central to an understanding of tragedy as response – one that serves as a coping strategy for the uncertainties, reversal, and defeats of our tragedy as condition – is "the notion of ambivalence ... the prevalence of duality over unity."[19] On this account, tragedy as response seeks to generate ambivalence in its audience as a productive response to tragedy as condition. It does not, of course, preclude – and may even *presume* – the existence of ambivalence in the text, the performance, or the author.[20]

[16] J. G. Finlayson, "Conflict and Reconciliation in Hegel's Theory of the Tragic," *Journal of the History of Philosophy*, 37(3), 1999, 494.

[17] Simon Goldhill, *Sophocles and the Language of Tragedy* (Oxford: Oxford University Press, 2006), 15. See also Steven Johnston, *American Dionysia: Violence, Tragedy, and Democratic Politics* (New York: Cambridge University Press, 2015), 4. "A tragic sensibility entails, accordingly, a newfound approach to remedial action and responsibility – a capacious sense of responsibility. Rooted in a deep sense of duality, this notion starts with the assumption that doing well in politics, with the best of intentions, offers no immunity from doing harm." And Steven Johnston, *The Truth About Patriotism* (Durham, NC: Duke University Press, 2007), 209.

[18] Paul Gilroy, *Darker than Blue: On the Moral Economies of Black Atlantic Culture* (Cambridge, MA: Belknap Press, 2010), 150. See also Honig, *Emergency Politics*, 11. This position builds on elements of Marcuse's understanding of tragedy as suffering. "Modern tragedy," wrote Marcuse, "is now only a cry of existence; not overcoming, not mitigation of suffering: only a compression and formulation as last and only reaction still possible." Ludwig Marcuse, *The World of Tragedy* (1923) cited in Mark W. Roche, "The Greatness and Limits of Hegel's Theory of Tragedy" in *A Companion to Tragedy* edited by Rebecca Bushnell (Oxford: Blackwell Publishing, 2005), 62.

[19] Richard Seaford, "Historicizing Tragic Ambivalence. The Vote of Athena" in *History, Tragedy, Theory: Dialogues on Athenian Drama* edited by Barbara Goff (Austin: University of Texas Press, 1995), 202. See also Jean-Pierre Vernant and Pierre Vidal-Naquet, *Myth and Tragedy in Ancient Greece* translated by Janet Lloyd (Cambridge: The MIT Press, 1988), 18–19. "Tragic ambiguity is to be found deep within the very language of tragedy."

[20] Seaford, "Historicizing Tragic Ambivalence," 204.

Nevertheless, this understanding of tragedy as response belongs to a group of theories concerned with tragedy's impact on its audience.[21] For the Greeks, tragic theater helped the citizenry negotiate the inevitable and irreconcilable tensions of democratic life. Key to its pedagogical function was the notion of "discrepant awareness": what one character sees and knows and what another does not or what the audience knows and the characters do not. Employing this mechanism, tragedy sought to train its democratic audience by demonstrating that any viewpoint is necessarily partial and illustrating the disastrous consequences of blindness, literal or figurative.[22] It was, however, not only the plays themselves that demanded their audiences reflect critically on all sides of complex issues – in the process embracing and learning to manage such conflict – but also their presentation at the Great Dionysia where the Festival's juxtaposition of celebration and critique performed and cultivated its own ambivalence toward the democratic city.[23] Thus, tragic mourning is predicated on and supportive of an understanding of the centrality of conflict and ambivalence to democratic politics, what a number of contemporary theorists have called "agonism."

Agonism understands democracy as a system in which there is no final solution – no *telos* – for political conflict, simply an always-ongoing battle between conflicting needs and desires. It is an understanding that draws on Nietzsche's insight about the centrality of conflict to human interaction. In this model, disagreement, not consensus, is understood to be at the heart of democratic politics. All parties to a disagreement recognize that there is no rational final solution to their conflict, only an ongoing debate. Such parties nevertheless seek to recognize the legitimacy of their opponents in the perpetual contest that is constitutive of the democratic polity – a feature that, it will be argued, demands a certain kind of political humanism.[24] Somewhat fittingly, perhaps, there is disagreement about the extent to which the major theorists of agonistic democracy – William Connolly, Bonnie Honig, and Chantal Mouffe – share a single understanding of how a commitment to *agon* as the central value of democratic

[21] Richard H. Palmer, *Tragedy and Tragic Theory: An Analytical Guide* (Westport, CT: Greenwood Press, 1992), 17–52.

[22] Froma I. Zeitlin, "Playing the Other: Theater, Theatricality, and the Feminine in Greek Drama," *Representations*, 11, 1985, 75.

[23] Simon Goldhill, *Love, Sex & Tragedy: How the Ancient World Shapes Our Lives* (Chicago: University of Chicago Press, 2004), 220–232.

[24] Mouffe, *On the Political*, 20.

politics shapes its outcomes.[25] Here, however, little turns on this debate, and these differences will largely be bracketed. Instead, the focus will be on what all three share: most obviously, a commitment to a particular way of being or understanding that is necessary for meaningful agonistic politics. Connolly, for example, identifies an ethos of "critical responsiveness" appropriate to agonism, one that offers a *"form of careful listening and presumptive generosity"* to political opponents that generates a "bicameral orientation to ... political life straddling two or more perspectives to maintain tension between them."[26] It is an ambivalent perspective partly constituted by the recognition of the partiality, incompleteness, and contingency of the agent's own position. Connolly labels this perspective "tragic"[27] and suggests that it emerges from a reflection on death and the finitude of life.[28] While ambivalence is an attitude appropriate to agonistic democracy, its proponents are far from ambivalent about democracy itself, even though, as Mouffe makes clear, they can disagree about the proper interpretation and application of its principles.[29]

Although democratic agonism is sometimes subject to Baconian-style critiques about the supposed implausibility of its worldview or the likelihood of its implementation, Andreas Kalyvas notes, "[d]emocratic agonism does not seek to describe real existing democracies but rather to point at a normative vision."[30] This positive and aspirational vision of

[25] See, for example, David R. Howarth, "Ethos, Agonism, and Populism: William Connolly and the Case for Radical Democracy," *British Journal of Politics and International Relations*, (10) 2008: 171–193. Agonism is a theme in nearly all of Honig's work. It first appears in her book *Political Theory and the Displacement of Politics* (Ithaca, NY: Cornell University Press, 1993).

[26] Connolly, *Pluralism*, 126, 4.

[27] William Connolly, *Identity/Difference: Democratic Negotiations of a Political Paradox* (Minneapolis: University of Minnesota Press, 1991), 179, 183.

[28] Ibid., 20, 167. For Mouffe, such a perspective is central to moving beyond the friend/enemy distinction that marks human antagonism and toward an agonistic politics marked by a struggle between opponents understood as adversaries. "Adversaries fight against each other," she writes, "because they want their interpretation...to become hegemonic, but they do not put into question the legitimacy of their opponent's right to fight for the victory of their position." Chantal Mouffe, *Agonistics: Thinking the World Politically* (New York: Verso, 2013), 7.

[29] "Consensus is needed," she writes, "on the institutions that are constitutive of liberal democracy and on the ethico-political issues that should inform political association. But there will always be disagreement concerning the meaning of those values and the way they should be implemented. This consensus will therefore always be a 'conflictual consensus.'" Ibid., 8.

[30] Andreas Kalyvas, "The Democratic Narcissus: The Agonism of the Ancients Compared to that of the (Post) Moderns" in *Law and Agonistic Politics* edited by Andrew Schaap (Burlington, VT: Ashgate Publishing, 2009), 33.

democracy as agonism might, then, be understood as something akin to the Ship of Theseus: an ongoing process in which the constituent parts of the polity change and reorganize themselves in different ways to maintain liberal democracy's core functions of popular representation and minority protections in the face of both quotidian and catastrophic challenges to its continued existence. *Pace* Jonathan Lear's *Radical Hope*, tragic mourning is concerned with what it might mean to go on as a democratic people, in the face of mass death, and how this "going on together" might be achieved.[31] As the history of African American death and public mourning in the United States suggests, the tragic condition of black life has served to cultivate a worldview and set of practices embodying just such a tragic set of responses to loss.

"AN AWFUL GLADNESS": BLACK EXPERIENCES OF DEATH

In *The Souls of Black Folk*, W.E.B. Du Bois extends his discussion of "the Veil" of race to the experience of his child's death.[32] He notes that amid his grief "sat an awful gladness in my heart" arising from the recognition that his son would not have to grow up in a world beset by racial discrimination: "my soul whispers ever to me, saying 'Not dead, not dead, but escaped; not bond, but free.'"[33] His experience was far from unique. Former slave John Washington's 1865 eulogy for his son Johnnie expressed similar sentiments,[34] and the work of Ronald K. Barrett suggests that African Americans are more *"death accepting"* than whites.[35] It is an ambivalent

---

[31] Jonathan Lear, *Radical Hope. Ethics in the Face of Cultural Devastation* (Cambridge, MA: Harvard University Press, 2008); and Josiah Ober, *Athenian Legacies: Essays on the Politics of Going on Together* (Princeton, NJ: Princeton University Press, 2005).

[32] An experience that, he notes, failed to save him from white America's scorn, even on the day of his son's burial. W.E.B. Du Bois, W.E.B. 2003. *The Souls of Black Folk* (New York: Barnes and Noble, 2003), 150. For evidence of the continued relevance of Du Bois's experience, see Bob Herbert, "Arrested While Grieving," *The New York Times*, May 26, 2007. www .nytimes.com/2007/05/26/opinion/26herbert.html?_r=0. Accessed Jan 17, 2014.

[33] Du Bois, *Souls*, 151.

[34] David W. Blight, *A Slave No More: Two Men Who Escaped To Freedom Including Their Own Narratives Of Emancipation* (New York: Harcourt, 2007), 259–260; see also Harriet Jacobs, *Incidents in the Life of a Slave Girl, Written by Herself* edited by Jean Fagin Yellin (Cambridge, MA: Harvard University Press, 1981), 62; and Elizabeth Keckley, *Behind the Scenes or, Thirty Years a Slave and Four Years in the White House* (New York: Penguin Books, 2005), 12.

[35] Ronald K. Barrett, "Sociocultural Considerations for Working with Blacks Experiencing Loss and Grief" in *Living with Grief: Who We Are, How We Grieve* edited by Kenneth J. Doka and Joyce D. Davidson (Washington, DC: The Hospice Foundation of America,

perspective captured by the frequent description – much in evidence at the service for Mrs. King – of African American funerals as "homegoings." Emerging from the slave tradition that held that death meant a return to the homeland, the term suggests that amid the sadness of a passing, there is a kind of joy about the release from pain and the movement to a better place.[36] It is a perspective further suggested by significantly higher suicide rates among African Americans, especially among black males.[37] Both Frederick Douglass and Martin Luther King are said to have contemplated killing themselves,[38] and suicide was so prevalent under slavery that some owners took to denying burials to and mutilating the bodies of slaves who took their own lives in order to discourage others from doing the same.[39] Indeed, the public suicide of a slave named Romain in Philadelphia in 1803 was widely considered to be a statement against the inhumanity of slavery, and much was made of it in abolitionist tracts.[40] In this, black experiences of death offered African Americans an ambivalent and bicameral orientation toward life: a double consciousness that was expressed in and reinforced by black burials and the rituals of mourning.

Orlando Patterson argues that the experience of slavery and segregation created a "social death" for African Americans.[41] It was one reflected in and reinforced by black experiences of physical death. Drawing on a widely held view that heaven too would be segregated, segregation in death extended well beyond the end of slavery and was evidenced by the

1998), 89; and Ronald K. Barrett, "Contemporary African American Funeral Rites and Traditions" in *The Path Ahead: Readings in Death and Dying* edited by Lynne Anne de Spelder and Albert Lee Strickland (Mountain View, CA: Mayfield Publishing Co, 1995).

[36] David R. Roediger, "And Die in Dixie: Funerals, Death, and Heaven in the Slave Community, 1700–1865," *Massachusetts Review*, 22, 1981, 177.

[37] This is no mere historical oddity. Between 1980 and 1992, when suicide rates among white males declined, the rates for African Americans increased dramatically (Karla F.C. Holloway, *Passed On: African American Mourning Stories. A Memorial* (Durham, NC: Duke University Press, 2003), 89–90). Similarly, average death rates in the United States are higher for blacks than for whites, a gap that has increased since 1960. David Satcher, George E. Fryer, Jr., Jessica McCann, Adewale Troutman, Steven H. Woolf, and George Rust, "What If We Were Equal? A Comparison of the Black-White Mortality Gap in 1960 and 2000," *Health Affairs*, 24(2), 2005: 459–464.

[38] Frederick Douglass, *Narrative of the Life of Frederick Douglass, American Slave, Written by Himself* (New York: Penguin Books, 2013); Taylor Branch, *Parting the Waters. America in the King Years 1954–1963* (New York: Simon & Schuster, 1988), 48–49.

[39] Max Cavitch, *American Elegy: The Poetry of Mourning from the Puritans to Whitman* (Minneapolis: University of Minnesota Press, 2007), 212.

[40] Mark S. Schantz, *Awaiting the Heavenly Country: The Civil War and America's Culture of Death* (Ithaca, NY: Cornell University Press, 2008), 143–144.

[41] Orlando Patterson, *Slavery and Social Death: A Comparative Study* (Cambridge, MA: Harvard University Press, 1982).

geographical marginality of black burial grounds and by the existence of distinct hierarchies of internment.[42] Even when slaves and servants were buried with their masters, it was in a way that indicated their lower status, often at the feet of their owners; indeed, some slaves simply refused the opportunity to be buried in otherwise white burial grounds for fear that they would continue to be terrorized by their masters in death.[43] In the national cemeteries established to commemorate the Union dead, black Civil War veterans were buried separately from their white counterparts,[44] and, more recently, the struggles of the families of black veterans of the Korean and Vietnam Wars to have their loved ones buried in the cemeteries of their choice provided a parallel to the civil rights struggle among the living.[45] This double consciousness of death found cultural and political expression in – and reinforcement by – the "blues sensibility" of the "Sorrow Songs."[46]

The Sorrow Songs, observes Du Bois, "are the music of an unhappy people, of the children of disappointment; they tell of death and suffering and an unvoiced longing toward a truer world."[47] Although the Sorrow Songs have been a controversial subject for some black intellectuals – Zora Neale Hurston rejects any view of the songs that associates them with the stigma of death[48] – Max Cavitch argues such a viewpoint

[42] David Robertson, *Denmark Vesey: The Buried Story of America's Largest Slave Rebellion and the Man Who Led It* (New York: Vintage Books, 2000), 19; Roediger "And Die in Dixie," 179; and Timothy B. Tyson, *Blood Done Sign My Name* (New York: Three Rivers Press, 2004), 183.

[43] Angelika Krüger-Kahloula, "On the Wrong Side of the Fence: Racial Segregation in American Cemeteries" in *History and Memory in African American Culture* edited by Geneviève Fabre. (Cary, NC: Oxford University Press, 1994), 137–138.

[44] Drew Gilpin Faust, *This Republic of Suffering: Death and the American Civil War* (New York: Knopf, 2008), 236.

[45] Krüger-Kahloula, "On the Wrong Side of the Fence," 130. The eventual success of these families did not always solve the problem of postmortem segregation. In the South in the early 1970s, some white families removed their relatives' remains from recently integrated cemeteries. Harmon Perry, "Whites Remove Dead from Cemetery Now Owned by Black Man," *Jet*, May 6, 1985: 38–40.

[46] Stanley Crouch, *The All-American Skin Game, Or, The Decoy of Race* (New York: Pantheon Books, 1995); and Angela Y. Davis, *Blues Legacies and Black Feminism: Gertrude "Ma" Rainey, Bessie Smith, and Billie Holiday* (New York: Vintage, 1999).

[47] Du Bois, *Souls*, 179.

[48] Zora Neale Hurston, "Spirituals and Neo-Spirituals" in *Folklore, Memoirs, and Other Writings* edited by Cheryl Wall (New York: Library of America, 1995). Hurston was not, however, unaware of the importance of death to African American politics. In a 1945 letter to W.E.B. Du Bois, she suggested the construction of a cemetery for black luminaries, including Frederick Douglass and Nat Turner. "You must see," she wrote, "what a rallying spot that would be for all we wish to accomplish and do." Michael Kammen, *Digging*

misses the complexity of the genre and that the songs display a hope within a sadness that is reflective of the tragic sense embodied by African American mourning traditions.[49] For some theorists of tragedy such as Ludwig Marcuse, any suggestion of hope is, of course, an anathema.[50] Certainly Cornel West's formulation of the tragic as a kind of insight that emerges from the conditions of black life – what Du Bois called "second sight"[51] – and an impetus to the action required to overcome them has been the subject of much criticism.[52] For this reason, any attempt to identify black public mourning as a tragic response seems doomed to failure. Nevertheless, as Nietzsche suggests in *Human, All Too Human*, hope and tragedy are not only not inimical but may actually be bound up in one another.[53] The resolution of this apparent tension lies in understanding the *nature* of the hope expressed by the Sorrow Songs and, indeed, by the broader black mourning tradition of which they are a part.

"Through all the sorrow of the Sorrow Songs," writes Du Bois, "there breathes a hope – a faith in the ultimate justice of things."[54] Such hope as a tragic response does not, however, entail an expectation of fulfillment. Eddie Glaude Jr. identifies a "hope against hope" captured "by the commonsensical understanding that a radical transformation of American society was implausible." It is, he says, grounded "in a regulative ideal toward which we aspire but which ultimately defies historical fulfillment."[55] As Du Bois himself asked, "Is such a hope justified? Do

Up the Dead: A History of Notable American Reburials (Chicago: Chicago University Press, 2010), 26.

[49] Max Cavitch, *American Elegy: The Poetry of Mourning from the Puritans to Whitman* (Minneapolis: University of Minnesota Press, 2007), 205.

[50] See Mark W. Roche, "The Greatness and Limits of Hegel's Theory of Tragedy" in *A Companion to Tragedy* edited by Rebecca Bushnell (Oxford: Blackwell Publishing, 2005), 62.

[51] Du Bois, *Souls*, 9.

[52] Cornel West, *The Cornel West Reader* (New York: Basic Books, 1999), 101–105; 435–439); Lorenzo Simpson, "Evading Theory and Tragedy?: Reading Cornel West," *Praxis International*, 13(1), 1993: 32–45; and Robert Pirro, "Remedying Defective or Deficient Political Agency: Cornel West's Uses of the Tragic," *New Political Science*, 26(2), 2004: 147–170.

[53] "Hence he looks upon the one evil still remaining as the greatest source of happiness – it is hope – Zeus intended that man, not withstanding the evils oppressing him, should continue to live and not rid himself of life, but keep on making himself miserable. For this purpose he bestowed hope upon man: it is, in truth, the greatest of evils for it lengthens the ordeal of man." Friedrich Nietzsche, *Human All Too Human: A Book for Free Spirits* translated by Alexander Harvey (Chicago: Charles H. Kerr & Company, 1915), 102.

[54] Du Bois, *Souls*, 186.

[55] Eddie Glaude, Jr., *Exodus! Religion, Race, and Nation in Early Nineteenth-Century Black America* (Chicago: Chicago University Press, 2000), 112. See also Cornel West,

the Sorrow Songs sing true?"[56] Reflecting an understanding of tragedy as condition, the Songs and the hope that they expressed were a response to it. The ambivalence of such hope is, however, largely obscured by popular narratives of U.S. racial history in which its fulfillment is considered a function of the inexorable logic of liberalism rather than the product of precarious human struggle.[57] The historical persistence of this misunderstanding is suggested by Frederick Douglass's astonishment at white Northerners who saw the slaves' songs as "evidence of their contentment and happiness. It is impossible to make a greater mistake. Slaves sing when they are most unhappy."[58] In this, the songs were both a lamentation and an expression of resistance with their political significance suggested by the fear they struck into whites and by the attempts of white authorities to regulate the funerals of which they were part.[59]

By necessity and often by homeland tradition, slave funerals often took place at night, frequently unnerving slave owners. Georgia plantation resident Francis Kemble recounts how the "first high wailing notes of a spiritual" emanating from a slave funeral "sent a chill through my nerves."[60] Consequently, they were subject to heavy restriction. In New York alone, nighttime slave funerals were prohibited by laws passed in 1722, 1731, 1748, and 1763; and those that were permitted were tightly regulated, limited to twelve mourners and deprived of all ceremonial trappings.[61] Funerals offered slaves an opportunity to experience themselves as a people in a ritualized setting, one that preceded and later promoted the emergence of black Christianity.[62] Indeed, Albert Raboteau's work stressing the importance of slave agency to abolition and David Roediger's work

The American Evasion of Philosophy: A Genealogy of Pragmatism (Madison: University of Wisconsin, 1989), 229.

[56] Du Bois, *Souls*, 186.

[57] Bonnie Honig, *Emergency Politics: Paradox, Law, Democracy* (Princeton, NJ: Princeton University Press, 2009), 47.

[58] Sterling Stuckey, "Ironic Tenacity" Frederick Douglass's Seizure of the Dialectic" in *Frederick Douglass: New Literary and Historical Essays* edited by Eric Sundquist (Cambridge: Cambridge University Press, 1990), 35.

[59] Roediger, "And Die in Dixie," 168.

[60] Frances Anne Kemble, *Journal of a Residence on a Georgian Plantation in 1838–1839* (Athens: University of Georgia Press, 1984), 147.

[61] Krüger-Kahloula, "On the Wrong Side of the Fence," 143.

[62] When the first African Methodist Episcopal Church was established in Charleston, South Carolina, in 1815, its initial meeting was held in a hearse house near the city's black cemetery. Robertson, *Denmark Vesey*, 146; see also Roediger, "And Die in Dixie," 176. This account complicates West's suggestion that black Christianity was the source of the African American tragic sense. See West, *Reader*, 425–434; 435–439; and Pirro, "Remedying Defective or Deficient Political Agency," 156.

on the role of funeral rites in generating black solidarity both suggest the ways in which black loss was made productive.[63] Gabriel Prosser's attempted slave revolt and assault on Richmond in 1800 is, for example, said to have gained momentum from a meeting held at the funeral of a child.[64] As such, the delicate economy of slave funeral restrictions, permissions, and transgressions politicized black burials even before the founding of the nation. Under a system in which the humanity of slaves was so much in doubt that those who died during transportation were simply thrown overboard and certain masters had to be reminded to bury their dead slaves, *any* black burial had distinctly political connotations.[65] It was, moreover, a deeply self-conscious politics. Following Denmark Vesey's failed uprising in Charleston, South Carolina, in 1822, slaves were prohibited from wearing outward signs of mourning in the week following his execution.[66] Many nevertheless chose to do so and were imprisoned for their pains.

Black mourning rituals were thus a tragic response to a tragic condition, their complex duality finding expression in funeral services that often constituted "a posthumous attempt for dignity and esteem denied and limited by the dominant culture" and which frequently clashed sharply in both style and substance with those of white Americans.[67] In July 1863, for example, the elaborate burial in New Orleans of Captain André Cailloux – the first black officer to die during the Civil War – sought to overcome the indignities heaped on his body by Confederate sharpshooters, who prevented its recovery from the battlefield for forty-one days. Drawing an enormous crowd of soldiers and civic society members, Cailloux's highly political funeral featured a parade and a eulogy calling on others to follow his example in the fight against slavery.[68]

Seeking to make death more than a mere statistic, black funerals became festive celebrations of lives lived rather than simple lamentations

---

[63] Albert Raboteau, *Slave Religion. The "Invisible Institution" in the Antebellum South* (Oxford: Oxford University Press, 1978); Roediger, "And Die in Dixie," 168–171.

[64] Roediger, "And Die in Dixie," 168–171.

[65] Marcus Rediker, *The Slave Ship. A Human History* (New York: Viking, 2008), 4–5; Krüger-Kahloula, "On the Wrong Side of the Fence," 142.

[66] Robertson, *Denmark Vesey*, 98, 104.

[67] Ronald K. Barrett, "Psychocultural Influences on African American Attitudes Towards Death, Dying, and Bereavement" in *Personal Care in an Impersonal World: A Multidimensional Look at Bereavement* edited by J. D. Morgan (Amityville, NY: Baywood, 1993), 226.

[68] Stephen J. Ochs, *A Black Patriot and a White Priest: Andre Cailloux and Claude Paschal Maistre in Civil War New Orleans* (Baton Rouge: Louisiana State University Press, 2000), 4, 155–156.

of loss, frequently combining with another tradition of African American festivals and countermemorials, themselves often dominated by a concern with mortality.[69] Throughout the nineteenth century, African Americans developed an alternative festival calendar that ran parallel to that of the white majority but that was infused with entirely different significance. January 1, traditionally a day of despair marking another year of suffering for those in captivity, came to be celebrated for the abolition of the foreign slave trade in 1808 and July 5, as a counterpoint to white Independence Day. The mood of these events was, Geneviève Fabre notes, "*subjunctive*, the *ought* and *should*, prevailed over the *was*: with a feeling of urgency, of great impatience at the renewed delay, African Americans invented a future no one dared to consider and forced its image on black and white minds and spirits."[70] They were self-consciously political and highly critical of American practices, even as they demonstrated their ambivalence by both participating in and subverting the holidays. The modern Memorial Day grew out of this tradition when former slaves in Charleston, South Carolina, conducted a mock funeral for slavery and organized a parade to provide a proper burial for and decorate the graves of Union soldiers who had died in the city's prison camp. In so doing, they created what David Blight called "the Independence Day of the second American Revolution" and reinvigorated an older tradition.[71] "Due to Memorial Day," he writes, "the ancient art of funeral orations and sermons gained a new life in America. The Decoration Day speech became an American genre that ministers, politicians, and countless former soldiers tried to master."[72]

The undoubted master of this revival was Frederick Douglass, who offered several such speeches, including a series of eulogies for Abraham Lincoln starting in 1865 and culminating, most famously, in his 1876 speech at the unveiling of the Freedmen's Memorial in Washington, DC. The speeches reveal not only the ways in which Douglass inhabited the African American tragic tradition of public mourning – embodying an understanding of tragedy as both condition and response – but also the

[69] Joseph Roach, *Cities of the Dead: Circum-Atlantic Performance* (New York: Columbia University Press, 1996), 60–63, 277–281.
[70] Geneviève Fabre, "African American Commemorative Celebrations in the Nineteenth Century" in *History and Memory in African American Culture* edited by Geneviève Fabre (Cary, NC: Oxford University Press, 1994), 72.
[71] David W. Blight, *Beyond the Battlefield: Race, Memory, and the American Civil War* (Amherst: University of Massachusetts Press, 2002), 187.
[72] David W. Blight, *Race and Reunion: The Civil War in American Memory* (Cambridge, MA: Belknap Press, 2001), 72.

ways in which the tradition offered a distinct political position and a
pedagogical opportunity to its audience. If, as Du Bois suggests, the conditions of black life offered African Americans "second sight"[73] – "an
ability to see the world as it is disclosed to a social group different from
one's own ... thus as it is ordinarily not available to be seen"[74] – then the
expression of this dual perspective in the rituals of black mourning might
be thought to offer a pedagogical opportunity to its audience, one that
extends beyond the issue of race.

"LESSONS OF THEIR OWN HISTORY": PEDAGOGY
AND PUBLIC MOURNING

Frederick Douglass was well aware of the eulogy's pedagogical potential.
In his 1866 speech, "The Assassination and its Lessons," he declared,
"The masses are always engaged chiefly in the struggle for existence, and
have little time to give to theories. A few can comprehend a rule and the
reasons therfor [sic], but many require illustrations before they can be
instructed."[75] Douglass was equally aware, however, that he faced a postbellum American polity committed to romantic modes of remembrance
and the "Good Death." This deeply romantic understanding of mortality
was, however, fundamentally disrupted by the carnage of the Civil War.
For the first time, white America endured violent, sudden death on a
grand scale. Far from home, surrounded by strangers, white America had
its first encounter with what had hitherto been a predominantly black
experience. The unprecedented horror of the war opened a fissure in the
American understanding of death, creating uncertainty and disorientation
in its standard narratives of mortality. "The presence and fear of death,"
writes Drew Gilpin Faust, "touched Civil War Americans' most fundamental sense of who they were, for in its threat of termination and transformation, death inevitably inspired self-scrutiny and self-definition."[76]
Stepping into the explanatory void at Gettysburg, Abraham Lincoln
offered a tragic eulogy that made sense of the carnage: the serendipitous

---

[73] Du Bois, *Souls*, 9.
[74] Robert Gooding-Williams, *In the Shadow of Du Bois: Afro-Modern Political Thought in
America* (Cambridge, MA: Harvard University Press, 2009), 78.
[75] Frederick Douglass, "The Assassination and Its Lessons: An Address Delivered in
Washington, D.C., on February 13 1866" in *The Frederick Douglass Papers. Series One,
Speeches, Debates and Interviews*, v. 4 edited by John W. Blassingame (New Haven,
CT: Yale University Press, 1991), 108.
[76] Faust, *This Republic of Suffering*, xv; see also, Jenny Edkins, *Trauma and the Memory of
Politics* (Cambridge: Cambridge University Press, 2003), 5.

intersection of man, moment, and method. In what Garry Wills called "one of the most daring open-air sleight of hands ever witnessed by the unsuspecting,"[77] Lincoln took the opportunity of the fissure opened by mass death to employ a tragic mode of mourning – marking what was gained in liberty by what was lost in blood, and juxtaposing national celebration with national critique – that established the Declaration of Independence at the heart of the Constitution, fundamentally changing the nation and her self-understanding. It was, however, a fissure that soon closed.[78]

In the aftermath of the Civil War, the narrative of the "Good Death" was aggressively reasserted. Extraordinary efforts were made to retrieve and inter the bodies of the Northern fallen in national cemeteries, where they were lauded as heroes of liberty. The North's racism and complicity in slavery was all but forgotten in sentimentalized celebrations of the dead. In the South, this Northern mourning provoked an equal and opposite reaction. The North's refusal to bury the Confederate dead prompted the formation of Southern ladies' memorial associations that sought to raise funds for the internment of their fallen. Deliberately sectional, they offered an equally singular and romanticized account of the Lost Cause.[79] Both initially exacerbated ongoing tensions. Despite the rhetoric of reunion, the immediate aftermath of the war was often marked by bitterness, vindictiveness, and resentment between the two ostensibly former enemies.[80] Nevertheless, the ideological commitment to consensus embodied in romantic public mourning eventually served to suppress – if not entirely to erase – the conflict.[81] Indeed, with so much detail already jettisoned from their responses to loss – North *and* South – the final triumph of reconciliationism and the transition to a romantic narrative of higher unity predicated on national forgetting was, perhaps, all but

---

[77] Garry Wills, *Lincoln at Gettysburg: The Words that Remade America* (New York: Simon & Schuster, 1992), 38.

[78] As is suggested by the differences between the stark realism of the photographs of Matthew Brady's 1862 exhibit "The Dead of Antietam" and the romanticization of death in his assistant Alexander Gardner's 1866 *Photographic Sketchbook of the Civil War*. Laderman, *The Sacred Remains*, 148–151; Schantz, *Awaiting the Heavenly Country*, 163–206.

[79] Faust, *This Republic of Suffering*, 247.

[80] Michael Kammen, *Mystic Chords of Memory: The Transformation of Tradition in American Culture* (New York: Vintage Books, 1993), 110, 115; and Benjamin C. Cloyd, *Haunted by Atrocity: Civil War Prisons in American Memory* (Baton Rouge: Louisiana State University Press, 2010), 31–55.

[81] Kammen, *Mystic Chords of Memory*, 121, 13; Kammen, *Digging Up the Dead*, 86, 105; and Cloyd, *Haunted by Atrocity*, 79–80.

inevitable. Just as in Antiquity, where forgetting was achieved by literally whitewashing a stone tablet and inscribing on it new laws in the place of the old, Decoration Day and its later incarnation as Memorial Day were metaphorically washed white in a series of postwar commemorations in which the heroism of the war dead – on both sides – was celebrated at the expense of any discussion of the origins of the war or its enduring legacies.[82] Such mourning, as Douglass was well aware, threatened to undo Lincoln's refounding of the nation and boded ill for blacks. Thus, employing the tragic understanding of African American public mourning, and within only hours of Lincoln's death, Douglass began his fight against historical amnesia in Rochester, New York, on April 15, 1865.

Although this speech, coming so soon after Lincoln's passing, was peppered with many of the platitudes more commonly expected of the funeral oration – "A dreadful disaster has befallen the nation"; "I feel it as a personal as well as a national calamity"; and Douglass's most persistent if least-observed trope, "This is not an occasion for speech-making, but for silence" – it also offered the self-consciously political perspective of the black funeral tradition. "Only the other day," he declared, "it seemed as if the nation were in danger of losing a just appreciation of the awful claims of this rebellion. We were manifesting almost as much gratitude to General Lee for surrendering as to General Grant for compelling him to surrender." "Let us not," he stated, "be in too much haste in the work of restoration. Let us not be in a hurry to clasp to our bosom the spirit which gave birth to Booth."[83] Similarly, in 1866, Douglass warned the polity against the "desire to conciliate, and that maudlin magnanimity that is now our greatest danger," asking "When will the American people learn rightly the lessons of their own history?"[84] On May 30, 1871, on the first national celebration of Decoration Day – an event marked by the garlanding of the graves of Union soldiers – Douglass repeated the refrain, noting that the mourning manifested at such events served to obscure important distinctions between those who had fought for slavery and those who had fought against it.[85] It was a criticism that, as he made

[82] Blight, *Race and Reunion*, 64–97. See also Michael P. Rogin, "Washed White," *London Review of Books*, 15(11), June 10, 1993, 18.

[83] Frederick Douglass, "Our Martyred President: An Address Delivered in Rochester, New York, on April 15, 1865" in *The Frederick Douglass Papers: Series One, Speeches, Debates, and Interviews*, v. 4 edited by John W. Blassingame (New Haven, CT: Yale University Press, 1991), 78.

[84] Douglass, "The Assassination and Its Lessons," 108.

[85] Frederick Douglass, "The Unknown Loyal Dead, Speech Delivered at Arlington National Cemetery, Virginia, on Decoration Day, May 30, 1871" in *Frederick Douglass: Selected*

clear in an 1878 Decoration Day speech, was aimed not just at demonizing the South but also criticizing those "Good, wise, and generous men
at the North, in power and out of power, for whose good intentions and
patriotism we must all have the highest respect, [who] doubt the wisdom
of observing this memorial day, and would have us forget and forgive,
strew flowers alike and lovingly, on rebel graves."[86]

A historically precocious thinker who demonstrated a clear understanding of the difference between the sign and the signified, Douglass
recognized that establishing what Lincoln meant and how he was viewed
in the postbellum period was central to establishing the public memory
of the Civil War.[87] "Dying as he did," Douglass declared of Lincoln,
"his name becomes a text."[88] Such insight was matched by a call for
action. On April 15, 1865, embodying the subjunctive mood of the
African American countermemorial, Douglass declared, "Today, today
as never before the American people, although they know they cannot
have indemnity for the past – for the countless treasure and the precious
blood – yet they resolve today that they will exact ample security for the
future."[89] Similarly, he later imagined a better future recollection of the
Civil War in which subsequent generations would "marvel that men to
whom it was committed the custody of the Government, sworn to protect
and defend the Constitution and the Union of the states, did not crush
this rebellion in its egg; that they permitted treason to grow up under
their very noses."[90] Indeed, just as Lincoln employed the Declaration of
Independence as a standard against which to measure the nation and
find it wanting at Gettysburg, Douglass employed Lincoln to judge the
living and spur them to action. The president, Douglass declared, "would
have stood with those who stand foremost and gone with those who go
farthest, in the cause of equal and universal suffrage."[91]

Speeches and Writings edited by Philip S. Foner (Chicago: Lawrence Hill Books, 1999), 609–610.

[86] Frederick Douglass, "There was a Right Side in the Late War, Speech Delivered at Union Square, New York City, on Decoration Day, May 30, 1878" in *Selected Speeches and Writings*, 632.

[87] "It should be remembered that acts of Parliament and acts of Congress are but signs, and are less than the thing they signify." Frederick Douglass, "Emancipation Day speech in Rochester New York, 1883," *The Frederick Douglass Papers at the Library of Congress*. memory.loc.gov/cgibin/ampage?collId=mfd&fileName=24/24005/24005page. db&recNum=13&itemLink=/ammem/doughtml/dougFolder5.html&linkText=7. Accessed Jan. 27, 2014.

[88] Douglass, "The Assassination and Its Lessons," 111.

[89] Douglass, "Our Martyred President," 78.

[90] Douglass, "There Was a Right Side," 632.

[91] Douglass, "The Assassination and Its Lessons," 111.

Douglass did not, however, simply confine himself to specific criticisms of American policy and explicit calls to action; he also sought to generate an understanding of the tragic condition in his white audience. In this, however, there may appear to be something of a paradox. For while the title of Douglass's 1878 Decoration Day speech – "There Was a Right Side in the Late War" – demonstrates his unequivocal commitment to a definite view of the conflict, tragedy necessarily suggests ambivalence and the contingency of any particular perspective. On this account of Douglass's approach, the latter seems to undermine the former. If the demand for change is but one of several possibilities, it is not clear why an account of the war as a struggle for black freedoms should be embraced over an account of the war as a filial squabble. Resolving this tension reveals much about the ingenuity of Douglass's rhetorical and political strategy and, indeed, about the ways in which he sought to employ a tradition of tragic African American public mourning to disrupt a romanticized, distinctly white consensus that obscured the nation's tortured contradictions on race.

In his "What to a Slave is the Fourth of July?" address, argues George Shulman, Douglass reconciles the apparent conflict between his commitment to a definite political position and his recognition that any such position requires justification by offering a prophetic form of "democratic authority" that seeks to impel political change by modeling contrary practice. Unlike the prophecy of America's founding sermons, which closed down politics with oracular statements about right and wrong, Douglass's prophecy incited politics by uprooting conventions, "exposing them *as* conventions, hence as practices we have authored and could in principle change."[92] Thus, Shulman argues, by showing that what they took to be natural or God-given categories were human constructions and thus subject to change, Douglass sought to overcome whites' "motivated blindness" about race.[93] Expanding Shulman's argument beyond race and employing the language of recent democratic theory, Douglass's method can be characterized as seeking to shift America's democratic self-understanding from consensus to agonism.[94] Douglass's position required not that he recognize the legitimacy of white supremacy as a political doctrine, simply the legitimacy of those who held that position

---

[92] George Shulman, "Thinking Authority Democratically. Prophetic Practices, White Supremacy, and Democratic Politics," *Political Theory*, 36(5), 2008: 718.

[93] Ibid., 720.

[94] George Shulman, *American Prophecy: Race and Redemption in American Political Culture* (Minneapolis: Minnesota University Press, 2008), 242.

to *argue* for their viewpoint. His eulogies sought, in effect, to "level the playing field" by demanding that those who had hitherto considered their position natural, given, and unassailable defend it against his more compelling arguments.[95] By inviting his white audience to engage him in reasoned argument, moreover, Douglass enmeshed them in something of a performative contradiction, undermining white supremacist claims by forcing them to recognize him as a person worthy of engagement.

It might, nevertheless, be argued, that for Douglass, who famously declared in his Fourth of July Address, that "[a]t a time like this, scorching irony not convincing argument, is needed," such reasoned argument is an anathema.[96] Nevertheless, while scorching irony and powerful oratory were indeed tools in his considerable rhetorical toolkit – one that also included scorn, compelling metaphors, and all-out assaults on his audiences – it might also be noted that in that same Fourth of July Address, even as Douglass denies that he could or should argue for his position or that argument is in any way appropriate for his task, he nevertheless does exactly that. His speech sets out evidence to support his claims about the humanity of slaves, and he carefully picks apart the contradictions at the heart of America's claims to justice. Thus, Douglass wielded both argument *and* rhetoric – with each sometimes masquerading as the other – in his attempts to overcome and undermine the political and religious tenets of those to whom he was opposed. As such, the tragic tradition of African American public mourning offered Douglass a

---

[95] This does not commit Douglass, or indeed this author, to a Habermasian belief in an "ideal speech situation." For Habermas, the latter is marked by its aim of shared, rational truth seeking. Douglass was under no illusions about his opponents' commitment to truth, shared goals, or even rationality. The aim of Douglass's provocation was to draw his opponents into a debate in which the contradictions, hypocrisies, and alleged factual bases of their claims might be shown to be problematic and thus subject to amendment and/or rejection by the broader polity. As Robert Gooding Williams, channeling Nancy Fraser, notes about Douglass's political method, "In effect, Douglass ... project[s] his voice as the agent of what contemporary political theorists would call a 'subaltern counterpublic,' a discursive arena wherein the members of a subordinated social group 'invent and circulate counter-discourses, which in turn permit them to formulate oppositional interpretations of their identities, interests, and needs' – that is, interpretations that disrupt and challenge the interpretations advanced in 'official public spheres.'" Robert Gooding-Williams, *In the Shadow of Du Bois: Afro-Modern Political Thought in America* (Cambridge, MA: Harvard University Press, 2010), 203. See also, Nancy Fraser, *Justice Interruptus: Critical Reflections on the "Post Socialist" Condition* (Routledge: New York: 1997), 81–82. I am grateful to Andrew Poe for helping me to clarify this point.

[96] Frederick Douglass, "What to a Slave is the Fourth of July? Rochester, NY, July 5, 1852" in *Political Oratory from the Revolution to the Civil War* edited by Ted Wilmer (New York: Library of America, 2006), 538.

further pedagogical tool with which to seek to generate what Connolly calls a "critical responsiveness" in his white audience, potentially opening them up to the ambivalent and bicameral orientation of black life and forcing them to reconsider the certainty with which they held their own positions.[97] The approach is most evident in Douglass's 1876 eulogy for Lincoln at the unveiling of the Freedmen's Memorial in Washington, DC, where, by offering critical distinctions about even the "Martyr President" himself – when most were expecting to hear the platitudes of the funeral oration – Douglass brought complexity, ambivalence, and the subjunctive mood into mainstream mourning, challenging the nation to recognize that which its romantic commitment to national unity and consensus served to mask.

In Greek theatre, argues Simon Goldhill, seating arrangements marked out citizens according to their sociopolitical status, representing the city to itself in a manner conducive to democratic reflection.[98] Douglass's 1876 speech before Congress, the Supreme Court, the Chief Justice, the president, and many of the black citizens who had paid for the monument – the polity represented to itself – offered a similar possibility for a meaningful pedagogy of mourning.[99] Indeed, Lincoln's success at Gettysburg suggested that public mourning could be a moment of transformation, one that radically altered the nature of a public and its modes of deliberation. In 1876, America's centennial year, the negative consequences of romantic public mourning had already begun to manifest themselves: the majority of the former Confederate states were back under white Democratic control; the political and civil rights of blacks were in considerable jeopardy; and African Americans justifiably feared retribution from a white population embittered by the failures of Reconstruction.[100] As such, Douglass's speech called out for some acknowledgement of the circumstances facing those whose monies had been used to erect the "highly interesting object" that was the Freedmen's Memorial, itself something of a shrine to the romantic reconciliationism of the postwar years.[101] Nevertheless,

---

[97] William J. Connolly, *Pluralism* (Minneapolis: University of Minnesota Press, 2005), 126.

[98] Goldhill, *Love, Sex and Tragedy*, 224.

[99] Kirk Savage, *Monument Wars. Washington, D.C., the National Mall, and the Transformation of the Memorial Landscape* (Berkley: University of California Press, 2010), 87.

[100] Blight, *Beyond the Battlefield*, 84.

[101] Frederick Douglass, "Oration in Memory of Abraham Lincoln" in *American Speeches: Political Oratory from Abraham Lincoln to Bill Clinton* edited by Ted Wilmer (New York: The Library of America, 2006), 74. On the reconciliationism in the monument's design, see Kirk Savage, *Standing Soldiers, Kneeling Slaves: Race, War, and*

the occasion was still a memorial, and Lincoln's transformative words at Gettysburg notwithstanding, few expected the speech to be what James Oakes called "a scandalous rehearsal of all the criticisms Douglass had hurled at Lincoln during his Presidency."[102] In stark contrast to his 1865 claims that Lincoln was "emphatically the black man's president,"[103] Douglass offered what appeared to be an excoriating critique of the slain commander in chief:

> It must be admitted, truth compels me to admit even here in the presence of the monument we have erected to his memory, Abraham Lincoln was not, in the fullest sense of the word, either our man or our model. In his interests, in his associations, in his habits of thought, and in his prejudices, he was a white man. He was preeminently the white man's President, entirely devoted to the welfare of white men. He was ready and willing at any time during the last years of his administration to deny, postpone and sacrifice the rights of humanity in the colored people, to promote the welfare of the white people of this country.[104]

In coming metaphorically to bury Lincoln not to praise him, Douglass bucked the dominant trend of funeral rhetoric and performed something akin to the productive disorientation of tragic theater. Nevertheless, Oakes, among others, suggests that although Douglass began his speech in this critical vein, it did not last. "By the time Douglass reached his conclusion," he observes, "he had long since retreated from the provocative claims with which he had opened his speech."[105] Douglass declared, "... under his wise and beneficent rule we saw ourselves gradually lifted from the depths of slavery to the heights of liberty and manhood; and by measures approved and vigorously pressed by him, we saw the handwriting of the ages, in the form of prejudice and proscription, was rapidly fading from the face of our whole country."[106] He further noted that Lincoln's rule saw full recognition of Haitian independence, the abolition of the internal slave trade, the enforcement of the ban on the foreign slave trade, and the Emancipation Proclamation. "Though we waited long," Douglass declared, "we saw all this and more."[107] Oakes sees the speech

Monument in Nineteenth-Century America (Princeton, NJ: Princeton University Press, 1997), 898–128.
[102] James Oakes, *The Radical and the Republican. Frederick Douglass, Abraham Lincoln, and the Triumph of Antislavery Politics* (New York: Norton, 2007), 267.
[103] William Lee Miller, *President Lincoln: The Duty of a Statesman* (New York: Alfred Knopf, 2008), 307.
[104] Douglass, "Oration in Memory of Abraham Lincoln," 77.
[105] Oakes, *The Radical and the Republican*, 271–272.
[106] Douglass, "Oration in Memory of Abraham Lincoln," 79.
[107] Ibid., 79.

as a gradual progression, a rehearsal of Douglass's changing attitudes to Lincoln over the course of his own career. It is an ingenious reading but one that misses the bicameral orientation of Douglass's approach, an orientation arising from its connection to a tragic tradition of African American public mourning.

"The Freedmen's Memorial speech," observed David Blight, "is too easily dismissed as merely eulogistic or particularly negative."[108] Refusing the temptation to iron out its apparent inconsistencies, the eulogy can be seen as one whose ambivalence demands interpretation from its audience, presenting them with two different perspectives in the hope that they will develop the pluralistic perspective of the speech itself. Indeed, the sophistication of Douglass's speech is demonstrated by his attempt to achieve the perspective of his subject. "Though high in position," declared Douglass, "the humblest could approach him and feel at home in his presence. Though deep, he was transparent; though strong, he was gentle; though decided and pronounced in his convictions, he was tolerant towards those who differed from him, and patient under reproaches."[109] Employing the tragically ambivalent double consciousness of the African American funeral tradition, Douglass offered contrasting visions of Lincoln and demanded that his audience reflect on them both.[110] Given his concern about the masses' lack of opportunity for theoretical reflection, Douglass even demonstrated his method. "Viewed from the genuine abolition ground," he declared, "Mr. Lincoln seemed tardy, cold, dull, and indifferent: but measuring him by the sentiment of his country, a sentiment he was bound as a statesman to consult, he was swift, zealous, radical, and determined."[111] Demanding acknowledgment of Lincoln's complexity, Douglass disrupted the romantic narratives of reconciliation and consensus offered by both sides – North *and* South – and offered his audiences the opportunity for critical reflection not only on the passing of the deceased but also on the lives of those who mourned. His aim was "a renovation of the white American public mind," one that would "help to

---

[108] Blight, *Beyond the Battlefield*, 84.

[109] Douglass, "Oration in Memory of Abraham Lincoln," 81.

[110] Although many eulogies for Lincoln were marked by ambivalence, including Emerson's 1865 address or Woodrow Wilson's 1916 dedication of Lincoln's birthplace, Douglass's speech is distinguished by his use of ambivalence as a *method*. While Emerson and Wilson expressed their own personal conflicts about the meaning of Lincoln's death, Douglass's speech – though no doubt partly an expression of his own complicated relationship to the slain president – was more systematic in its approach and more oriented toward creating a public through speech.

[111] Douglass, "Oration in Memory of Abraham Lincoln," 81.

engender new political practices and, ultimately, a radical transformation of the fabric of the political habits constituting the nation."[112] Most obviously, Douglass sought to engender a mode of critical remembering, one that would return the questions of social and political justice for African Americans to the public sphere where, because of the failures of Reconstruction and the romantic quest for reconciliation, they had been all but erased. Moreover, he sought to do so in a way that would generate an ongoing "ethical insight into the untenability of one-sided positions."[113]

Further evidence for the claim that Douglass employed the tragic ambivalence of the black mourning tradition to demand a bicameral orientation from his audience is to be found in the qualifiers that pepper his speech. At the outset, he declares that he and his audience "stand today at the national centre [sic] to perform *something like* a national act"; he further offers that "Abraham Lincoln was not, in the *fullest sense* of the word either our man or our model"; "He was *preeminently* the white man's President" and, to the white audience, that "you and yours were the object of his *deepest* affection and *most earnest* solicitude" and that "we are *at best* only his step-children."[114] The effect of these qualifiers is to suggest that there is more going on in the speech than simple praise or blame. Much the same can be said for Douglass's invocation of the double consciousness of being black in a white society. In his eulogy for Lincoln, Douglass drew repeated attention to his insider/outsider status, demanding further recognition and reflection from those present. "In view then, of the past, the present, and the future," he observed, "and with liberty, progress, and enlightenment before *us*, I again congratulate *you* upon this auspicious day and hour"; further declaring that: "For the first time in the history of *our* people, and in the history of the *whole* American people, *we* join in this high worship." It was this ambivalent perspective of tragedy as response that, Douglass suggested, allowed African Americans "to take a comprehensive view of Abraham Lincoln, and to make reasonable allowance for the circumstances of his position"; the bicameral and tragic perspective, that is, of agonistic democracy.[115]

---

[112] Gooding-Williams, *In the Shadow of Du Bois*, 204.

[113] Roche, "The Greatness and Limits of Hegel's Theory of Tragedy," 57.

[114] Douglass, "Oration in Memory of Abraham Lincoln," 74–77. Emphasis added.

[115] Ibid., 75–78. Emphasis added. In this, the argument presented here shares Peter Myers's view that Douglass's 1876 speech employed ambivalence to pedagogical ends. Nevertheless, the different understanding of hope in African American political thought, rhetoric, and practice offered here – what Myers regards as optimistic and rational is seen as tragic and frequently performative – generates significantly different conclusions

Although mourning was but one of many sources and expressions of what Cornel West calls the "tragic sense" of black life, it was one that played a significant role in the expression and cultivation of the others. Nevertheless, it relied in part for its effect on an audience trained in or at least receptive to a polyphonic tradition.[116] At Gettysburg, Lincoln benefited from a social disorientation that opened up his audience to such a method. Douglass, by contrast, faced a polity consumed by a thirst for national reconciliation. Consequently, in his efforts to bring African American mourning into the American mainstream and to engender a more complex understanding of the war and its legacies, Douglass himself became a representative of tragedy as condition. Beginning with a steady stream of postwar literature, film and later television, that included Jefferson Davis's *Memoirs* through *Birth of a Nation*, *Gone With the Wind*, and Ken Burns's *Civil War*, the romantic myth of the Lost Cause and/or the idea of the conflict as a family squabble took a firm hold of the American imagination.[117] For white America, the brief window of

about Douglass's work and its implications for contemporary racial politics. Although Myers repeatedly invokes Douglass's "hopefulness," he does not say how he understands the term. Peter C. Myers, "A Good Work for Our Race To-Day": Interests, Virtues, and the Achievement of Justice in Frederick Douglass's Freedmen's Monument Speech," *American Political Science Review*, 104(2), 2010: 218, 219, 221; and Peter C. Myers, *Frederick Douglass. Race and the Rebirth of American Liberalism* (Lawrence: Kansas University Press, 2008), 7, 9, 12, 15, 48. The context of his usage strongly suggests, however, that he sees it as a synonym for "optimistic"; as does his observation that David Blight's work on Douglass and the Civil War "provides an excellent chronicling and analysis of Douglass's optimism." Myers, *Frederick Douglass*, 260, 216 *n.*5. In this, however, Myers seems to be underplaying the complexity both of Blight's argument and of Douglass's thought. In the work cited by Myers, Blight uses the word "optimism" less often than he uses the word "hope," a term which is, as Blight acknowledges, also compatible with anxiety and pessimism. David W. Blight, *Frederick Douglass's Civil War. Keeping Faith in Jubilee* (Baton Rouge: Louisiana State University Press, 1989), 6, 11, 23. Indeed, Blight repeatedly refers to the "*duty* of hope," and suggests a frequent tension between Douglass's private beliefs and the demands of his public rhetoric. Blight, *Frederick Douglass*, 22, 45, 18. If Douglass is *hopeful* in the African American tragic sense outlined here rather than simply *optimistic*, then Myers's attempt to position Douglass as being concerned with "the integrationist mainstream of African American protest thought" requires some qualification; as does his suggestion that Douglass's "theory of racial progress...challenges recent, pessimistic readings of American racial history and prospects." Myers, "A Good Work," 223, 209; and Myers, *Frederick Douglass*, 201.

[116] Garry Wills, *Under God: Religion and American Politics* (New York: Simon & Schuster, 1990), 195–206.

[117] Blight, *Race and Reunion*, 211–254, 211–220; and Eric Foner, "Ken Burns and the Romance of Reunion" in Eric Foner, *Who Owns History? Rethinking the Past in a Changing World* (New York: Hill and Wang, 2002), 189–204. See also Michael P. Rogin,

opportunity for tragic mourning offered by the carnage of the Civil War had closed. "The poetry of the 'Blue and Gray,'" lamented the African American *Christian Recorder* in July 1890, "is much more acceptable than the song of black and white."[118] The consequences of the triumph of romantic public mourning for those who had been "strangely told" by Lincoln that they "were the cause of the war" were disastrous.[119] "[T]his tearful, joyous, and spiritual family reunion," observed Bill Farrell, "could occur as it did only because the North abandoned black Americans in the South. As a result, this population faced disenfranchisement, lynchings, and pervasive violence, debt peonage, de jure segregation, lack of education, poverty and malnutrition."[120] Demonstrating the value of William Connolly's observation that the "drive to national unity" in consensus-based democracy "too readily fosters marginalization of vulnerable minorities,"[121] the romantic and reconciliationist mode of mourning embraced by both North and South helped rob African Americans of many of the gains of Reconstruction and the Thirteenth Amendment.[122] Consequently, the polity was forced to replay its racial conflicts, most obviously in the struggle over civil rights, conflicts in which the tradition of black tragic mourning played a significant role.

By establishing the continuity of this tradition of African American mourning – identifying its importance to the struggle *against* post-Reconstruction violence and *for* civil rights – it is possible to see how the response to Mrs. King's funeral is indicative of the decline of this tradition and its tragic ethos. Locating the funeral at a generational intersection, it is, moreover, possible to see the ways in which the successes of this tradition of black tragic mourning have helped bring about its near demise and generated significant changes in African American political thought and practice. It is, however, also to identify a tradition with a significant impact on the polity, one whose very ethos suggests the hopeful possibility of its own revival, even as a new and deeply political mode of mourning has begun to emerge out of more recent black experiences of death.

Ronald Reagan The Movie and Other Episodes in Political Demonology (Berkley: University of California Press, 1987), 190–235.

[118] Blight, *Race and Reunion*, 300.

[119] Douglass, "Oration in Memory of Abraham Lincoln," 78.

[120] Bill, Farrell, "All in the Family: Ken Burns's *The Civil War* and Black America," *Transition: An International Review*, 58, 1993, 170.

[121] William Connolly, *Pluralism* (Minneapolis: University of Minnesota Press, 2005), 7.

[122] See Douglas Blackmon, *Slavery by Another Name: The Re-Enslavement of Black Americans from the Civil War to World War II* (New York: Doubleday, 2008).

A TRAGIC HOMEGOING

Amid the racial violence that followed Reconstruction, rituals of mourning became one of the few venues for the expression of African American political protest. Although funerals for lynching victims were frequently political and transgressive of white authority, whites – perhaps betraying an increasing ignorance of black mourning traditions – were often content to let African Americans mourn unmolested.[123] Alternatively, bodies of lynching victims were left unburied as a protest against racial violence.[124] Embodying both of these political responses to loss, the 1955 funeral for lynching victim Emmett Till marked the intersection of the struggle against racial violence and the quest for civil rights. The funeral, at which Till's mother famously chose an open casket and eschewed the cosmetic work of the undertaker so that the world might see what racism had done to her son, was the spark that lit the civil rights fire, bringing the tragic black funeral tradition to bear on yet another iteration of America's racial conflicts.[125]

In much the same way that a funeral allowed Gabriel Prosser to organize his assault on Richmond, the impetus for the Selma-to-Montgomery march arose out of the funeral for slain black activist Jimmie Lee Jackson.[126] Aware that the black funeral tradition was a powerful weapon in the fight for equality, Martin Luther King employed it repeatedly, most obviously in his 1963 eulogy for the victims of the Sixteenth Street Baptist Church bombing. Indeed, recognizing the platform that the deaths of four little girls offered him both to gird African Americans for the fight and to reach out to white America by undermining claims about racial differences in suffering, King browbeat the parents of one of the girls, Carole Robertson, for refusing to allow her to be buried with her playmates, proving "to the point of callousness that he was anything

---

[123] W. Fitzhugh Brundage, *Under Sentence of Death: Lynching in the South* (Chapel Hill: University of North Carolina Press, 1997), 274; W. Fitzhugh Brundage, *Lynching in the New South: George and Virginia 1880–1930* (Champaign: University of Illinois Press, 1993), 46.

[124] Ashaf Rushdy, "Exquisite Corpse" in *The Best American Essays* (New York: Houghton Mifflin, 2001), 262.

[125] Frederick C. Harris, "It Takes a Tragedy to Arouse Them: Collective Memory and Collective Action During the Civil Rights Movement," *Social Movement Studies,* 5(1), 2006: 19–43. See also Heather Pool, "Mourning Emmett Till," *Law, Culture, and the Humanities,* May 2012: 1–31.

[126] Michael Eric Dyson, *April 4, 1968. Martin Luther King, Jr.'s Death and How It Changed America* (New York: Basic Books, 2008), 21; and David Remnick, *The Bridge: The Life and Rise of Barack Obama* (New York: Knopf, 2010), 8–9.

but squeamish about confronting the human costs of his leadership."[127] Among the many deaths that King used to his political advantage was his own. King constantly invoked his mortality for political effect in what Thomas Kane calls his "automortography,"[128] most famously at Mason Temple on the eve of his assassination but even at his own funeral where his "Drum Major Instinct" sermon was broadcast to the crowd.[129] Although self-conscious, it was not cynical. For the Kings, who spent their wedding night in a funeral home because hotels in Alabama were forbidden from serving blacks and who often used hearses to travel to and from rallies and church appearances, the connection between mourning and politics was especially tight. Much of Mrs. King's initial moral authority emerged, for example, from her status as Dr. King's widow. Beginning on April 8, 1968, when she marched with the Memphis sanitation workers only days after her husband's death, Mrs. King's presence invoked his absence and the tragic need to go on even in the face of death. It was, therefore, only fitting that her funeral service was very much in the civil rights tradition: part celebration, part jeremiad. That this was not broadly recognized suggests not only the decline of that tradition but also the complex consequences of its success.

Mrs. King's funeral took place in the 10,000-seat New Birth Missionary Baptist Church in Lithonia, Georgia, on February 6, 2006. In addition to then-President Bush, three of the four living former presidents, and numerous members of Congress, most of the six-hour service was attended by the governor of Georgia, the mayor of Atlanta, veterans of the civil rights movement, and a host of friends, dignitaries, and celebrities including Maya Angelou, Stevie Wonder, and Malaak Shabazz: the polity represented to itself.[130] It was, however, the eulogies by Joseph Lowery and former President Jimmy Carter that drew the most attention in the days after the funeral. Offering a eulogy in ragged verse, Reverend Lowery observed, "How marvelous that presidents and governors come to mourn and praise. But in the morning," the audience interrupting him

---

[127] Branch, *Parting the Waters*, 892.

[128] Thomas H. Kane, "Mourning the Promised Land: Martin Luther King, Jr.'s Automortography and the National Civil Rights Museum," *American Literature*, 76,(3), 2004: 549–577.

[129] Martin Luther King, Jr., *Testament of Hope: The Essential Writings and Speeches of Martin Luther King* edited by James M. Washington (New York: Harper, 1996), 279–286; and Dyson, *April 4, 1968*, 25.

[130] The presence of blue-eyed soul singer Michael Bolton was, perhaps, a somewhat more dubious honor. Bolton performed his heartfelt but cloying 2005 tribute to Mrs. King, *Courage in Your Eyes*.

with cheers and applause of anticipation, "will words become deeds that meet needs?"[131] Minutes later, he turned to the lines replayed most often in the subsequent furor:

> She extended Martin's message against poverty, racism, and war,
> She deplored the terror inflicted by our smart bombs on missions way-a-far.
> We know now there were no weapons of mass destruction over there,
> But ... but Coretta knew and we know there are weapons of misdirection
>   right down here:
> Millions without health insurance, poverty abounds.
> For war, billions more, but no more for the poor.[132]

Coming shortly after Lowery's eulogy, Jimmy Carter's comments were more restrained but remarkably similar in tone. Drawing out the virtues of the King family, including their peaceful commitment to encouraging democracy, Carter offered an implicit critique of the Bush administration's policies in Iraq, and, discussing the surveillance of the King family by the FBI during the civil rights struggle, drew attention to the administration's policy of warrantless wiretaps for those suspected of terrorist activity. Noting that there were "not yet equal opportunities for all Americans," Carter challenged the nation to carry on the Kings' work. The public response to the funeral fell into three main categories: two romantic and one tragic.

The first romantic response to Mrs. King's funeral simply aestheticized the event, celebrating the service in the manner of the nineteenth-century Northerners whose misunderstanding of the sorrow songs so vexed Frederick Douglass. Contrasting the King service with that held for Democratic Senator Paul Wellstone in 2002 – an event that provoked a considerable amount of partisan bickering[133] – Peggy Noonan declared, "The King funeral was nothing like this. It was gracious, full of applause and cheers and amens. It was loving even when it was political. It had spirit, not rage. That's part of why it was beautiful."[134] Similarly, in his

---

[131] All references to the funeral are taken from Columbia Broadcasting Service (CBS) 46 (Atlanta, GA), "In Memory: Coretta Scott King 1927–2006," February 6, 2006. Lowery's echoing of Pericles' (and Thucydides') concern about the relationship between words and deeds is, no doubt, coincidental. Thucydides, *History of the Peloponnesian War* translated by Rex Warner (London: Penguin Books, 1972), 147.

[132] Although Lowery did not acknowledge it, his final observation seemed to be borrowed from a Stevie Wonder song, "A Time to Live."

[133] "Tone of Wellstone memorial generates anger. Ventura blasts 'political rally,'" *CNN. com.* archives.cnn.com/2002/ALLPOLITICS/10/30/eleco2.memorial.fallout/. Accessed Feb. 6, 2008.

[134] Noonan's sentimentalization of African Americans was not confined to her appreciation of the service and her failure to recognize the various expressions of anger. "Blacks in America," she declared, "are not afraid to love Jesus the way they want to love him,

eulogy, former President George Herbert Walker Bush observed, "I come from a rather conservative Episcopal parish. I've never seen anything like this in my life ... It's absolutely wonderful ... the music, itself. It's just spectacular." Bush Sr. further praised the Kings for rejecting "race baiting" and observed that he had recently watched the movie *Glory Road* – about an integrationist basketball coach – with high school and college students who "didn't know what discrimination was until they saw this movie."[135] In burying Coretta Scott King, he seemed to suggest, America was burying the memory of its previous divides and, in so doing, demonstrating the closure of race as a political issue in the United States. It was a popular viewpoint summarized by CNN commentator Jeff Greenfield. "[T]he idea of civil rights has now become a consensus," he observed. "There's nobody arguing that Martin Luther King was on the wrong side of history."[136]

The second, more vociferous romantic response was summarized by Sean Hannity of Fox News. "The President of the United States came to honor this woman," he declared. "It should have been about her life, not ... using the occasion of her funeral to take a shot politically at the President ... I don't think that was the right thing to do in that environment."[137] Similarly, Georgia's *Augusta Chronicle* labeled Lowery and

to use the language and symbols they want to use. I want to kiss their hands for this." Peggy Noonan, "Four Presidents and a Funeral. A spirited tribute to Mrs. King – and to democracy," *The Wall Street Journal*, February 10, 2006. www.peggynoonan.com/2006/02/10/339/. Accessed Jan. 28, 2014.

[135] Bush senior later also expressed the second, more bellicose, romantic response to the funeral. "In terms of the political shots at the president who was sitting there with his wife, I didn't like it and I thought it was kind of ugly frankly," he observed in a subsequent interview. Dan Collins, "Dad Slams Attack on Bush at King Rite," CBSnews.com, February 10, 2006, www.cbsnews.com/news/dad-slams-attack-on-bush-at-king-rite/. Accessed Jan. 28, 2014.

[136] Jeff Greenfield, "Do You Really Do this at a Funeral?" *CNN.com*, February 8, 2006. www.cnn.com/2006/US/02/08/otsc.greenfield/index.html. Accessed Jan. 28, 2014.

[137] "Rev. Joseph Lowery Defends His Remarks at the King Funeral," *Hannity & Colmes*, February 9, 2006. www.foxnews.com/story/2006/02/10/rev-joseph-lowery-defends-his-remarks-at-king-funeral/. Accessed Jan. 28, 2014. In a previously published version of this chapter, I mistakenly suggested that the views of Colbert King of *The Washington Post* echoed those of Sean Hannity. They did not. The mistake arose from misreading of a transcript of King's February 7, 2006, appearance on MSNBC's *Hardball with Chris Matthews*. I am happy to correct the mistake here. For the mistake, see Simon Stow, "Agonistic Homegoing: Frederick Douglass, Joseph Lowery, and the Democratic Value of African American Public Mourning," *American Political Science Review*, 104(4), 2010: 691. For King's actual views on the funeral, see his article: "A Fitting Funeral for Mrs. King," *The Washington Post*, February 11, 2006. www.washingtonpost.com/wpdyn/content/article/2006/02/10/AR2006021001700.html. Accessed Jan. 28, 2014.

Carter "[u]tterly, absolutely, unendingly despicable."[138] Although hostility
to strong criticism of the racial status quo is a long-standing American
trope, the sheer *persistence* of the claim that a funeral was no place for
politics nevertheless suggested a genuine concern with propriety. While it
is possible that the concern with form was simply a mask for a concern
with content, the similar hostility generated by political critique at the
Wellstone memorial, or at that for Arizona-Cardinal-turned-U.S.-Army-
Ranger Pat Tillman, suggests that the response to Mrs. King's funeral
was part of a broader commitment to romantic public mourning and
to the ideology of consensus in the American polity.[139] What made the
response to the King funeral so remarkable was, however, that this commitment was expressed by so many African Americans. For although the
media controversy over the King funeral may have meant little to most
Americans, the hostility to the "politicization" of the event expressed
by numerous black pundits, scholars, and citizens suggests a significant
change in the understanding of the tragic mourning tradition among the
black citizenry.

The views of Mark Jordan of the conservative African American think
tank Project 21 directly echoed those of Sean Hannity. Jordan declared
of Lowery and Carter, "At an event to celebrate the achievements of one
of America's greats, these two men conducted themselves in a disgrace-
ful manner. They descended into the muck to take poorly-timed shots at
the President." His colleague Geoffrey Moore revealed a similar commitment to consensus, one equally redolent of a romantic worldview.
"As Americans of all colors and creeds gathered in Atlanta and in front
of televisions across the nation to honor the life and works of Mrs.
King," he declared, "liberals such as Reverend Joseph Lowery and former
President Jimmy Carter used her funeral as a stage for their politics of
division."[140] Roy Innis, chairman of the considerably more progressive
Congress on Racial Equality, expressed a similar demand for propriety
over politics. "Regardless of their political persuasions or their animus
for President Bush, they should have known that the solemn funeral of

---

[138] "Beyond Contemptible; Dignified Funeral Lapses into Shameful Partisan Slams,"
Augusta Chronicle, February 9, 2006. chronicle.augusta.com/stories/2006/02/09/edi_
54368.shtml. Accessed Jan. 28, 2014.

[139] See Mike Fish, "An Un-American Tragedy. Part Three: Death of An American Ideal,"
ESPN.com, 2009. sports.espn.go.com/espn/eticket/story?page=tillmanpart3. Accessed
Jan. 28, 2014.

[140] "Black Activists Outraged by Politicization of Coretta Scott King's Funeral," February
8, 2006. www.nationalcenter.org/P21PRPoliticizingFuneral206.html. Accessed Jan. 28,
2014.

Mrs. King was the wrong place and the wrong time for their critique."[141]
Indeed, blogging for *The New York Times* and attempting to pre-empt
the suggestion that "no white can criticize anything blacks do 'for one
of their own,'" University of Washington in St. Louis literature professor Gerald Early observed that "When Mr. Lowery [sic] defended his
remarks later by talking about 'speaking truth to power' and how Mrs.
King would have approved and how what he said, was, in fact, her position, it sounded like a lot of pious, self-serving flapdoodle from an old
civil rights leader."[142] Outside of the pundit class, several self-identified
African American citizens expressed their dismay with the manner
in which Mrs. King's funeral was conducted. In *USA Today*, E. Alfred
Johnson of Troy, Michigan, complained, "[t]o take a cheap shot at our
president, who graciously accepted the invitation to attend the funeral,
was callous, mean-spirited and even vicious."[143] Writing from the dou-
bly evocative location of Stone Mountain, Georgia,[144] *Atlanta Journal-
Constitution* reader Venetia Poole spoke for many when she declared,

[141] "Roy Innis, Blasts President Jimmy Carter and Rev. Joe Lowery for Behavior at the
Funeral of Coretta Scott King," News Release Wire, February 14, 2006. www.expert-
click.com/NRWire/Releasedetails.aspx?id=11656. Accessed Jan. 29, 2014. Likewise,
Adrienne T. Washington, writing in *The Washington Times*, declared that "Partisan
bickering has no place at the funeral of a woman whose entire public persona symbol-
ized grace, poise, dignity and tolerance. One expects homilies and hymns in the house of
the Lord, not daggers and diatribes." Anticipating the suggestion that her concern was
about the values that were expressed, not the expression itself, Washington asserted,
"Don't get me wrong: My political ideology is not at issue here. What has been called
into question is my belief that there is an appropriate 'season' for everything." Adrienne
T. Washington, "Southern manners sadly lacking at King rites," *The Washington Times*,
February 10, 2006.

[142] Gerald Early, "Trash Talking Funeral Talk," February 9, 2006, www.nytimes.com. early.
blogs.nytimes.com/2006/02/09/trash-talking-funeral-talk. Accessed Sept. 24, 2008.
Early's remarks were more nuanced than most – noting, for example, the strangeness
of political conservatives trying to appropriate Mrs. King as one of their own – and
were less concerned with funeral etiquette than with the suggestion that Lowery and
his fellow travelers belonged to an age of racial politics and political agitation that had
long since passed. As such, they do not undermine the claim being made here about the
decline of the tragic mourning tradition among African Americans but rather support
it. Early, perhaps, embodies the view that the politics of struggle that produced the tradition of politically infused public mourning among African Americans has now been
supplanted.

[143] E. Alfred Johnson, "Funeral Politics were 'mean-spirited and even vicious,'" *USA Today*,
February 10, 2006, 12A.

[144] The site of the largest monument to the Confederacy in the United States, a bas-relief
sculpture of Robert E. Lee, Stonewall Jackson, and Jefferson Davis carved into the
mountainside. The site of the founding of the second Ku Klux Klan in November 1915,
the mountain was memorably referenced in the closing section of Martin Luther King's
speech to the March on Washington in August 1963. King, *Testament of Hope*, 223.

"As an African American, I was somewhat appalled by the fact that some of our 'black leaders' used the funeral as a political platform to scold President Bush concerning the war...I appreciate the fact that speakers had a captive audience with the President, but I disagree with the time and place."[145] Both romantic responses to the funeral nevertheless overlooked the very real conflicts of the civil rights struggle –conflicts in which, as Lowery and others noted, the tradition of African American tragic mourning had played a central role.

For many, perhaps, Lowery's eulogy might simply appear to be a form of democratic leftist patriotism.[146] Nevertheless, it is clear that Lowery saw himself as embodying a definite inheritance. In a speech at a peace rally in Atlanta, Georgia, on April 1, 2006, Lowery situated himself firmly within a tradition:

> By what moral authority do they tell us how to conduct a black funeral? How many black funerals has George W. run in his life? ...for over half a century in the ministry I have buried hundreds of black people and I think I know more about how to conduct a black funeral than...Sean Hannity. In the black church, at a funeral, we celebrate the life of the dead, but then we challenge those who are living to pick up the mantle and carry on the work ... George W.... didn't come to celebrate Coretta's life because she made good girl-scout cookies. He came to celebrate her life because she was an advocate for peace and a warrior for justice, and if he didn't expect to hear about peace and justice he should have kept his Whitehouse-Texas self home.[147]

Such heated language – itself no doubt exacerbated by the tensions between America's romantic commitment to consensus and its very real political conflicts – was not, however, uncommon during the intensely antagonistic atmosphere of the second Bush administration, and that Lowery saw himself as a part of a tradition does not make it so. Nevertheless, to miss the tragic understanding expressed in Lowery's eulogy is, perhaps, to buy into the romantic understanding of racial politics expressed by his critics. For although it is clear that there has been considerable progress toward

---

[145] Venetia Poole, "Readers Write," *Atlanta-Journal-Constitution*, February 8, 2006, 10A. See also, D. R. Tucker, "Cheap shots at King funeral," *The Washington Times*, February 9, 2006, A20.

[146] That it should appear this way is, of course, unsurprising. The language of democratic leftist patriotism is made up of coalition of values emerging from multiple different traditions, including those of African American political activism. Moreover, to make such a claim would be to ignore the possibility of the kind tragic patriotism – predicted on a Dionysian juxtaposition of national celebration and critique – set out in the previous chapter.

[147] Joseph Lowery, "Remarks at Peace March, Atlanta, GA, April 1, 2006." www.youtube .com/watch?v=jYo1BnWfr4c. Accessed Jan. 30, 2014.

racial justice in the United States, to see the hope that underpins the black mourning tradition as having been fulfilled is to miss the contingency of those gains and the continuing injustices that Lowery identified in his speech, to miss the recognition that the gains of the civil rights movement not only came at the cost of those still hampered by racial inequalities but that these very gains made the alleviation of remaining inequalities all the more unlikely. Acutely aware that Americans do not yet live in a world in which "men judge men by their souls and not by their skins,"[148] Lowery continued his tragically hopeful push not only for racial justice but also for the possibly even-more-quixotic goal of peace. That Lowery recognized the costs of his approach and the likelihood of his success is suggested by his adoption of a dualistic and semicomic persona.

Before offering his initial salvo against the political luminaries present, a chuckling Lowery turned to the assembly of presidents and first ladies behind him and promised "I'm gonna behave." The duality embodied in this theatrical performance – itself echoed in the juxtaposition of his critique with the celebratory aspects of the event – found repeated expression in Lowery's eulogy. He quickly followed up his opening remarks about the disconnection between words and deeds with good-natured zings of Al Sharpton and Jesse Jackson, and the most searing – and most frequently replayed – lines of Lowery's speech were immediately prefaced with a joking reference to his own poetry presented as a faux apology to Maya Angelou. Not immune, furthermore, to romanticized reverie about the heavenly reunion of the Kings – "Together at last! Together at last! Thank God Almighty, together at last!"[149] – Lowery nevertheless went out of his way to note that King had her critics, pointedly referencing her opposition to homophobia, itself a rebuke to Bernice King, who had led an anti–gay-rights march that had culminated in an address at her father's grave.[150] In the performance of this ambivalence toward the event, and indeed, to the presence of many of the political notables,

---

[148] Du Bois, *Souls*, 186.

[149] Unsurprisingly, perhaps, this romantic reverie was one of Peggy Noonan's favorite moments in the service. "The Rev. Joseph Lowery gave a beautiful poem about Martin being with Rosa in heaven and then finding out that Coretta was coming, and rushing to greet her at the pearly gates. Strike you as corny? Not me. It was beautiful because it was not only full of unselfconscious faith, it assumed unselfconscious faith on the part of the audience, and so was both an implicit compliment and a declaration of shared assumptions." Noonan, "Four Presidents and a Funeral."

[150] Andrew Clark, "Martin Luther King's daughter Bernice takes up mantle as U.S. civil rights leader," *The Guardian*, November 1, 2009. www.guardian.co.uk/world/2009/nov/01/bernice-king-sclc-female-leader. Accessed Jan. 30, 2014.

Lowery offered – as did Douglass for Lincoln – a counternarrative to the largely hagiographic accounts of King's life that dominated the event and the subsequent commentary. His purpose was not, of course, to denigrate King but rather to complicate the story of racial reconciliation offered by the dominant narratives of U.S. history, seeking, like his historical forbear, to force his audience to recognize the limitations on the progress made toward racial justice. In so doing, he aimed to provide an agonistic antidote to the democratically poisonous ideological commitment to consensus on racial politics that has, for example, permitted the cooption of Dr. King's words by opponents of affirmative action.[151] That Lowery should become, like Douglass before him, an emblem of tragedy as condition is, perhaps, suggested by the ways in which the successes of the black mourning tradition help explain its contemporary decline.

While older civil rights activists grumbled that Mrs. King's funeral should have taken place in the Ebenezer Baptist Church where Dr. King had preached, the choice of the New Birth Missionary Baptist Church was highly significant. "[T]he funeral's location in an arena-sized church," observed Cameron McWhirter in the *Atlanta Journal-Constitution*, "set in the heart of an affluent section of black suburbia spoke volumes about how much the civil rights movement has transformed the political, economic and social landscape of the United States since the 1960s and the demise of segregation."[152] The African American population has become younger and, in many cases, more affluent in the years since the civil rights struggle. Half of the African American population of the United States is under thirty-five, and there are numerous indicators that they are less involved in electoral politics and civic organizations than the previous generation.[153] The emergence of a black middle class – a product of the increased opportunities generated by the successes of the civil rights movement – has produced significant socioeconomic, political, and theological changes in the African American population. As Allison Calhoun-Brown notes, the "end to legalized racism has allowed class differences among blacks to gain greater salience," with an increasingly suburbanized black middle class geographically and political separating from a "black underclass decaying in urban areas."[154] A cause and a consequence of this

[151] Eric J. Sundquist, *King's Dream* (New Haven, CT: Yale University Press, 2009), 203–206.
[152] Cameron McWhirter, "'Good night, my sister'; Coretta King laid to rest after spirited funeral," *The Atlanta Journal-Constitution*, February 8, 2006, 1A.
[153] R. Drew Smith, *Long March Ahead: African-American Churches and Public Policy in Post-Civil Rights America* (Durham, NC: Duke University Press, 2004), 224.
[154] Allison Calhoun-Brown, "What a Fellowship: Civil Society, African American Churches, and Public Life" in *New Day Begun. African-American Churches and Civic Culture in*

separation has been the declining social and political salience of the black church and the dramatic rise of the "prosperity gospel."[155]

Although there is a "troubling lack of research" on the role of the church in contemporary black politics,[156] the efforts of the Public Influences of African-American Churches project and Frederick Harris both suggest a decreased political efficacy for an "increasingly un-churched" African American population.[157] As Aldon Morris and others point out, the church was the institutional center of the civil rights movement, offering a democratic pedagogy that was both generated and reinforced by the church's rituals and traditions.[158] However, whereas a generation ago, somewhere in the region of 80 percent of African Americans attended church, the number is now believed to be as low as 40 percent.[159] Among those who do attend church, theological changes have had a significant impact on their political orientation. Foremost among them has been the mainstreaming of the "prosperity gospel," that which embraces personal enrichment and individual rather than social change.[160] This viewpoint – which Harris describes as "a complete reversal from the mission of the black church

---

Post-Civil Rights America edited by R. Drew Smith (Durham, NC: Duke University Press, 2003), 47.

[155] Dyson, *April 4, 1968*, 128. See also F. C. Harris, "Entering the Promised Land? The Rise of the Prosperity Gospel and Post Civil-Rights Black Politics" in *Religion and Democracy: Danger or Opportunity?* edited by Alan Wolfe and Ira Katznelson (Princeton, NJ: Princeton University Press, 2010), 255–278.

[156] Smith, *New Day Begun*, ix

[157] Frederick C. Harris, *Something Within: Religion in African-American Political Activism* (New York: Oxford University Press, 1999); and Melissa V. Harris-Lacewell, "Righteous politics: the role of the black church in contemporary Politics," *Cross-Currents*, June 22, 2007.

[158] Aldon Morris, *The Origins of the Civil Rights Movement: Black Communities Organizing for Change* (New York: The Free Press, 1984), 10. See also, Harris, *Something Within*.

[159] Calhoun-Brown, "What a Fellowship," 48.

[160] Although growing out of the Protestant ethic identified by Max Weber (1992) that sees the acquisition of wealth as a sign of God's grace, the prosperity gospel deviates from this tradition in two key ways. First, whereas the former sees wealth as a by-product of hard work, the prosperity gospel sees it as an unearned blessing. Second, while the Protestant ethic has traditionally eschewed ostentatious displays of wealth and the enjoyment of riches – promoting, as Weber points out, both saving and capital investment – the prosperity gospel promotes the values of consumerism and the idea that God wishes his followers to enjoy the success bestowed on them. See Hanna Rosin, "Did Christianity Cause the Crash?" *The Atlantic Monthly*, December, 2009. www.theatlantic.com/magazine/archive/2009/12/did-christianity-cause-the-crash/7764. Accessed Jan. 30, 2014; and Max Weber, *The Protestant Ethic and the Spirit of Capitalism* translated by Talcott Parsons (London: Routledge, 1992). Bishop Eddie Long, then pastor of the New Birth Missionary Baptist Church, who presided over Mrs. King's funeral service, is a staunch proponent of the prosperity gospel. Asked in 2005 to justify his annual salary

during slavery, Reconstruction and civil rights"[161] – has reduced political activism in the black church, with those who embrace the prosperity gospel less likely to vote, contact public officials, sign petitions, or attend public demonstrations than those holding more traditional views about the black church and social justice.[162] Indeed, Preston Smith argues that the prosperity gospel has had the effect of "valorizing privatism" and "making public action increasingly illegitimate,"[163] with the remaining obstacles to social progress being seen as more attitudinal than structural.[164] At Mrs. King's funeral, the African American class schism manifested itself when a finger-wagging former President Clinton noted – to rapturous applause from *some* of those present – that there were "more rich black folks in this county" except one in the United States and asked, "Atlanta, what's your responsibility for the future of the King Center? What are you going to do to make sure this thing goes on?" Although such self-critique – albeit by proxy – suggests that the black tragic tradition of mourning in America is not yet fully exhausted, the social changes reflected in and reinforced by the rise of the prosperity gospel have, nevertheless, served to undermine the conditions under which this tradition emerged and prospered.

As Karla Holloway argues, the emergence of an African American middle class in the early part of the twentieth century was closely connected to the rise of the funeral home. Undertaking was one of the first black businesses to prosper after the Civil War, largely because segregation and a lack of interest and expertise among white undertakers in dealing with black skin – frequently bearing the marks of racial violence – all but ensured prosperity for black undertakers. That many funeral homes were owned and operated by ministers permitted the merging of the sacred and the secular in a way that gave impetus to the movement for social and political equality.[165] Throughout that century, however, as incomes

of more than a million dollars, Long responded by claiming, "Jesus wasn't poor." Harris, "Entering the Promised Land?" 255.

[161] Ira J. Hadnot, "Politics Toned Down at Black Churches," *Dallas Morning News*, July 31, 2004, 1G. See also Cheryl Hall-Russell, "The African American Megachurch: Giving and Receiving," *New Directions for Philanthropic Fundraising*, 48, Summer, 2005: 21–29; and Dyson, *April 4, 1968*, 129–130.

[162] Harris-Lacewell, "Righteous politics."

[163] Smith, *Long March Ahead*, 5.

[164] Smith, *New Day Begun*, 6–7. See also, R. Drew Smith and Corwin Smidt, "System Confidence, Congregational Characteristics, and Black Church Civic Engagement" in Smith, *New Day Begun*, 73.

[165] Karla C. Holloway, *Passed On: African American Mourning Stories. A Memorial* (Durham, NC: Duke University Press, 2003), 36–37. See also Suzanne E. Smith, *To Serve the Living* (Cambridge, MA: Harvard University Press, 2010).

rose, middle-class African Americans started to patronize white funeral homes. "For some black folk," noted Holloway, "white funeral homes became a new option and a visible mark of a certain status."[166] In order to compete, historically black funeral homes increasingly dissociated themselves from their traditional clientele, often by removing pictures of civil rights icons such as Dr. and Mrs. King from their walls. Similarly, white funeral homes made successful outreaches to the black community, with many black funeral services becoming less elaborate and more staid in the process.[167]

The changing nature of black funerals, the increasing discomfort of the black church with the theodicy of the emancipationist and civil rights struggles, and the decreasing loyalty of the black population to African American undertakers, appeared, then, to have combined to create a largely class and generational division in black responses to loss. At Mrs. King's funeral, this divide was clear. Those steeped in the tragic tradition of black mourning, such as Joseph Lowery and Bernice King, embraced agonism, celebrating the deceased by both highlighting her achievements and recognizing the limitations on her success, using the occasion to disrupt the problematic narratives of racial closure and to push for further social and political change. Those with shorter memories and a different theology embraced the consensus politics of romantic mourning by rejecting the critique and focusing solely on the advantages they had accrued from the – to them at least – entirely-historical struggle for civil rights. As the typology of public mourning offered at the outset suggests, the consequences of this shift away from tragic mourning for the American polity are likely to be largely negative.

The tragic irony of the decline of tragic black mourning in the American polity is, of course, that it has been fueled in part by the prior successes of the tradition, most obviously in the growth of a prosperous black middle class. Indeed, this emergence suggests that for some, at least, tragedy as response has been successful in making productive the suffering of black life, offering an African American political thought and practice that moves beyond the fetishism of political struggle.[168] Nevertheless, the decline of this mourning tradition and its tragic ethos

---

[166] Holloway, *Passed On*, 38.
[167] See Angelo B. Henderson, "Death Watch? Black Funeral Homes Fear a Gloomy Future as Big Chains Move in," *The Wall Street Journal*, July 18, 1997, A1; and Kamika Dunlap, "New Orleans' black funeral tradition dying out," *The Oakland Tribune*, March 29, 2006. www.highbeam.com/doc/1P2-7042934.html. Accessed Jan. 30, 2014.
[168] Glaude, *In a Shade of Blue*, 134–135.

suggests that the theological and class schism on display at Mrs. King's funeral will continue to expand to the detriment of those at the lower end of the socioeconomic scale, precisely those for whom the church and its rituals of mourning have been a traditional source of political strength. This is, perhaps, what Eddie Glaude meant when he declared that "the black church is dead."[169] If, however, this chapter itself constitutes something of a eulogy for a tradition of tragic and self-consciously political responses to loss, it is a eulogy very much in the same tradition, one that demands that instead of lamenting, the polity pick up the mantle and carry on the work. Certainly there would seem to be something of this 'going on together' in the approach of Black Lives Matter, a movement that is likewise predicated on a form of public mourning and a concomitant demand for social and political change.

MICHAEL BROWN'S BODY

A little after midday on August 9, 2014, Michael Brown, an unarmed eighteen-year-old African American man, was shot dead by a white police officer, Darren Wilson, in Ferguson, Missouri. Wilson fired twelve shots, hitting Brown in the torso, the arms, and the head. Brown's body lay face down in the street, uncovered, blood pouring from his head, for at least ten minutes, during which time a large crowd of neighborhood residents gathered. Eventually a firefighter partially covered Brown's body with a sheet, but it remained publicly visible on the street for more than four hours, further inflaming an already angry black community. In much the same way that photographs of Emmett Till's body galvanized African Americans to strive for civil rights nearly sixty years earlier, and in the similar way that the treatment of deceased black bodies under slavery and the domestic terrorism of lynching precipitated the emergence of a politically motivated mourning tradition, images of the disrespect shown to Brown in death produced the first national public protest by the nascent Black Lives Matter (BLM) movement. The movement had begun in 2013 following the acquittal of George Zimmerman, a neighborhood watch volunteer from Sanford, Florida, who shot to death an unarmed black teenager, Trayvon Martin, in February of 2012. Mobilizing their grief and anger, three black women, Alicia Garza, Patrisse Cullors, and Opal Tometi, began an online campaign pointing to the ways in which

---

[169] Eddie Glaude, Jr., "The Black Church Is Dead," *The Huffington Post*, August 23, 2012. www.huffingtonpost.com/eddie-glaude-jr-phd/the-black-church-is-dead_b_473815 .html. Accessed Feb. 20, 2016.

Martin's humanity had been denied, in both his murder and a subsequent media vilification that seemed – in a pattern repeated following the deaths of a number of other African Americans at the hands of law enforcement – to make the victim responsible for his own demise. The hashtag #blacklivesmatter began to trend on Twitter and elsewhere.

Given America's history with strong pushbacks against racial violence and social injustice, much of the popular response to BLM was, perhaps, all too predictable. The consensus-oriented, misperceived legacy of Martin Luther King became, once again, a standard against which to judge BLM and find it wanting and a stick with which to beat it. On the political right, the usual media suspects attacked the organization for its views and its tactics. "[C]ommandeering the microphone and bullying people and pushing people out of the way I think really isn't a way to get their message across," observed perennial Republican presidential candidate Rand Paul.[170] Likewise, Wisconsin Governor Scott Walker declared, "We need to change the tone in America from chants and rallies that fixate on racial division."[171] Similarly, the black conservative commentator Juan Williams lamented, "If only the energy and passion of #BlackLivesMatter protesters could be harnessed in something constructive rather than destructive."[172] Even the African American Democratic Congressman Keith Ellison took issue with the movement's approach, supporting the call by Minneapolis mayor Betsy Hodges to end the occupation of an area near the Fourth Precinct Police Station following the shooting death of another African American male, Jamal Clark.[173] Ellison followed up with a tweet suggesting that the movement read Dr. King's "Letter from a Birmingham Jail," noting that King "didn't just sit on Edmund Pettus Bridge" but "[m]oved to 1965 Voting Right [sic] Act."[174]

[170] Rosie Gay, "Rand Paul: Black Lives Matter Should Change Its Name," *Buzz Feed News*, August 27, 2015. www.buzzfeed.com/rosiegray/rand-paul-black-lives-matter-should-change-its-name#.luroNeAj9X. Accessed Feb. 28, 2016.

[171] Jenna Johnson, "Scott Walker alleges a 'rise in anti-police rhetoric' under Obama," *The Washington Post*, September 2, 2015. www.washingtonpost.com/news/post-politics/wp/2015/09/02/scott-walker-alleges-a-rise-in-anti-police-rhetoric-under-president-obama/. Accessed Feb. 28, 2016.

[172] Juan Williams, "Juan Williams: #BlackLivesMatter is playing with fire," *The Hill*, September 7, 2015. thehill.com/opinion/juan-williams/252672-juan-williams-blacklivesmatter-is-playing-with-fire. Accessed Feb. 28, 2016.

[173] Betsy Hodges, "A Message from the Community to End the Occupation," November 30, 2015. mayorhodges.com/2015/11/30/a-message-from-the-community-to-end-the-occupation/. Accessed Feb. 28, 2016.

[174] twitter.com/keithellison/status/671499919375638530?ref_src=twsrc%5Etfw. Accessed Feb. 28, 2016.

At the heart of many of these attacks was a view, expressed by former Arkansas governor Mike Huckabee, that "All lives matter. It's not that any life matters more than another ... That's the whole message that Dr. King tried to present, and I think he'd be appalled by the notion that we're elevating some lives above others."[175]

The persistent claim that Black Lives Matter was a racist organization – Bill O'Reilly of Fox News repeatedly called it a "hate group" and compared it to the Ku Klux Klan[176] – that sought to elevate some people over others might arise, in part at least, from the tenets of liberal democratic theory, which demand a commitment to the universal over the specific. Nevertheless, the perceived deviance in the demands of the Black Lives Matter movement might also be seen as a product of America's ongoing commitment to the politics of consensus, both in terms of its broader democratic understanding and, more specifically, with regard to the issue of race. Certainly, the claim that Martin Luther King and especially the Martin Luther King of "Letter from a Birmingham Jail" might have been opposed to both the disruptive tactics and civil disobedience of BLM is misplaced, for it is precisely these tactics that most clearly suggest a continuity between BLM and its civil rights precursor.[177] Likewise, the movement's commitment to a certain type of ethical humanism as the basis for a future politics – itself a rejection of the claim that to say some lives matter is necessarily to say that others do not – also suggests a continuity between BLM and its forebear. That both emerged from and employed public mourning as a political tool is a further structuring affinity. There are, however, significant differences between the historical tradition of African American public mourning employed by King and his forebears and that embodied by Black Lives Matter: differences in leadership, personnel, and approach. Nevertheless, both share a commitment to a certain kind of mortalist humanism – the claim that, in the face

[175] Julie Kliegman, "Martin Luther King III said his dad would be proud of the Black Lives Matter Movement," *The Week*, August 24, 2015. theweek.com/speedreads/573499/martin-luther-king-iii-said-dad-proud-black-lives-matter-movement. Accessed Feb. 28, 2016. Indeed, Rand Paul spoke for many when he suggested that the organization change its name to "All Lives Matter." Gay, "Rand Paul."

[176] "Bill O'Reilly Says Black Officers Lives Matter Is A 'Hate Group' That Wants Police Officers Dead," *Media Matters for America*, August 31, 2015. mediamatters.org/video/2015/08/31/foxs-bill-oreilly-says-black-lives-matter-is-a/205288. Accessed Feb. 29, 2016.

[177] See, for example, Mark Engler and Paul Engler, "MLK was a disruptor: How Black Lives Matter carries on Martin Luther King's legacy of effective activism," *Salon*, January 18, 2016. www.salon.com/2016/01/18/mlk_was_a_disruptor_how_black_lives_matter_carries_on_martin_luther_kings_legacy_of_effective_activism/. Accessed Feb. 29, 2016.

of death, human beings achieve a form of equality as moral and political agents[178] – to democracy and, indeed, to democratically productive responses to loss.

Writing about the death of Michael Brown, Eddie Glaude observed,

> Of course, Reverend Al Sharpton sought to get ahead of the protests. As he did with the outrage over the death of Trayvon Martin...Sharpton sought to channel the energies of mass demonstrations into 'legitimate' forms of black political behavior ... in the name of a kind of fidelity to a particular and narrow understanding of the civil rights movement.[179]

"Sharpton and the Brown family together," he continued, gave "... voice to their grief and to the demands for justice. But, as if split screened, those images stood alongside the actions of young people and organizers in the streets of Ferguson – and amid the violence of the state. In so many ways, the protests exceeded the disciplines of non-violence [and] ... called to mind a more complex picture of black struggle." In this split screen, perhaps, it is also possible to see how the ethos of the tragic mourning tradition embodied by Du Bois's expression of a "hope, not hopeless but unhopeful" has been supplanted by a "fiercely intelligent, and organized" form of anger.[180] Such anger is not yet the excessive anger of *mênis* – some looting and destruction of property not withstanding – but rather a disciplined and focused anger strategically employed to definite political ends: its democratic orientation is suggested by its commitment to a certain form of humanism that is, it will be argued in the next chapter, a necessary precursor to democratic politics. It is one that recognizes that African Americans must first count as people before they can count as citizens, a claim that, like the movement's righteous anger, was also present in Frederick Douglass's activism and ire. Like Douglass, King, and others, BLM seeks to establish that humanity through a politically focused form of mourning.

Darren Wilson explained his decision to open fire on Michael Brown by claiming that Brown looked "like a demon" and that as, such he feared for his life. He further claimed that Brown

made like a grunting, like aggravated sound ... it looked like he was almost bulking up to run through the shots, like it was making him mad that I'm shooting

---

[178] For an illuminating discussion of this claim, see, for example, Bonnie Honig, "Antigone's Two Laws: Greek Tragedy and the Politics of Humanism," *New Literary History*, 41(1), 2010, 1–33.

[179] Eddie Glaude, Jr., "A Requiem for Michael Brown/A Praisesong for Ferguson," *Theory & Event*, 17(3) Supplement, 2014.

[180] Glaude, "A Requiem."

at him. And the face he had was looking straight through me, like I wasn't even there, I wasn't even anything in his way.[181]

Thus, the trope – ubiquitous in American history – of black beastliness and inhumanity was once again employed to explain disciplinary violence against African Americans. Such discipline was, perhaps, reinforced by the failure – deliberate or otherwise – to remove Brown's body from public view, itself a disturbing echo of the terror evoked in black communities by the exposed bodies of slave suicides and lynching victims. It was this denial of humanity that provoked many of BLM's activists to take part in the Ferguson protests.

"Unlike the civil rights movement," observed Frederick Harris, "the focus of Black Lives Matter – on policing in black and brown communities, on dismantling mass incarceration – is also being articulated less as a demand for specific civil or political rights, and more as a broader claim for 'black humanity.' This insistence on black humanity has repeatedly been used by Black Lives Matter activists as a catalyst for political action."[182] Indeed, Ferguson activist Ashley Yates argued that such appeals to black humanity are both an expression of anger and an appeal to others to act. "And at the very core of this is humanity – Black Lives Matter," she observed. "We matter. We matter. Black lives matter because they are lives. Because we are human. Because we eat. Because we breathe. Because he [Michael Brown] had a dream, because he made rap songs, they may have had cuss words in them. Yeah. He was human. And when we neglect to see that we end up where we are today."[183] This commitment to establishing black humanity was the impetus behind the submission, in November 2014, by Michael Brown's parents of a statement to the United Nations Committee Against Torture. It declared, in part, "The killing of Mike Brown and the abandonment of his body in the middle of a neighborhood street is but an example of the utter lack of regard for, and indeed dehumanization of, black lives by law enforcement personnel."[184]

Black Lives Matter is, then, a movement that employs a politically oriented public mourning that eschews the tragic understanding of hope

---

[181] Josh Sanburn, "All the Ways Darren Wilson Described Being Afraid of Michael Brown," *Time*, November 25, 2014. time.com/3605346/darren-wilson-michael-brown-demon/. Accessed Mar. 1, 2016.

[182] Frederick C. Harris, "The Next Civil Rights Movement?" *Dissent*, Summer 2015. www .dissentmagazine.org/article/black-lives-matter-new-civil-rights-movement-fredrick-harris. Accessed Mar. 1, 2016.

[183] Ibid.

[184] Ibid.

embodied by its precursor – certainly it would be hard to describe its members as in any way seeking to inculcate ambivalence in their audience – in favor of a more focused and vehemently expressed anger. The movement nevertheless embodies another key element in the tragic mourning tradition: a democratically oriented politics of humanism. Such humanism was as evident in black funerals that sought to celebrate lives lived as it was in Frederick Douglass's attempts to establish African Americans as being worthy of political consideration. Mortalist humanism of this sort is, however, the subject of some debate in contemporary political thought, with Bonnie Honig, in particular, rejecting it as a basis for democratic politics. It may be, however, that Black Lives Matter suggests that such humanism is a necessary precursor to democratic politics: that the agonism that Honig and others seek requires it to establish the legitimacy, as opponents, of those currently excluded by the polity's commitment to a democratic and racial consensus. It is the latter that suggests that those who exist outside of the misperceived legacy of Dr. King – who has, in dying, like Lincoln before him, become a text on which to write the concerns of those who invoke him[185] – are illegitimate and, often, less than human.

Thus, while the older black mourning tradition embodied by Frederick Douglass and on display at Coretta Scott King's funeral would now appear to be in decline, it nevertheless suggests the possibilities of a tragic and democratically productive set of responses to loss that might yet be revived. Even as the political mourning of the Black Lives Matter movement seems to have moved away from cultivating the bicameral

---

[185] As the work of Francesca Polletta and Jacquelyn Dowd Hall demonstrates, the manner in which the polity chooses to remember Martin Luther King profoundly affects its attitudes toward contemporary racial politics. Indeed, Hall's work further suggests the tragic nature of the hope that permeates black politics (1251). Similarly, Polletta notes that the tension between the politically necessary acknowledgment of black political gains and the more difficult recognition that African American hopes remain unfulfilled is evident in contemporary congressional debate. She identifies the problem of "black legislators rhetorically *struggling* to represent the purpose of memorializing King and the movement, to retell the past in a way that neither deprecates the movement's accomplishments nor claims that its aims have been fulfilled" (483). Francesca Polletta, "Legacies and Liabilities of an Insurgent Past. Remembering Martin Luther King, Jr., On the House and Senate Floor," *Social Science History*, 22(4), 1998: 479–512; and Jacquelyn Dowd Hall, "The Long Civil Rights Movement and the Political Uses of the Past," *The Journal of American History*, 91(4), 2005: 1233–1263. See also Larry J. Griffin and Kenneth A. Bollen, "Civil Rights Remembrance and Racial Attitudes," *American Sociological Review*, 74(4), 2009: 594–614.

orientation and tragic ambivalence of that earlier tradition, it nevertheless suggests, in the face of opposition from critics of mourning as a form of political action, that humanism is a necessary element of or precursor to meaningful democratic agonism. Turning to the death of a figure who most Americans have repeatedly placed outside of the human community – Osama bin Laden – might be thought to provide a useful test case for this claim.

3

Mourning bin Laden: Aeschylus, Victory, and the Democratic Necessity of Political Humanism

> People who treat other people as less than human must not be surprised when the bread they have cast on the waters comes floating back to them, poisoned.
>
> – *James Baldwin, No Name in the Street*

Two scenes:

A pregnant woman speaks on the telephone to her husband moments before she sees the building in which he is trapped crumble to the ground on live television. Later she watches as groups of Arabs celebrate the raid that made her a widow.

A young girl is woken in the night to find a team of foreign soldiers searching her home. They kill her father and remove his body. Later she watches on television as groups of Americans celebrate his death.

At the heart of this chapter is a no doubt distasteful suggestion: that Americans should mourn the death of Osama bin Laden, seeking to tell a complex story about him and his motivations in much the same way that Lincoln told a complex story about America at Gettysburg, Douglass about Lincoln in Washington, DC, or Joseph Lowery about Coretta Scott King and the politics of race in Atlanta. In a world where political theory was widely read, such a suggestion would undoubtedly bring disapprobation from some quarters and eye rolling from others – further evidence, perhaps, for those who do not need it, of the way in which academia divorces its practitioners from reality and/or commits them to a virulent anti-Americanism.[1] Even among those attentive

[1] This view is, perhaps, best captured by Jonathan Yardley's suggestion that liberal academics compete in an "America sucks sweepstakes," in which they seek to find better and bitterer ways to describe the failings of the United States. See Richard Rorty, *Philosophy*

to contemporary theoretical debates and/or sympathetic to employing outlandish claims to generate political reflection, the suggestion might still encounter a significant degree of resistance, less, perhaps, for its content than for what it might be thought to imply about mourning as a political strategy. From either perspective, practical or theoretical, the suggestion that America should mourn its enemies might be seen as a politically objectionable form of humanism, the philosophical doctrine that holds that human beings *qua* human beings are united by certain qualities that make them equally worthy of moral consideration.[2] In this, the conservative historian Victor Davis Hanson and the far-from-conservative political theorist Bonnie Honig might find themselves in heated agreement.

Rejecting any attempt to engage with America's enemies as equals, the Hoover Institute's Hanson suggests that, as a matter of practical politics and military strategy, the writings of al Qaeda should "serve as a wake-up call to an often naïve and therapeutic West that believes that enemies are to be understood rather than defeated."[3] Similarly, he suggests, any attempt to contextualize the activities of terrorist groups such as, al Qaeda or "rogue" nations such as Iran, should be resisted. Doing so, he argues, merely empowers extremists who wish to destroy and destabilize America. Indeed, offering a scornful characterization of the position of those who claim otherwise, he suggests they believe that "[h]uman nature is better understood through a therapeutic perspective. Most nations, in fact, interpret outreach as magnanimity leading to reciprocity, not as weakness deserving of contempt." Indeed, possibly capturing – albeit ironically in his case – the argument of this chapter better than its author, Hanson suggests that "[p]olarizing and out-of-date labeling such as calling ISIS or the Taliban 'terrorists' or 'Islamists,' ... serve no purpose other than to simplify complex issues in ways that caricature those from whom we differ."[4]

---

and Social Hope (London: Penguin, 1999), 4. Yardley's view nevertheless raises the philosophical problem of whether a sweepstakes can legitimately be considered as such when Noam Chomsky has already won.

[2] "Humanism" is, of course, a term with multiple possible meanings. Here I employ it in the way in which it is formulated by some of its most recent critics, most notably by Bonnie Honig.

[3] Victor Davis Hanson, "Introduction" in *The Al Qaeda Reader: The Essential Texts of Osama Bin Laden's Terrorist Organization* edited by Raymond Ibrahim (New York: Doubleday, 2007), Kindle Edition, location 378–379.

[4] Victor Davis Hanson, "Obama Does Have a Strategy," *The National Review*, February 3, 2015. www.nationalreview.com/article/397720/obama-does-have-strategy-victor-davis-hanson. Accessed Apr. 13, 2015. See also Victor Davis Hanson, "How to Empower Violent

In a more theoretical register, Honig identifies two reasons why mortalist humanism – the view that in facing death, human beings achieve a form of equality as moral agents – is an inadequate basis for politics. First, she argues, by embracing the universal, the mortalist humanism suppresses the conflict at the heart of the political.[5] Second, she suggests, the practice of politics is undermined by an ethical turn that frequently accompanies this focus on mortality. Irrespective of whether that ethic is a Foucauldian care of the self or a Levinasian care of the other, Honig argues, such approaches merely seek to cultivate a particular worldview at the expense of the "action in concert on behalf of collective life" that constitutes democratic politics.[6] It should, of course, be noted that Honig – unlike Hanson – is not denying the humanity of those with whom she might disagree, simply suggesting that focusing on a shared humanity offers a false unity that denies the political. Here, however, it will be argued that it is precisely the acknowledgement of this shared humanity that makes politics possible: that all politics is a form of conflict, but not all conflict is political. Following Aristotle, it will be suggested that politics can only take place between equals and that the absence of humanism makes conflict something occurring between different species: precisely that which, perhaps, Hanson suggests when he calls for the hunting down and destruction of America's enemies.

Drawing on a reading of Aeschylus' *The Persians* – a play depicting the grief of Athens' defeated enemy – this chapter seeks to demonstrate the political worth of the humanism that both Hanson and Honig eschew and, with it, the ongoing value of tragic public mourning as a resource for democratic politics. It argues that the manner in which ethical insight is cultivated by the tragic complicates both Hanson's distinction between understanding and defeating the enemy and Honig's divorcing of ethic from action. This argument aims to recover a democratically productive form of humanism that anticipates Honig's and Hanson's objections

Extremism," victordavishanson.com, February 24, 2015. victorhanson.com/wordpress/?p= 8239. Accessed Apr. 13, 2015.

[5] "Finitude is said to soften us up for the call of the other, to open us up to the solicitations of ethics and bypass the intractable divisions of politics. I argue ... that even this humanism is implicated in political divisions it claims to transcend and, moreover, that an ethics of mortality and suffering is no adequate replacement for a (post)humanist politics with agonistic intent." Bonnie Honig, "Antigone's Two Laws: Greek Tragedy and the Politics of Humanism," *New Literary History*, 41(1), 2010: 1.

[6] Bonnie Honig, *Antigone, Interrupted* (Cambridge: Cambridge University Press, 2013), xiii. For a wonderfully insightful discussion of the differences between these types of ethic, see Ella Myers, *Worldly Ethics: Democratic Politics and Care for the World* (Durham, NC: Duke University Press, 2013).

while making the case for a politics of ethos that does not turn away from
action or seek to overcome conflict. Far from being antithetical to politics, it suggests, such humanism is a necessary precursor to its practice.
Indeed, it traces the connection between the dehumanization of America's
enemies embodied in and perpetuated by both the nation's contemporary mourning practices and its triumphalist response to bin Laden's
death, and the problematic politics – both foreign and domestic – of the
postplanes era.

Befitting its engagement with Honig's work as both influence and
inspiration, the chapter begins by drawing on a distinction she identifies
between two forms of Ancient mourning: the Homeric and the democratic.[7] The latter, corresponding to the nationalist mourning identified
in the discussion of Pericles' Funeral Oration, focused on the city's loss
of its anonymous defenders, while the former focused on family losses of
specific individuals. In Antiquity, Honig notes, the democratic, or what
is here being termed the nationalist, was employed to temper the emotional excesses of the Homeric, thereby creating the preconditions for
Athenian democracy. It will, however, be suggested that modernity has
been marked by the emergence of a neo-Homeric response to loss focused
on the individual and marked by the public expression of private grief.
It is one that, far from being tempered by the nationalist, embraces it
in a way that exacerbates the negative aspects of each for the practice
of American democracy. This unfortunate symbiosis generates a moralized response to loss and a commitment to consensus that dehumanizes,
excludes, and/or makes deviant minority voices in a way that suppresses
a potentially productive agonism in democratic politics. Indeed, the combination cultivates a form of mourning without end – an *álaston pénthos* – that afflicts the citizenry with a grief-wrath the Ancients called
mênis. Most commonly associated with the protagonists of Greek tragedy, *mênis* manifests itself in a particular form of blindness that prevents
its sufferers from comprehending either their interests or their actions.
Identifying the complex ways in which this blindness undermines the
political and strategic capacities of the afflicted, the chapter points to
the ways in which America's postplanes response was undone by the
grief it embraced and assiduously cultivated in the years following the
attacks.[8] The aim here is not to rehearse the now well-known errors made

---

[7] Bonnie Honig, "Antigone's Laments, Creon's Grief: Mourning, Membership, and the
Politics of Exception," *Political Theory*, 37(1), 2009: 5–43.

[8] On such blindness, see Mark Button, "Accounting for Blind Spots: From Oedipus to
Democratic Epistemology," *Political Theory*, 39(6), 2011: 695–723.

by the U.S. in its ongoing War on Terror but rather to demonstrate the links between these errors and its response to the losses that precipitated its postattacks bellicosity. Both the neo-Homeric and the nationalist, it argues, served to dehumanize "the other" in a way that posed problems for American domestic politics and its strategies of foreign engagement, not least, perhaps, by helping to create the Islamic State, a more violent and sadistic form of opposition to America and its policies than that which precipitated its initial responses to loss.

By turning to Aeschylus' *The Persians* as an example of a tragic mourning, the chapter seeks to suggest the political efficacy of a complex mobilization of grief predicated on a mortalist humanism of the sort that Honig rejects. *The Persians*, it argues, not only helped cultivate an ethos conducive to democratic life and politics, it also provided a set of compelling reasons for embracing that ethos. As such, Honig's account of the relationship between ethic and action appears to separate the lightning from the flash, failing to capture the way in which the two are cultivated and emerge together. Honig, it is suggested, while undoubtedly right to embrace the democratic possibilities of the natal, is too quick to discount the political potential of the mortal. Indeed, returning to Loraux's later work on tragedy and loss suggests that Honig's rejection of the "antipolitics" of mourning may be predicated on a misreading of the classicist's argument. "Antipolitical" – as Loraux employs the term – is not, it will be argued, necessarily anticonflictual. As such, Loraux's mortalist humanism is much closer to Honig's agonism than the latter allows and that for this reason, the classicist might be thought to provide a model for the political revival of the humanist aspects of tragedy that Honig seems to overlook. Although the argument about the value of humanism to politics does not turn on whether Honig's reading of Loraux is a faithful one, exploring the relationship between the two theorists' work suggests the ways in which such humanism makes politics possible, not least by distinguishing mere conflict from the conflict of politics.

Having addressed the theoretical debate underpinning the turn to mortality and mourning in contemporary political thought, the chapter then turns to the practical. Situating its argument amid the triumphalism that engulfed the polity in the aftermath of bin Laden's death, this section suggests the ways in which the excesses embraced in victory mirrored those embraced in loss. Drawing on its reading of *The Persians*, the chapter identifies the political and strategic benefits that might accrue to the American polity if it were to temper this triumphalism by engaging in a tragic mourning for its enemies both old and new. It is not a demand that America mourn the whole world nor that it mourn its enemies out of a bleeding heart too liberal – in Robert Frost's phrase – to take its own side in an argument. Rather, it argues that cultivating and employing an ethos of tragic mourning for its enemies in a time of war will serve the interests of the polity far more faithfully than an orgiastic celebration of their losses. The chapter then turns to considering the cultural resources available for cultivating this ethos. Lest its argument prove insufficiently offensive to those repulsed by its structuring conceit, the chapter concludes by suggesting that a possible model for such mourning might be found in the Islamic world.

TEARS OF GRIEF, TEARS OF RAGE

Antigone, argues Bonnie Honig, "explores the clash in 5th century Athens between Homeric/elite and democratic mourning practices. The former … memorialize the unique individuality of the dead, focus on the family's loss and bereavement, and call for vengeance. The latter … memorialize the dead's contribution to the immortal polis and emphasize (as in the Funeral Oration) the replaceability of those lost."[9] Many scholars, she notes, point to Solon the Lawgiver's sixth-century BCE funeral reforms – aimed at reining in the excesses of Homeric mourning – as a necessary precursor to the emergence of the Athenian democracy. The fear that overwrought individually focused mourning practices might undermine democratic politics was a further manifestation of the Greek concern with excess rather than a fear of public emotion *per se*.[10] Democracy was considered especially susceptible to such excess because it demands a mode of engagement – one of productive discussion and careful deliberation – that can be undone by excessive emotion. In the absence of effective mechanisms for restraint, writes Loraux, such emotions can all too easily become *álaston pénthos* or "unforgettable grief."[11] When grief cannot be forgotten, she continues, it becomes the indelible anger that the Greeks called *mênis*,[12] one which, by erasing considerations of justice, reciprocity, and self-interest in favor

---

[9] Honig, "Antigone's Laments," 5.
[10] See, for example, James Davidson, *Courtesans and Fishcakes: The Consuming Passions of Classical Athens* (New York: Harper Perennial, 1999).
[11] The translation is from Athena Athanasiou and Elena Tzlepis, "Mourning (as) Woman: Event, Catachresis, and 'That Other Face of Discourse'" in *Rewriting Difference: Luce Irigaray and "the Greeks"* edited by Elena Tzlepis (Albany: State University of New York Press, 2010), 110. Corinne Pache translates the term as "mourning that cannot forget." Loraux, *Mothers in Mourning*, 54.
[12] Loraux, *Mothers in Mourning*, xii. Although predominantly associated with women, *mênis* also affected men. See also Leonard Muellner, *The Anger of Achilles: Mênis in*

of its own singular perspective, becomes the "worst enemy of [democratic] politics."[13] Evidence for the continued relevance of Loraux's claims is to be found in America's postplanes policy making.

In September 2001, CIA counterterrorism chief Coffer Black promised President Bush that he would deliver Osama bin Laden's "head in a box."[14] While such anger and bravado are, no doubt, understandable in the immediate aftermath of one of the bloodiest days in U.S. history, it was an anger and bravado that continued to structure the nation's response to the 2001 attacks long after the rubble had been cleared from Ground Zero. It was fueled, in part, by the nationalist mode of mourning – embodied by the choice of a decontextualized Gettysburg Address as a eulogy for New York City's dead – embraced by the polity in the wake of the attacks. Such mourning championed a narrative of American innocence and an unquestioning commitment to the nation, one that bolstered state power and silenced dissenting voices, not least by promoting a purely rhetorical commitment to the question "Why do they hate us?"[15] Historically, nationalist responses to loss served to temper the excessive laments of Homeric mourning and to undermine its commitment to revenge, thereby turning the focus away from the individual and toward the state. In modernity, however, far from tempering such excesses, this nationalist mode of mourning combined with a neo-Homeric response to loss that exacerbated the worst aspects of each for democratic politics. The neo-Homeric took many forms but found its most obvious expression in the memorialization of the victims of al Qaeda's attacks.

Starting on September 17, 2001, and ending fifty-one weeks later, *The New York Times* published a series of individual obituaries for the great majority of al Qaeda's New York City victims under the heading "Portraits in Grief."[16] Suggesting the *álaston pénthos* at the heart of the

Greek Epic (Ithaca, NY: Cornell University Press, 1996). I am grateful to Danielle Hanley for helping me clarify this point.

[13] Loraux, *Mothers in Mourning*, 98.

[14] Evan Thomas, "The Trouble with Assassination" in *Beyond Bin Laden: America and the Future of Terror* edited by Jon Meacham (New York: Random House, 2011), eBook, Kindle edition, loc. 938.

[15] Simon Stow, "Pericles at Gettysburg and Ground Zero: Tragedy, Patriotism, and Public Mourning," *American Political Science Review*, 101(2), 2007: 195–208.

[16] The series initially offered 1,910 of sketches of lives lived and lost. The sketches were collected together in 2002 and published as a book entitled *Portraits of Grief 9/11/01*. A second edition of the book, published in 2003, offered a total of 2,310 obituaries, providing additional details of those whose families chose to cooperate with the project once the initial series was over and, in one case, removing from the official record an individual whose existence and victim status could no longer be verified. New York

collection, the *Boston Herald* described "Portraits" as "a memorable way to engrave the costs of terrorism on American hearts for the rest of our days."[17] Indeed, possibly confirming Hannah Arendt's claims about the "rise of the social," many commentators fell over themselves to provide public testaments of the private tears provoked by the series, a claim that was as true for the audience of the obituaries as it was for those who produced them.[18] "Never before in my forty-plus years as a reader," observed Jack Bodanski in a letter to the *Times*, "have I been moved to close my eyes, place my palm on the page of a newspaper, shed a tear, and say a prayer."[19] Even Susan Sontag, who had initially objected to the way in which "the politics of a democracy" had been "replaced by psychotherapy" in the immediate aftermath of the attacks, felt obliged to embrace the postplanes consensus.[20] "I read the 'Portraits in Grief,' every last word, every single day," she wrote. "I was tremendously moved. I had tears in my eyes every morning."[21] Likewise, the design of the museum and memorial complex at Ground Zero was a further manifestation of the neo-Homeric, offering a focus on each person killed and commitment to what Loraux called the never-ending "pleasure of tears" that "the afflicted can find in weeping for himself or a loved one."[22] First among the "Guiding Principles" for the memorial's design was that it "[r]ecognize each individual who was a victim of the attacks,"[23] while

Times, *Portraits: 9/11/01: The Collected "Portraits of Grief" from The New York Times,* Revised Edition (New York: New York Times Books, 2003). See Simon Stow, "*Portraits 9/11/01: The New York Times* and the Pornography of Grief" in *Literature After 9/11* edited by Jeanne Follansbee Quinn and Ann Keniston (New York: Routledge, 2008), 224–241.

[17] "Victims live in our hearts," Editorial, *Boston Herald*, January 1, 2002, 20. See also the ubiquitous postattacks bumper sticker that declared "We Will Never Forget."

[18] *The Human Condition* (Chicago: Chicago University Press, 1998), 43. Mirta Ojito, one of the *Portraits'* authors, recalls crying over the phone as she spoke to the father of two daughters killed in the Twin Towers and then going into the women's bathroom at the *Times*, where she found a colleague also sobbing from the strain. Samuel F. Freedman, *Letters to a Young Journalist* (New York: Basic Books, 2006), 31.

[19] New York Times, *Portraits: 9/11/01: The Collected "Portraits of Grief" from The New York Times* (New York: New York Times Books, 2002), xi.

[20] Susan Sontag, "Talk of the Town," *The New Yorker*, September 24, 2001, 32. www.newyorker.com/archive/2001/09/24/010924ta_talk_wtc. Accessed Apr. 13, 2014.

[21] Janny Scott, "A Nation Challenged: The Portraits, Closing a Scrapbook Full of Life and Sorrow," *The New York Times*, December 31, 2001, B6.

[22] Nicole Loraux, *The Mourning Voice: An Essay on Greek Tragedy* translated by Elizabeth Trapnell Rawlings (Ithaca, NY: Cornell University Press, 2002), 47.

[23] Lower Manhattan Development Corporation, *World Trade Center Memorial Competition Guidelines* (New York: Lower Manhattan Development Corporation, 2003), 19.

the museum's designers promised that "[t]he lives of every victim of the 2001 and 1993 attacks will be commemorated as the visitors have the opportunity to learn about the men, women, and children who died."[24] Indeed, such is the memorial's focus on cultivating public manifestations of private grief that some have expressed fears the cavernous reflecting pools at the site might become a magnet for those moved to suicide by personal or national losses.[25] The commitment to *álaston pénthos* at the heart of the complex is, however, most clearly evidenced by the presence of a repository in the museum for the nearly 22,000 pieces of unidentified human remains recovered from the site. The repository serves not as a final resting place for the remains but rather as a way station for their preservation until forensic technology improves enough for them to be formally identified. In many cases, additional body parts have been returned to families long after those initially presented to them in the months and years following the attacks.[26] This commitment to the perpetual reopening of old wounds serves as a perfect metaphor for the politically problematic mourning of *álaston pénthos* that has gripped the polity since 2001.

The direct connection between *álaston pénthos* and the *mênis* embodied by America's response to the attacks is suggested by the American major in Afghanistan who began his daily briefings with an announcement of the number of days since "terrorists murdered three thousand innocent people when they attacked the World Trade Center in New York"; a reading from *Portraits*; and the declaration that "The hunt goes on. The war on terrorism in Afghanistan continues."[27] Likewise, the nation's emotions found physical manifestation in the commission of three navy vessels commemorating the locations of the attacks, one of which – the *U.S.S. New York* – was partly forged out of steel recovered from the World Trade Center.[28] Far from being tempered, moreover, by

[24] www.911memorial.org. Accessed Feb. 16, 2012.
[25] Al Baker, "At 9/11 Memorial, Police Raise Fears of Suicide," *The New York Times*, February 12, 2012. www.nytimes.com/2012/02/16/nyregion/at-9-11-memorial-police-raise-suicide-fears.html?_r%022&_r=0. I am grateful to Char Miller for drawing this article to my attention.
[26] Jo Craven McGinty, "As 9/11 Remains Are Identified, Grief Is Renewed," *The New York Times*, November 12, 2011. www.nytimes.com/2011/11/13/nyregion/as-remains-from-9-11-are-identified-no-end-to-grieving.html?pagewanted=all. Accessed Jun. 18, 2013. For a fuller discussion of the memorial and its relationship to American politics, see Simon Stow, "From Upper Canal to Lower Manhattan: Memorialization and the Politics of Loss," *Perspectives on Politics*, 10(3), 2012: 687–700.
[27] Jason Burke, *The 9/11 Wars* (New York: Penguin Global, 2011), 84–85.
[28] www.ussnewyork.com/. Accessed Jun. 19, 2013.

the dominant democratic-nationalist mode of mourning, the impact of
the neo-Homeric response was intensified by its merger with the same.[29]
In the postplanes polity, the combination of the nationalist and the neo-
Homeric generated a narrative in which the innocence of the attack
victims was merged with an assumption – ubiquitous in American history –
of national innocence, generating a *mênis*-fueled response that was both
deeply moralized, and dehumanizing of America's enemies. As such, the
attacks could only be seen through the lenses of loss and injustice, rather
than geopolitics.

President Bush's White House address to the nation on the day of the
attacks invoked evil four times in a speech lasting four and a half minutes. "Thousands of lives were suddenly ended by evil, despicable acts of
terror"; "Today our nation saw evil, the very worst of human nature";
"The search is under way for those who are behind these evil acts"; and,
quoting the 23rd Psalm, "Even though I walk through the valley of the
shadow of death, I fear no evil, for You are with me."[30] The first and third
uses employed "evil" as an adjective, the second and fourth as a noun.
While both were commonplace after the attacks, the latter was frequently
imbued with explanatory power: bin Laden was understood to be the
personification of an insidious force recurrent in human history.[31] "We do
not believe that Americans are fighting this evil to minimize it or to manage it," wrote David Frum and Richard Pearle, capturing the Manichean
worldview at the heart of the American response. "We believe they are
fighting to win – to end this evil before it kills again and on a genocidal
scale. There is no middle way for Americans. It is victory or holocaust."[32]
Nor was this understanding of bin Laden confined to the political right.
In 2011, John Brennan, Barack Obama's chief counterterrorism adviser,

[29] It is ironic then that many regarded the neo-Homeric "Portraits" as decidedly democratic. Harold Raines, executive editor of *The New York Times*, asserted, for example,
that "'Portraits in Grief' reminds us of the democracy of death, an event that lies in the
future of every person on the planet." New York Times, *Portraits*, vii.

[30] "Text of Bush's Address," CNN.com, September 11, 2001. archives.cnn.com/2001/US/
09/11/bush.speech.text/. Accessed Jun. 8, 2013.

[31] See also Bush's 2002 State of the Union Address, in which he unveiled the term "Axis of
Evil," revived the notion of America's Christian mission into the wilderness, and invoked
the word "evil" five times. George W. Bush, "Bush State of the Union address," January
29, 2002. archives.cnn.com/2002/ALLPOLITICS/01/29/bush.speech.txt/. Accessed Jun.
4, 2013.

[32] David Frum and Richard N. Pearle, *An End to Evil: How to Win the War on Terror*
(New York: Ballantine Books, 2004), 7. See also President's Bush's declaration during
the joint session of Congress on September 20, 2001, that "Either you are with us, or
you are with the terrorists." georgewbush-whitehouse.archives.gov/news/releases/2001/
09/20010920-8.html. Accessed Mar. 7, 2014.

declared, "We seek nothing less than the utter destruction of this evil that calls itself Al Qaeda."[33] Indeed, the Bush administration's frequent paralleling of fascism and Islamic fundamentalism was foreshadowed by no less a leftist hero than Jacques Derrida.[34]

"The absolute," wrote Hannah Arendt in *On Revolution*, "... spells doom to everyone when it is introduced into the political realm."[35] While theorists of agonistic democracy are divided over the value of the friend/enemy distinction, there is, nevertheless, widespread agreement on the political problems posed by the moralization of these categories. "At times," observes Richard Bernstein, "we do need to make a clear distinction between friends and enemies. But there is a danger that distinctions become reified and rigid in ways that obscure complex issues."[36] Drawing on Augustine and Leibniz, Bernstein argues that although the concept of evil has traditionally "been intended to provoke thinking, questioning, and inquiry," in modernity, "the appeal to evil is being used as a political tool to obscure complex issues, to block genuine thinking, and to stifle public discussion and debate."[37] Domestically, the moralized postattacks consensus served to muzzle Congress, the national press, and the citizenry in a way that marginalized dissent. The moral replaced the political in a way that drowned out, excluded, and frequently demonized alternative voices, narrowing the range of acceptable options and opinions and suppressing the conflict central to democratic agonism. That a Democratic president should be able to conduct a drone program that deliberately killed – at the time of writing – at least one U.S. citizen and inadvertently killed three more, without any meaningful legislative or judicial oversight

[33] William Shawcross, *Justice and the Enemy: Nuremburg, 9/11, and the Trial of Khalid Sheik Mohammed* (New York: Public Affairs, 2011), 213.

[34] The term *Islamofascism*, employed by George Bush in 2006, was invoked as early as 2002. See Martin Wolf, "A Free World," *The Financial Times*, September 3, 2002; Thomas L. Friedman, *Longitudes and Attitudes: Exploring the World After September 11* (New York: Farrar, Strauss, and Giroux, 2002), 189). Likewise, Victor Davis Hanson noted that Hitler's *Mein Kampf* is translated in Arabic as "*Jihadi*, or 'my *jihad*'" and declared: "Millions died as a result of the world's indifference to Hitler's straightforward words...the same mistake should not be made twice." Ibrahim, *Al Qaeda Reader*, loc. 536. On Derrida's paralleling of Islam – which he defined as democracy's "other" – with fascism, see Jacques Derrida, *Rogues: Two Essays on Reason* translated by Michael Naas and Pascale-Anne Brault (Stanford, CA: Stanford University Press, 2005), 28–37. For a discussion of this position, see Anne Norton, *On the Muslim Question* (Princeton, NJ: Princeton University Press, 2013), especially 118–139.

[35] Hannah Arendt, *On Revolution* (New York: Viking Books, 1963), 79.

[36] Richard J. Bernstein, *The Abuse of Evil: The Corruption of Politics and Religion Since 9/11* (Malden, MA: Polity: Kindle Edition), loc. 284–285.

[37] Bernstein, *Abuse of Evil*, 61–65.

or significant public outcry, suggests the entrenchment of this seemingly permanent American national consensus in its response to terror.[38]

To point to the ways in which the 2001 attacks were situated in a moralized narrative is not, of course, to deny that those killed in the attacks were the victims of a cruel and horrendous act or that, *pace* former University of Colorado professor Ward Churchill, they somehow deserved their fate.[39] It is, however, to suggest the ways in which the grief-wrath cultivated by America's mourning shaped its postplanes conduct: destroying the possibility of politics at home and/or abroad by dehumanizing the enemy. "The very idea of fighting a war for humanity," observed Carl Schmitt, "...makes the enemy into someone not quite human who must be sacrificed without scruple."[40] Indeed, Ahmed Rashid suggests that America's response to its losses effectively collapsed the distinction between foreign and domestic politics. "Bush's depiction of a war between good and evil," he wrote, "and more talk of a war between civilizations conjured up strong feelings of revenge and retribution. There was little discussion in the media or Congress as to how this war would be carried out, as people wanted the administration to get tough with terrorism."[41] Thus, the grief-wrath of *mênis* embodied in and cultivated by the nation's responses to loss dehumanized the enemy, making them something to be destroyed rather than someone with whom to engage. As such, the polity denied itself the possibility of a measured response to the attacks, one based on careful deliberation, good judgment, and reasoned debate, values central to the democratic ideal. It led to blindness and the eliding of important distinctions that, among other things, paved the way for the Bush administration to shift – in a tragically self-defeating way – the focus of the War on Terror to Iraq.[42] America's mourning practices thus helped undermine domestic politics, denied the possibility of a politics beyond the polity, and adversely affected the execution

---

[38] Charlie Savage and Peter Baker, "Obama, in a Shift, to Limit the Target of Drone Strikes," *The New York Times*, May 22, 2013. www.nytimes.com/2013/05/23/us/us-acknowledges-killing-4-americans-in-drone-strikes.html?_r=0. Accessed Apr. 14, 2015.

[39] Ward Churchill, "Some People Push Back: On the Justice of Roosting Chickens." www.kersplebedeb.com/mystuff/s11/churchill.html. Accessed Jan. 7, 2014.

[40] Carl Schmitt, *The Concept of the Political* translated by George Schwab (Chicago: Chicago University Press, 1996), 54.

[41] Ahmed Rashid, *Descent into Chaos: The U.S. and the Disaster in Pakistan, Afghanistan, and Central Asia* (New York: Penguin Books, 2009), 295.

[42] See, for example, Fawaz A. Gerges, *The Rise and Fall of Al-Qaeda* (New York: Oxford University Press, 2011), 105; and Bruce Riedel, *The Search for Al Qaeda: Its Leadership, Its Future, and Its Ideology* (Washington, DC: The Brookings Institution, 2008), 87.

and formulation of the military strategy it adopted as an alternative to political engagement.

In *Trauma and the Memory of Politics*, Jenny Edkins suggests that a lesson we can take from Primo Levi is "his insistence that we do not disregard the humanity of those who plan and organize unilateral, deliberate slaughters of innocent and defenseless people. Despite their utter contempt for life," she suggests, "they are nevertheless human like the rest of us. If we demonize them we are taking the easy way out."[43] Indeed, Terry Eagleton observes that "it is precisely the fact that they are human that makes what terrorists do appalling. If they really were inhuman, we might not be in the least bit surprised by their behavior."[44] In this instance, at least, what is true for the moral is true for the political. In order to evaluate the actions of "others" on either rubric, it is imperative that we regard those "others" as fully human, thereby preventing such "othering" from destroying the possibility of political engagement.[45] Acknowledging shared humanity does not, of course, commit one to the sort of soft-headed relativism identified by Victor Hanson. Indeed, in response to the type of antihumanism espoused by Hanson, Eagleton notes that for "some commentators, trying to grasp what motivates Islamic suicide bombers by, say, pointing to the despair and devastation of the Gaza Strip, is to absolve them of their guilt." It is nevertheless, he argues, possible to "... condemn those who blow up little children in the name of Allah without assuming that there is no explanation for their outrageous behavior – that they pulverize people simply for kicks. You do not have to believe the explanation in question is sufficient reason to justify what they do."[46] It is only by recognizing the humanity of those who perpetrate such actions, he suggests, that we can look for causes.[47] The epistemological limitations engendered by America's nationalist and neo-Homeric responses to loss

---

[43] Jenny Edkins, *Trauma and the Memory of Politics* (Cambridge: Cambridge University Press, 2003), 228. Such dehumanization is common to America's approach to its current and former enemies. In 1995, the Smithsonian Institution's plans to display the *Enola Gay* in a way that both honored the crew and depicted the suffering of the Japanese were scrapped after a public outcry. Edward T. Linenthal and Tom Engelhardt (editors), *History Wars: The Enola Gay and Other Battles for America's past* (New York: Henry Holt, 1996).

[44] Terry Eagleton, *On Evil* (New Haven, CT: Yale University Press, 2010), 9.

[45] Few would, for example, be prepared to consider the actions of even high-functioning nonhuman primates as being morally or politically motivated.

[46] Eagleton, *On Evil*, 7

[47] Eagleton notes that the word "evil" "has come to mean, among other things, 'without a cause.'" Likewise, he observes, "If some people are born evil, however, they are no more responsible for this condition than being born with cystic fibrosis." Ibid., 3, 5.

serve, then, to obscure more complex understandings of the motivations of America's enemies, be they sociological, historical, psychological, or political. It is precisely these motivations that the embrace of a tragic mode of mourning – such as that embodied by Aeschylus' *The Persians* – seeks to make visible.

The most convincing case for understanding tragedy as a genre of mourning is made by Nicole Loraux, whose later work contrasts tragedy with the Funeral Oration, the focus of her earlier work.[48] "The place of mourning," she declares, "is on the stage, not the city-state."[49] Paradoxically, perhaps, given the long history of criticism that seeks to identify the importance of Greek theater to democratic life and politics, Loraux describes tragedy as an "antipolitical" genre. "As I see it," she writes, "spectators of Greek tragedy were being solicited, whether individually or collectively, less as members of the political body than as members of that entirely apolitical body known as the human race, or to give it its tragic name, 'the race of mortals.'"[50] For Bonnie Honig, this suggests that mortalist humanism undoes the political by committing Loraux to the universal. "Rather than impress citizens into polis identification," writes Honig, "tragedy may overcome political divisions by way of non-discursive sound, inciting spectators into a mortalist humanism of universal voice, cry, or suffering."[51] Such an approach, she argues, depoliticizes tragedy by moving its claims from the civic to the ethical.[52]

It may be, however, that Honig misreads Loraux and/or overstates the extent to which the turn to the human and the ethical is a move away from conflict, action, and/or the political. Reconstructing Loraux's argument through a reading of *The Persians* – a play central to her account of tragedy as a genre of mourning – suggests, first, that Honig's assertion that the humanist is necessarily antipolitical is misplaced and, second,

---

[48] Nicole Loraux, *The Invention of Athens: The Funeral Oration in the Classical City* (New York: Zones Books, 2006).

[49] Loraux, *Mourning Voice*, 53.

[50] Ibid., 89.

[51] Honig, *Antigone, Interrupted*, 25–26.

[52] Honig is also responding to the work of Judith Butler. "[We] each have the power to destroy and be destroyed, and that we are bound to one another in this power and this precariousness. In this sense, we are all precarious lives." Judith Butler in *Frames of War: When Is Life Grievable?* (New York: Verso, 2009), 43. See also Judith Butler, *Precarious Life: The Powers of Mourning and Violence* (New York: Verso, 2006). The argument presented here does not seek to defend Butler's position – she is more than capable of defending herself – but rather to articulate an alternative formulation of mortalist humanist.

that such an ethical turn is predicated on and generative of the kind of action in concert that Honig sees as central to democratic politics.

AESCHYLUS, *THE PERSIANS*, AND THE
"ANTIPOLITICS" OF MOURNING

Aeschylus' *The Persians* is the first extant Attic tragedy. Initially performed in 472 BCE with a young Pericles as its patron, it is unusual in that it deals with relatively contemporaneous events: the defeat of the Persian army by the Athenians at the Battle of Salamis in 480. Even more unusually, it is set in Susa in the court of the Persian King Xerxes. No Greeks appear in the play. Rather, it details the Persian laments for their fallen and the consequences of their defeat for Xerxes and his people. Unsurprisingly, the play has been the subject of some controversy, with scholars divided into two more or less distinct camps: those who see in the play an Athenian triumphalism, with every Persian lament a hymn to the Athenian victory, and those who offer a reading in which, while acknowledging the elements of Athenian nationalism in the play, nevertheless see an expression of empathy for the shared suffering of fellow mortals. Establishing the validity of this second reading is central to showing that Aeschylus offers a politically generative form of tragic mourning for a fallen enemy.

Edith Hall and Thomas Harrison both argue that *The Persians* is largely a paean to Athenian success.[53] For Hall, the play is part of a larger exercise in Greek self-definition. By depicting their enemy as barbarians, she writes, the Athenians were able to define themselves and their values – most notably democracy – as the epitome of civilization.[54] That the Greek depiction of the other may have had little correspondence to the actuality of the Persians' values and way of life was, she argues, less important for the Greeks than its ideological function in Athens. Indeed, she sees *The Persians* as "the first unmistakable file in the archive of Orientalism."[55] As evidence for her claims, she points to the excessive laments offered by the Persians for their war dead, a strangeness compounded by their being performed not by women – as was the Greek custom – but by men.[56] Indeed,

[53] Edith Hall, *Inventing the Barbarian: Greek Self-Definition through Tragedy* (Oxford: Clarendon Press, 1989); and Thomas Harrison, *The Emptiness of Asia: Aeschylus' Persians and the History of the Fifth Century* (London: Duckworth, 2000).
[54] Hall, *Inventing the Barbarian*, 1–2.
[55] Ibid., 99. See also Edward Said, *Orientalism* (New York: Vintage Books, 1979), 21.
[56] "[E]xcessive mourning practices," she notes, "were considered 'barbaric' and discouraged at Athens." Hall, *Inventing the Barbarian*, 84.

Hall argues that this concern with Persian excess offered the "moral lesson – destruction attends upon hubris – [that] informs the whole play."[57] Although Hall is prepared to concede that *The Persians* incorporates elements that work against a purely nationalistic reading – identifying "a genuinely tragic *pathos*, which precludes the nineteenth century interpretation of the drama as mere xenophobic self-congratulation"[58] – she nevertheless rejects the view that the play is primarily about an empathetic identification with Athens' enemy.[59] Given that Aeschylus' brother had been killed at Marathon, she argues, giving "the Persians a sympathetic hearing was probably not [his] priority."[60] Similarly, she cites Aristophanes' depiction of Aeschylus in *The Frogs* as evidence of the tragedian's antipathy towards Athens' enemy.[61] Finally, she suggests some of the Persian barbarians escape denunciation – something quite different from eliciting sympathy – for reasons of dramatic expediency. "An aim of tragedy was to inspire pity," she writes, "...certain kinds of *pathos* must produce pity...and the emotional response of an audience is heightened in proportion with the moral worth of the victim."[62]

The most strident critique of the claim that *The Persians* is a form of mourning for Athens' enemy is, however, offered by Thomas Harrison, who sees Hall's reading as "an uncomfortable balancing-act" between understandings of the play as merely xenophobic and subtly empathetic.[63] For Harrison, the "Greeks were apparently quite comfortable in seeing the war from the Persian point of view; only the themes highlighted are those that stress the devastation wrought on the Persians, not their common humanity."[64] Like Hall, Harrison points to the death of Aeschylus' brother, Aristophanes' depiction of Aeschylus, and the excessive lamentation of the Persian chorus as evidence for his position.[65] More fundamentally, however, Harrison argues that the sympathy some critics see in *The Persians* "is the product of wishful thinking, a projection of modern values onto the

57 Ibid., 70.
58 Ibid., 100.
59 Edith Hall, "Aeschylus' *Persians* via the Ottoman Empire to Saddam Hussein" in *Cultural Responses to the Persian Wars: Antiquity to the Third Millennium* edited by Emma Bridges, Edith Hall, and P. J. Rhodes (Oxford: Oxford University Press, 2007), 170 *n*.9.
60 Edith Hall, *Aeschylus Persians* (Warminster, UK: Aris & Phillips, 1996), 3.
61 "[B]y putting on my *Persians*, an excellent work, I taught my audience always to yearn for victory over their enemies." *The Frogs*, in Hall, *Inventing the Barbarian*, 100.
62 Ibid., 212.
63 Harrison, *The Emptiness of Asia*, 21.
64 Ibid., 55.
65 Ibid., 51, 52, 91.

Greeks, and a prejudice that art, especially great art, must be free from any traces of nationalism."[66] The play is, he says, "part of concerted strategy of patriotic stimulation."[67] As such, he rejects readings that see the list of the Persian war dead recounted in the play as evidence of an empathetic identification with Athens' enemy, offering "a more obvious, though less palatable, possibility: that such passages reflect a relish in the details of the slaughter of the Persians."[68] Indeed, he points to the historical context of the play as evidence against the empathetic interpretation. "Is it plausible," he asks, "...that Aeschylus, himself a veteran of Salamis, would have chosen to express his sympathy for the consequences of the Persians' defeat in a city, indeed, in a theater that still bore the scars of Persian occupation, in front of an audience that had experienced evacuation from Attica, and who sat (possibly) on seats made from the timber of the shipwrecked Persian fleet?"[69] Readings of the play that resist the "zero-sum game" between sympathy and patriotism, he argues, tend "to be markedly vague."[70]

"[T]he tragic genre," notes Nicole Loraux, "in its complexity, is not uni-dimensional."[71] Similarly, Christopher Pelling argues that a central problem of writing about Greek tragedy is that it is "all too easy ... to speak as if the audience would respond as a monolithic whole."[72] Thus, any reading – such as Harrison's – that adopts a "zero-sum" approach would appear to be problematized by the complexity of both the genre and its audience.[73] Indeed, Harrison's assertion that those who see sympathy and/or complexity of perspective in the play are guilty of imposing modern values on it seems to be mistaken on two counts. On the first, sympathy is a fundamental concern in both Plato's and Aristotle's reading of tragedy, and – as Simon Goldhill points out – other Greek tragedies, including *Medea, Philoctetes,* and *Trojan Women,* problematize sympathy as a theme.[74] Indeed, Paul Woodruff observes that: "Caring

[66] Ibid., 111.
[67] Ibid., 53.
[68] Ibid., 112.
[69] Ibid., 51.
[70] Ibid., 103.
[71] Loraux, *Mourning Voice,* 46.
[72] Christopher Pelling, "Aeschylus' *Persae* and History" in *Greek Tragedy and the Historian* edited by Christopher Pelling (Oxford: Clarendon Press, 1997), 14.
[73] While Harrison at one point acknowledges the claim that the play is "pure jingoism" is "an absurd suggestion," he never elaborates on what he might mean by this qualification and gives short shrift to those readings that do. Harrison, *The Emptiness of Asia,* 56.
[74] Additionally, Goldhill notes, Harrison fails to recognize the role of sympathy in Homeric epic, including that shown to "the Eastern Hector, Andromache, Astyanax, [and] Priam." Simon Goldhill, "Fifth Century Persians Review of *The Emptiness of Asia. Aeschylus'*

for the enemy in defeat is one of the moral triumphs of Ancient Greek culture."[75] On the second, Harrison's desire for a clear-cut account of the play's meaning – a desire perhaps echoed by Hall's identification of the play's "moral lesson" – would seem to do great violence not only to the ambivalences and ambiguities of tragedy's texts but also to the social and political context in which they were presented. Tragedy was a questioning not a didactic genre, one that sought to provoke theoretical reflection on the values and conflicts that the audience faced as democratic citizens. Indeed, Sara Monoson employs the term "audience performance" to capture "the active manner in which Athenian spectators experienced the theater."[76] Central to this activity was the questioning ambivalence cultivated by both the plays and the festival of which they were a part. In the case of *The Persians*, such ambivalence is suggested by the juxtaposition of pride over the Greek victory with the expression and cultivation of sympathy for the enemy in defeat.

Even among those critics who identify Aeschylean sympathy for the enemy, there is a widespread agreement that *The Persians* praises Athens' victory and values. The Persian Queen initiates an exchange with the Chorus in which she is told that Athens has a great army that has already achieved victories at Medes and elsewhere. Similarly, the Chorus details the Athenian mode of warfare, their wealth, their form of government, and its implications for their previous military successes, leading the Queen to conclude, "What you say is fearful to think about for the

Persians and the History of the Fifth Century by T. Harrison," *The Classical Review,* New Series, 51(1), 2001: 10. Alan Sommerstein suggests, furthermore, that *The Persians* was modeled on an earlier play – *The Phoenician Women* – by Phrynichus that invited the "audience to view the war from the enemy's standpoint, not as a triumph for the Greeks but as a disaster for the Persians." Sommerstein also notes that Aeschylus borrowed the first line of *The Persians* from the *Phoenician Women,* an allusion that might suggest a thematic connection between the plays. Alan H. Sommerstein, "Preface to *The Persians*" in Aeschylus, *The Persians and Other Plays*" translated by Alan Sommerstein (New York: Penguin Books, 2009), Kindle edition, loc. 579, 589. Noting the same allusion, Susan Letzler Cole goes further. "If, as thought," she writes, "Phrynichus's play focused on the Greek victory (and Persian defeat) at Salamis, the chorus of Phoenician women is a chorus of widows. Thus, Aeschylus's probable model for *The Persians* would have been at least as much, if not more, a tragic performance centered on ritual mourning." Susan Letzler Cole, *The Absent One: Ritual, Tragedy, and the Performance of Ambivalence* (University Park, PA: Penn State University Press, 1991), 30. See, however, Rush Rehm, *Greek Tragic Theater* (New York: Routledge, 2004), 22.
[75] Paul Woodruff, *The Necessity of Theater: The Art of Watching and Being Watched* (Oxford: Oxford University Press, 2008), 162.
[76] Sara Monoson, *Plato's Democratic Entanglements: Athenian Politics and the Practice of Philosophy* (Princeton, NJ: Princeton University Press, 200), 238, *n.29.*

parents of those who have gone there."[77] It is hard to parse such passages as anything other than an expression of Athenian pride; a similar list of virtues would make up the nationalist mourning of Pericles' Funeral Oration. The Greeks would have also taken considerable pleasure in the messenger's account of the Battle of Salamis in which a fleet of three hundred routed a Persian navy more than three times its size.[78] Although there appears to be considerable support for the readings offered by Hall and Harrison, both nevertheless underestimate the extent to which such pride and patriotism are compatible with the cultivation and expression of sympathy for the enemy.

For moderns, the suggestion that one can both celebrate victory over an enemy and feel their suffering in defeat might seem hopelessly confused. For the Greeks, by contrast, such complexity would have been commonplace. Indeed, in suggesting that those who seek to identify sympathy for the enemy in *The Persians* are imposing modern values on the text, Harrison appears to be guilty of that which he accuses others, for the cultivation of ethos capable of entertaining conflicting perspectives was central not only to the pedagogical function of tragedy but also to the theatrical festival in which the plays were presented. The juxtaposition of opposites – so central to Greek life – helped to generate the questioning integral to tragedy, with the Dionysian patriotism of the festival making possible the plays' pointed critique of the city's politics.[79] Pedagogically, this served to draw attention to certain dangers to the polity such as hubris, personified in the *Persians* by Xerxes, whose overreach is a persistent theme of the text.

Upon hearing of the Persian defeat, Xerxes' mother declares, "My son has found his vengeance upon famous Athens to be a bitter one; the Eastern lives that Marathon had already destroyed were not enough for him."[80] Similarly, the ghost of Xerxes' father laments of his son, "He thought, ill-counseled as he was, that he, a mortal, could lord it over all the gods and Poseidon. Surely this was a mental disease that had my son in its grip."[81] On two separate occasions, Darius ascribes Xerxes' behavior

[77] Aeschylus, *The Persians and Other Plays* translated by Alan Sommerstein (New York: Penguin Books, 2009), 245.

[78] Ibid., 337–433.

[79] "Greek conceptualization found it unproblematic to retain a strong polarity while recognizing the existence of marginal cases, or cases which belong on both sides of the divide, just as here human suffering and fragility is common to both Greek and Barbarian." Pelling, "Aeschylus' *Persae*," 17. See also Davidson, *Fishcakes and Courtesans.*

[80] Aeschylus, *Persians*, 474–475.

[81] Ibid., 751–752.

to his son's youth, a dramatic license employed by Aeschylus – Xerxes was probably about forty years old at the time of Salamis – to emphasize the rashness of his actions.[82] Indeed, Aeschylus tells us not only that the war against Athens was carried out in a hubristic fashion – he details the plundering of the Greek temples and the destruction of their altars[83] – but that it was carried out for the wrong reasons: Xerxes' overweening ambition was fueled by the taunts of his countrymen, who unfavorably compared his comfortable life with the heroic exploits of his father.[84] In this sense, Xerxes, in his desire for vengeance, proved himself incapable of the complexity of vision that the tragic theater sought to cultivate in its audience as a response to their tragic condition. In the absence of a capacity to move beyond his singular perspective, Xerxes came to ruin. The pedagogical function of tragedy as a response was to help its audience avoid a similar fate. Here, "discrepant awareness" – what one character knows that the others do not or what the audience knows the tragic protagonists do not – was key.[85] Prior to the news of the Persian defeat, the Chorus declares that no one could withstand the might of the Persian army,[86] while the Queen's dream, which, for the audience, clearly foreshadows the Persian defeat,[87] is interpreted by the Chorus to suggest "things will turn out well for you in every way."[88] In each instance, the audience – already familiar with the battle's outcome – is made acutely aware of humanity's capacity for self-delusion, its willingness to base its worldview on incomplete information, and the disastrous consequences of so doing.[89]

If one of the aims of *The Persians* was to alert its audience to the dangers of hubris, it nevertheless faced the possibility that the audience would see only the hubris of Xerxes and fail to connect it to the dangers

---

[82] Ibid., 744, 784.

[83] Ibid., 810–812.

[84] Aeschylus, *Persians*, 753–758. There is, perhaps, something of a parallel here to George W. Bush, who is said to have targeted Iraq, in part at least, because of an assassination attempt on his father orchestrated by Saddam Hussein. Daniel Lieberfield, "Theories of Conflict and the Iraq War," *International Journal of Peace Studies*, 10(2), 2005: 14.

[85] Froma I. Zeitlin, "Playing the Other: Theater, Theatricality, and the Feminine in Greek Drama," *Representations*, 11(63), 1985: 75.

[86] Aeschylus, *Persians*, 87–92.

[87] Ibid., 195–200.

[88] Ibid., 225.

[89] In this, tragedy demonstrates the dangers of what Mark Button calls "second-order" blindness – humanity's blindness to its own blindness – that prevents it from seeking to compensate for its necessarily partial vision in other ways. Mark Button, "Accounting for Blind Spots: From Oedipus to Democratic Epistemology," *Political Theory*, 39(6), 2011: 695–723.

hubris posed to Athens: taking pleasure in the downfall of others might blind them to their own susceptibility to the same. Aeschylus attempts to overcome this by repeatedly tying the Greeks to the Persians, noting, for example, that Xerxes was of Greek ancestry; that the two women – one Greek, one Persian – in the Queen's dream were "sisters of the same stock" and that the only difference between them was "one, by the fall of lot, was a native and inhabitant of the land of Greece, the other of the Orient."[90] Most forebodingly, perhaps, he lists the territories conquered by Darius then lost by his son, a list that corresponds almost exactly – with the exception of Cyprus – to the alliance known as the Delian League, which was aligned with and controlled by Athens by 472.[91] Nevertheless, an audience buoyed by the triumphalism of military victory might dismiss such parallels. It is one thing to *tell* an audience to avoid hubris but quite another to try to cultivate an ethos that will help them do so. Understanding the ways in which Aeschylus makes his play a form of mourning for the Persian fallen demonstrates how tragedy might serve his *polis* in both domestic and foreign relations, cultivating both an ethic and action in the face of loss.

Central to the claims of those who would see *The Persians* as little more than Athenian triumphalism are the passages in which the messenger to the court at Susa recounts, in great detail, the deaths of individual Persians, "Artembares, marshal of ten thousand horse"; "Dadaces, captain of a thousand men"; "Metallus the Chrysean"; and so on.[92] It is in these details, Harrison suggests, that the Athenians would have taken the pleasure that comes from defeating one's enemies. While there is, perhaps, something to be said for this interpretation, Mary Ebbott offers a reading of these passages more in line with Loraux's account of tragedy as an act of mourning. She notes that the lines evoke the conventions of the Athenian casualty lists, thereby potentially resonating with an audience who would recognize their own practices of honoring the dead, especially so in the case of veterans like Aeschylus himself. It creates, she suggests, not an antithesis but a humanistic connection between Greek and Persian. Ebbott argues that such a connection would have

[90] Aeschylus, *Persians,* 79–80; 186–189.
[91] Sommerstein, "Preface," loc. 676. The paralleling of Athens with the Persians would also be employed by Thucydides in his *History of the Peloponnesian War.* If Aeschylus was concerned about the *possibility* of Athens becoming Persia, Thucydides would identify the ways in which it *had* become so. See Richard Ned Lebow, "Thucydides the Constructivist," *American Political Science Review,* 95(3), 2001: 550.
[92] Aeschylus, *Persians,* 303–331.

been lent further resonance by the Greek fear of leaving bodies – even those of one's enemy – unburied.⁹³ Thus, Ebbott suggests, the "familiarity in this setting would produce an eerie effect, since this listing of casualties is of dead warriors who are not buried at all but are instead exposed corpses – an opposite and abhorrent plight."⁹⁴ Indeed, Aeschylus expends considerable effort in detailing the horrors of those who die without the appropriate rites.

The Chorus lament, "the dead bodies of our loved ones are floating, soaked and constantly buffeted by salt water, shrouded by mantles that drift in the waves!"⁹⁵ Similarly, the messenger lists, in great detail, the names of the commanders and the fate of their bodies – "to wander around the wave beaten island of Ajax,"⁹⁶ or "beating their heads against the hard rocks round the islands where doves breed"⁹⁷ – declaring, "All this I report about the commanders; but I have mentioned only a small part of the great suffering that there was."⁹⁸ The theme of bodies in the water that will never be recovered is one that the playwright returns to again and again.⁹⁹ While it is always possible that the Athenians might have taken pleasure in such scenes, the Greek concern with proper burials and the sheer repetition of the horrific experiences of the Persian sailors suggests that the effect of the play was something more than nationalistic stimulation. While the first few scenes of Persian suffering might have excited the audience, the graphic detail, the breaking of taboos, and the constant return to the theme may have served to temper that excitement and to transform it into humanist sympathy as the play progressed. Even for those members of the audience who were unwilling to go so far as to mourn the Persian losses, Aeschylus' repeated and graphic presentation of Persian suffering might have served to draw their attention to the costs of victory and, perhaps, to have problematized their previous pride and celebrations.¹⁰⁰ Much the same might be said for Aeschylus' repeated

⁹³ In Greek warfare, it was common practice for the winners to grant a truce to allow both sides to recover their dead for burial, hence the horror engendered by the sacrilegious treatment of Hector's body in the *Iliad*.
⁹⁴ Mary Ebbott, "The List of the War Dead in Aeschylus' *Persians*," *Harvard Studies in Classical Philology*, 100(2000), 96.
⁹⁵ Aeschylus, *Persians*, 275–278.
⁹⁶ Ibid., 311.
⁹⁷ Ibid., 313.
⁹⁸ Ibid., 331.
⁹⁹ Ibid., 420–423, 424–431, 568–578, 595–597, and 977.
¹⁰⁰ It is, perhaps, hard to imagine that even America's postplanes bloodlust might not be somewhat tempered by extensive footage of the enemy war dead – as well as the bodies of those civilians caught in the crossfire – being played repeatedly on television.

reference to the Persian "parents and wives [who] count the days and tremble as the time stretches out."[101] While it is no doubt possible that the Greeks would have taken pleasure in the suffering of bereaved Persian wives and parents, it is, perhaps, more likely that a warrior culture that knew the suffering of war might be moved to reflect on the costs of victory. "For an Athenian audience watching the suffering of a dignified enemy," writes Peter Euben, "the *Persae* unites loss and gain in a single instant, bringing to their victors in their exultation a wisdom born of suffering and loss."[102]

What Harrison sees as the "markedly vague" interpretations of those who identify an empathetic understanding of the enemy in the play might, then, better be seen as attempts to account for the complexity of the genre, one that makes the existence of such apparently conflicting emotions of patriotism and empathy for others integral to tragedy. The parsimony of Harrison's explanation simply cannot account for the ambivalence embodied in and engendered by tragic theater. Indeed, much of Harrison's critique rests on speculations about Aeschylus's biography – the death of his bother – or the always-problematic attempt to read the words of a comic poet straight, and a number of rhetorical questions.[103] "Is it really plausible," he asks, "that in the year 472, so shortly after the conclusion of hostilities in Greece, and a time when the battle of Eurymedon and other hostilities still lay in the future, Aeschylus would have thought to stage a domestic tragedy centered, just incidentally, on the Persian royal family?"[104] Harrison might have attempted to answer his own question. Doing so suggests the ways in which the ambivalence toward Persia – the Athenian celebration of victory and the simultaneous lamenting of its costs to their enemy – generated by the play might have cultivated action by alerting Athens to its pressing political and strategic interests.

Edith Hall argues that the moral lesson of the play is the danger of hubris. By looking to the excesses of Xerxes, it is suggested, the Athenian audience would be moved to avoid the same. The paradox of this reading of the play is that if it is indeed what Hall and Harrison suggest – a

---

[101] Aeschylus, *Persians,* 63–64, 245, 579–583.

[102] J. Peter Euben, "The Battle of Salamis and the Origins of Political Theory," *Political Theory,* 14(3), 1986: 365.

[103] Claims also offered by Hall.

[104] Harrison, *The Emptiness of Asia,* 51. Phrynichus had, however, already produced a play on the same subject. As such, it would not have been too novel or painful for its audience. Dana LaCourse Munteanu, *Tragic Pathos: Pity and Fear in Greek Philosophy and Tragedy* (Cambridge: Cambridge University Press, 2011), 155.

celebration of Athenian triumph with little to no empathy for the enemy fallen – then *The Persians* is a play that undermines itself by cultivating an ethos more conducive to hubris than careful reflection. The mere *depiction* of hubris is, moreover, insufficient to teach its audience to avoid it, not least when they could easily ascribe such hubris to some fault in the Persian character. Aeschylus' attempts to tie the Greeks to the Persians – by pointing to Xerxes' ancestry or recounting the Queen's dream – may have been an attempt to avoid such a reading. Nevertheless, his most thoroughgoing method of teaching the Athenians to avoid the dangers of hubris was to offer a play whose ambivalence about the Greek victory sought to cultivate in his audience an ethos conducive to avoiding Xerxes' excesses. In this sense, just as the juxtaposition of nationalism and critique embodied by the Great Dionysia sought to generate in its audience an ethos appropriate to democracy – one capable of embracing conflicting viewpoints – the agonistic juxtaposition of nationalism and empathy in *The Persians* sought to cultivate in its audience an ethos appropriate to an increasingly imperialistic democracy. *The Persians* offers up triumphalism and warns about its dangers, calling into question any attempt to see the victory as an unalloyed good.[105] This is not to suggest, of course, that Aeschylus would have preferred that the Greeks had lost the battle, simply that the play celebrates victory while foreshadowing a possible downfall that might occur should the Greeks become carried away by their success. While the play ends with Xerxes stripped of his godlike aura and reduced like those around him – both on stage and in the audience – to the status of a mortal, a status that, Richard Kuhns argues, the purely nationalistic Athenian might enjoy, it actually serves as a reminder to the Athenians of their long-standing political wisdom "that the Greeks honor humanity in its humanness, while barbarians misplace veneration, elevating the human to divine status."[106] "That in itself," he continues, "is a tragic mistake. And it is a mistake the Athenians can appreciate *politically*, as it thereby allows them to mourn with and alongside the Persians."[107]

---

[105] Aeschylus "is talking to his fellow citizens about their own history, simultaneously stimulating their pride in their great victory and disciplining that pride by the recognition of the terrible losses brought to others. He is also warning the Athenians that they should guard against the heady overconfidence that might otherwise naturally arise from the victory." James Boyd White, *Living Speech: Resisting the Empire of Force* (Princeton, NJ: Princeton University Press, 2006), 172.

[106] Richard Kuhns, *Tragedy: Contradiction and Repression* (Chicago: University of Chicago Press, 1991), 28.

[107] Ibid. Author's emphasis.

For Athens, the cultivation of this productive ethos of ambivalence was all the more important because it was highly likely that they would, at some point, be pulled back into war. As H. C. Avery observes, "Themistocles was probably still in Athens. Xerxes was still on the Persian throne. The Battle of Eurymedon was still some four or five years in the future. The victories of 480 and 479 had been magnificent, but it had taken the Persians ten years to return to Greece after Marathon. What guarantee was there that the Persians would not come back again?"[108] In such circumstances, the dangers of overconfidence emanating from the Greek victory at Salamis were all the more pressing. *The Persians* not only sought to warn of these dangers, it offered a tragic pedagogy of mourning that might help its audience avoid them. Indeed, both Hall and Harrison make much of the death of Aeschylus' brother at the hands of the Persians, but it is far from clear that a desire for revenge is the only possible reaction to such a loss. It is equally plausible that, having lost a brother in a conflict in which he himself had taken part, Aeschylus was concerned that Athens not engage in an ill-advised or poorly thought-out war that would bring similar sorrow to his countrymen.

The Persians served, then, as a form of mourning for Athens' enemies in a way that problematizes Honig's claims about ethic and action. While the play sought to generate empathy in his audience for the losses of "the other," its humanism was far more complex than Honig's account of tragedy allows. For although the play did indeed seek to tie the Persians to the Athenians by highlighting a shared capacity for grief – the cultivation of mortalist humanism – this was not its only pedagogical mechanism. The play simultaneously offered pragmatic reasons for its audience to adopt the theoretical position of tragedy, seeking to motivate them to action by identifying their interests, such as avoiding the strategic and military consequences of hubris. This is, perhaps, what Ella Myers means when she points to a concern with "worldly things" as a prerequisite for an ethics-based politics.[109] Indeed, drawing on Myers's use of Bruno Latour's distinction between "a matter of fact" and a "matter of concern," it might be suggested that Honig's account of the ethical mistakenly sees the sort of empathy engendered by tragedy as generating only an awareness of fact – "our enemies suffer" – when Aeschylus also shows us how tragedy engenders a concern for the self – "we do not wish to suffer what our

---

[108] Harry C. Avery, "Dramatic Devices in Aeschylus' *Persians*," *The American Journal of Philology*, 85(2), 1964: 183. See also Ippokratis Kantzios, "The Politics of Fear in Aeschylus' 'Persians,'" *The Classical World*, 98(1), 2004: 19.

[109] Myers, *Worldly Ethics*, 98.

enemies suffered" – that is enhanced by and gives reasons for embracing and cultivating the concern for fellow human beings that marks the ethical turn in mourning.[110] It is here, perhaps, that Honig separates the lightning from the flash. The claim is not that the awareness of fact cultivates concern in the linear way that Honig's account of Judith Butler's work suggests – that recognizing a shared capacity for grief leads us to see the other as human and thus to care for her in a way that destroys politics – but rather that the fact of mortality and the concern for political action are each implicated in the other. Indeed, given that tragedy was a mourning genre and theater a shared activity, the worldview cultivated by public mourning might best be understood as an ethic of action, one that demands a communal response to loss rather than merely passive private laments.

Against this background, *The Persians* might be thought to illustrate the dangers to humanity of hubristic excess in a way that seeks to engender Athenian action to avoid the same as a matter of self-preservation. Simultaneously, however, it also seeks to cultivate a humanistic sympathy for the enemy that multiplies the efficacy of its illustration of the dangers of excess. By demanding that its audience imagine themselves as "the other," those dangers become even more of a "matter of concern" for themselves in a way that solicits political action. As such, the cultivation of the ethic and the cultivation of political action that tragic humanism seeks to engender in its audience emerge together and reinforce one another in a way that suggests Honig's distinction between ethic and action is far too sharply drawn.[111] It is, as Aristotle observes, "by doing just acts that the just man is produced, and by doing temperate acts the temperate man."[112] This is not to argue that the cultivation of such empathy was purely instrumental – though, as Aristotle suggests, such instrumentalism could, over time, help cultivate the ethos necessary to the mourning of one's enemies – simply to suggest that such mourning could benefit the polity: an explanation that neither Hall nor Harrison considers. Indeed, while the classical dilemmas of moral theory most often pit the actions demanded by self-interest against those of ethical behavior, the two more commonly point in the same direction.

"Socrates," observes Peter Euben, "argued that what we do to another we do to ourselves; that if we kill another we must live with the killer

---

[110] Ibid., 94.

[111] Oddly, Honig, who takes so much from Nietzsche, adopts a rather more linear conception of causality than he would allow.

[112] Aristotle, *Nicomachean Ethics* (II.4 1005b 9–12).

we have become; that if we harm someone we need to be aware of the harm that we are doing to ourselves in the process. This has always been regarded as a *moral* argument, and indeed it is, but it is also a *political* one."[113] As such, tragedy encompasses and engenders a complexity of motives and motivations, pedagogy and prodding that is best captured by Loraux's observation that "the reception of a tragedy such as *The Persians* has to do with a subtle mix of patriotism and compassion, pleasure and pain."[114] The patriotic is, as Steven Johnston reminds us, always political, and – as George Kateb suggests – essentially nationalistic, while the compassionate is necessarily ethical.[115] Even here, however, each is implicated in the other, as are the pleasure and the pain engendered by the enemy's losses. The type of tragic patriotism displayed at and cultivated by the Great Dionysia, as opposed to the merely nationalist, incorporates both the triumphalism of the Athenian victory and also the self-concern – arising from its far more clear-sighted self-love – that the polity not fall prey to the excesses that brought down its enemies.[116] Such excesses, it suggests, can best be seen and understood through the cultivation of compassion for the humanity of those same enemies.

Given the way in which tragedy as a form of mourning not only generates an ethic and political action but also an ethic that informs political action, Loraux's description of it as an "antipolitical" genre is, perhaps, somewhat surprising. Certainly Honig might point to Loraux's frequent use of this term as evidence for the claim that Loraux sees mortalist humanism as a way of bringing politics to an end. The veracity of Honig's reading of Loraux is, of course, considerably less important than its plausibility as an account of the political pedagogy of tragic mourning. Indeed, the argument presented here could be predicated on a creative misreading of Loraux that nevertheless offered compelling insights into the value of tragic responses to loss. It is, however, worth teasing out the possible sources of confusion in Honig's reading of Loraux because they

[113] J. Peter Euben, "Thucydides in the Desert," *When Worlds Elide: Classics, Politics, Culture* edited by Karen Bassi and J. Peter Euben (Lexington, KY: Lexington Books, 2010), 170. Author's emphasis.

[114] Loraux, *Mourning Voice*, 50.

[115] Steven Johnston, *The Truth About Patriotism* (Durham, NC: Duke University Press, 2007); George Kateb, *Patriotism and Other Mistakes* (New Haven, CT: Yale University Press, 2006).

[116] Although Johnston rejects the role that patriotism might play in democratic critique, he seems to employ precisely that in his suggestion for an American Dionysia on the National Mall. Steven Johnston, "American Dionysia," *Contemporary Political Theory*, 8(3), 2009: 255–275.

suggest that tragedy's mortalist humanism provides the glue that makes politics – rather than just conflict – possible.

In his foreword to Loraux's *Mourning Voice* – the text in which she sets out her mature understanding of the politics of public loss in Athens – Pietro Pucci identifies the twofold implications of the term "antipolitical." First, he writes, "it designates positions and stances that go beyond politics, and second, it indicates practices and representations that are consciously or unconsciously opposed or foreign to the ideology of the polis."[117] Honig focuses on the former at the expense of the latter, failing to recognize the ways in which the two positions constitute an agonistic juxtaposition that she might otherwise be inclined to embrace. Part of the problem here is that the term "antipolitical" is somewhat misleading given that there are – at least – two different understandings of the term "political" in Loraux's work: politics understood as conflict and politics understood as consensus. "'Antipolitical,'" she writes, "can mean two very different things, depending on whether we define politics as a practice of consensus – currently the most widely accepted definition – or instead define politics, beginning with Athenian democracy during the most fertile period of the tragic genre, as essentially conflictual, with the conflict almost always repressed."[118]

For Honig, politics is necessarily conflictual, and there are moments when Loraux clearly shares this viewpoint. She refers to "those forces of conflict that found the political" and suggests that conflict "lies at the heart of" politics.[119] As such, Honig might seem justified in her assumption that Loraux believes that the "antipolitical" humanism of tragic mourning – that which, according to Pucci, "goes beyond politics" – appeals to the universal in a way that negates conflict. Even here, however, it should be noted that Loraux's claim is somewhat more nuanced than Honig suggests. The spectators of Greek tragedy were, writes Loraux, solicited "*less* as members of the political body than as members of that entirely apolitical body known as the human race."[120] She does not say that there is *no* appeal to audience as members of a political body, only that, at

---

[117] Pietro Pucci, "Foreword" in Loraux, *Mourning Voice*, xi.

[118] Loraux, *Mourning Voice*, 27.

[119] "Conflict is thus the missing link, this hidden dimension, which I tend, if not to identify with the political as a whole, at least to see as indispensable to any thought about its workings." Nicole Loraux, *The Divided City: On Memory and Forgetting in Ancient Athens* translated by Corinne Pache with Jeff Fort (New York: Zone Books, 2002), 61, 55, 52.

[120] Loraux, *Mourning Voice*, 89. My emphasis.

this particular moment, this appeal is a *lesser* one. For this reason, there would appear to be a potentially agonistic tension between the appeal to the conflictual aspects of the political and the universalistic appeal to the human, a movement that might transform conflict without necessarily negating or overcoming it. Indeed, pointing to a shared characteristic such as finitude or mortality is, perhaps, no more likely to end conflict than pointing out to squabbling adults that they are all members of the same family, even as it might – potentially, at least – serve to change the nature of that conflict.[121] "Antipolitical" is not, as Loraux makes clear, synonymous with "apolitical."[122] As such, *contra* Honig, seeking to cultivate an awareness of the possibility of shared suffering through tragedy does not necessarily seek to negate or overcome the conflict at the heart of the political. This can be seen even more clearly on those – far more frequent – occasions when Loraux employs "political" as a synonym for "consensus."

In *The Divided City*, Loraux notes that Athens was marked by a public commitment to consensus and unity.[123] "Grounded in the *meson*," she notes, "the political is conceived as having gone beyond conflicts – once and for all."[124] In this, she argues, the Greeks defined politics in opposition to the conflict implied by the word *stasis*, a term "which is always rejected in Greek thinking on the political."[125] Indeed, Loraux more frequently employs the term "antipolitics" to indicate conflict than she does to indicate the universal. In this, it might be argued, Loraux's argument about tragedy and humanism is fatally flawed: logic dictates that opposing assertions cannot both be true at the same time. Honig resolves this apparent tension by identifying the antipolitics of humanism solely with consensus. Vidgis Songe-Møller suggests a more complex approach. Loraux, she observes:

…is playing on two senses of the Greek word *anti*: "in the place of"/"instead of" and "opposed to." Tragedy goes far beyond the political and reminds us first and foremost of our mortality; thus it was something other than politics. But this very point – human mortality was something that was suppressed in the ideology of the democratic city-state, a circumstance that tragedies convey by taking issue

---

[121] See Kennan Ferguson, *All in the Family: On Community and Incommensurability* (Durham, NC: Duke University Press, 2012).
[122] Loraux, *Mourning Voice*, 26.
[123] Loraux, *The Divided City*, 27–28.
[124] Loraux, *Divided City*, 53.
[125] Ibid., 29.

with that ideology. In other words, the tragedies offer an alternative voice to that of the political discourse while at the same time opposing it.[126]

Athenian politics was, as Loraux notes, an always-ongoing tension between the forces of unity and disunity. It was a tension reflected in the institution of tragedy itself: while the rituals of the Dionysia stressed the unity and exceptionalism of the city, the plays exposed the fault lines and tensions of the same. As Charles Segal observes, "The actual content of these works denies what their ritual context affirms."[127] Thus, tragedy's antipolitical humanism does not negate politics in the way Honig suggests but rather provides a unity that is essential to it. The antipolitical, writes Loraux, "can designate the other of politics, but also another politics, no longer based on consensus and living together, but on what I call the 'bond of division.'"[128] In a city-state riven by divisions of class, age, tribe, and region, the humanism of tragedy offered a unity that sought to regulate that conflict in constructive ways, creating what Loraux elsewhere calls "the bond of conflict" and Chantal Mouffe a "conflictual consensus."[129] Humanism does not then deny conflict, but rather makes that conflict one between fellow human beings: some versions of which we might call politics. In this, Jacques Rancière is right to suggest that a political community is one united by its divisions.[130]

Humanism is then a necessary precursor to the practice of politics, suggesting, in the manner of William Connolly, that agonism has an ethical foundation. Ethical humanism creates the essential but paradoxical bond that makes a conflict one between members of an imagined or actual community rather than the anthropologically interesting but politically irrelevant differences between solitudes or species. Mortality is not, of course, the only possible basis for such a politics. Some of Honig's hostility to the humanism embraced by both Judith Butler and Stephen White seems to rest on the view that each is advocating a politics predicated on mortality because it constitutes the thinnest ontological basis for shared

---

[126] Vigdis Songe-Møller, "Antigone and the Deadly Desire for Sameness: Reflections on Origins and Death" in *Birth, Death, and Femininity: Philosophies of Embodiment* edited by Robin May Schott (Bloomington, IN: Indiana University Press, 2010), 217.

[127] Charles Segal, *Dionysiac Poetics and Euripides' Bacchae* (Princeton, NJ: Princeton University Press, 1982), 14.

[128] Loraux, *Mourning Voice*, 23.

[129] Loraux, *Divided City*, 113; Chantal Mouffe, *Agonistics: Thinking The World Politically* (London: Verso Books, 2013), Kindle Edition, loc. 55–56.

[130] Jacques Rancière, "The Ethical Turn of Aesthetics and Politics," *Critical Horizons*, 7(1), 2006, 6.

engagement.[131] The argument presented here makes no such claim. It simply suggests that humanism can be politically productive, a claim it seeks to demonstrate with practical examples. It is, as *The Persians* suggests, an argument with a considerable historical pedigree, one that illustrates the political and strategic importance of mortalist humanism in both victory and defeat.

GERONIMO E-KIA

President Obama's announcement from the East Room of the White House on May 1, 2011, that Navy Seals had killed Osama bin Laden during a raid on a private compound in Pakistan set off a wave of national celebration. In addition to the crowds gathered at the White House and Ground Zero, throngs of students – many of whom had spent half their lives living under the threat of terror that bin Laden personified – engaged in spontaneous demonstrations marked by singing and flag waving on college campuses across the country.[132] For those unwilling or unable to take to the streets, the Internet became a focal point for national celebration, with the comments section of the YouTube site for Miley Cyrus's song "Party in the U.S.A." becoming an unlikely gathering point for the jubilant, leading one commentator to declare the song "the Osama bin Laden Death Anthem."[133] There were, nevertheless, voices of dissent from within the polity. Intellectual gadfly Noam Chomsky imagined a parallel universe in which Iraqi commandos kidnapped and killed former president George W. Bush before dumping his body in the Atlantic,[134] while the social media sites Facebook and Twitter registered the ambivalence of at least some Americans about the celebration of bin Laden's death with a quote – "I will mourn the loss of thousands of precious lives, but I will not rejoice in the death of one, not even an enemy" – that was apocryphally attributed to the Reverend Martin Luther King, Jr..[135] Such voices were

[131] See Bonnie Honig, "The Politics of Ethos," *European Journal of Political Theory*, 10(3), 2011, 422–429.
[132] See, for example, "Patriotic Celebration Erupts in Sunken Garden," *The Flat Hat* (The College of William and Mary), May 2, 2011. flathatnews.com/2011/05/02/75554/. Accessed Jun. 2, 2013.
[133] Nitsuh, Abebe, "Why Miley Cyrus's 'Party in the U.S.A.' Became the Osama Bin Laden Death Anthem," *The Vulture.Com*, May 2, 2011. www.vulture.com/2011/05/why_miley_cyruss_party_in_the.html. Accessed Jun. 2, 2013.
[134] Noam Chomsky, "My Reaction to Osama bin Laden's Death," May 6, 2011. www.guernicamag.com/daily/noam_chomsky_my_reaction_to_os/. Accessed Feb. 19, 2013.
[135] Jonathan Haidt, "Why We Celebrate a Killing," *The New York Times*, May 7, 2011. www.nytimes.com/2011/05/08/opinion/08haidt.html?_r=0. Accessed Feb. 19, 2013.

largely concerned with the propriety of celebrating bin Laden's death rather than with the act of killing itself.[136] Likewise, many foreign news organizations expressed distaste for American triumphalism, frequently drawing a parallel between the pictures of the Palestinians celebrating al Qaeda's attacks on America and similar conduct by Americans following bin Laden's death.[137] Americans remained largely undeterred by such criticism.

In an editorial entitled "Killing Evil Doesn't Make Us Evil," Maureen Dowd of *The New York Times* rejected any parallel between the Arabs who had celebrated the attacks on America and the triumphant response to the death of bin Laden. "Those [Arabs] who celebrated...were applauding the slaughter of American innocents," she wrote. "When college kids spontaneously streamed out Sunday night to the White House, ground zero and elsewhere, they were the opposite of bloodthirsty: they were happy that one of the most certifiably evil figures of our time was no more."[138] Similarly, psychologist Jonathan Haidt – who oddly described the American response as "altruistic" – declared that the "celebrations were good and healthy. America achieved its goal – bravely and decisively – after ten painful years. People who love their country sought out one another to share collective effervescence. They stepped out of their petty and partisan selves and became briefly, just Americans rejoicing together."[139] This celebration – embodying as it did a commitment to nationalism, unity, and consensus – was not just confined to the streets, newspapers, or Internet. In a flurry of electronic books rushed out in the immediate aftermath of the killing, a plethora of public intellectuals fell over themselves to celebrate bin Laden's death and revive a trope ubiquitous in the aftermath of the 2001 attacks.

[136] See also Jess Coleman, "Bin Laden's Death: When a Killer Dies," *The Huffington Post*, September 11, 2012. www.huffingtonpost.com/jess-coleman/when-a-killer-dies_b_1872410.html?. Accessed Jun. 3, 2013.
[137] An editorial in *The Tehran Times* written by an Iranian immigrant to the U.S. noted that "Americans are so fond of describing other people's customs, the Burkha, for example, as barbaric, and yet I can find nothing more barbaric than dancing over the death of another human being, nothing more macabre than teaching children that this is good thing." Ru Freeman, "Osama bin Laden and America's Celebration of Death," *The Tehran Times*, May 10, 2011. old.tehrantimes.com/Index_view.asp?code=240292. Accessed Aug. 25, 2012.
[138] Maureen Dowd, "Killing Evil Doesn't Make Us Evil," *The New York Times*, May 7, 2011. www.nytimes.com/2011/05/08/opinion/08dowd.html?_r=0. Accessed May 10, 2014.
[139] Jonathan Haidt, "Why We Celebrate a Killing," *The New York Times*, May 7, 2011. www.nytimes.com/2011/05/08/opinion/08haidt.html. Accessed Jun. 3, 2013.

"Osama bin Laden was a near-flawless personification of the mentality of a real force," wrote Christopher Hitchens, "the force of Islamic jihad ... this force absolutely deserves to be called evil, and ... the recent decapitation of its most notorious demagogue and organizer is to be welcomed without reserve."[140] Similarly, Jon Meacham referred to bin Laden as "That fanatic – the rich, elusive embodiment of an ancient evil in a new century."[141] Karen Hughes, former White House advisor to George W. Bush, quoted Mark Antony's eulogy from Shakespeare's *Julius Caesar* and declared that the "evil [bin Laden] unleashed is still with us."[142]

In the face of such celebration, any attempt to mobilize a mortalist humanism of the sort embraced and engendered by Aeschylus' *The Persians* on behalf of al Qaeda's leader seems quixotic at best. No amount of information about bin Laden's love for his children, enthusiasm for soccer, or pride in his cultivation of sunflowers could possibly erase the stain of the nearly three thousand American deaths engineered by the jihadist organization of which he was head, nor indeed should it.[143] For, contrary to Honig's claims about mortalist humanism, seeking to recognize the human in the "other" does not mean eradicating all conflict or disagreement or even seeking to do so. As Michael Scheuer observed in the introduction to his biography of bin Laden, "I have tried not to make him seem like an admirable man (though, as might have become clear, I respect his piety, integrity, and skills) but instead like a formidable enemy, one whom we have almost willfully misunderstood."[144] Tragedy's mortalist humanism seeks not to overcome conflict but rather to frame it in a more productively agonistic fashion, moving away from a moral or existential register to a political one. Although such a movement may seem unlikely in the contemporary polity, with bin Laden's death, as with Aeschylus' *Persians*, there are nevertheless good reasons for embracing that ethic and the action it demands.

[140] Christopher Hitchens, *The Enemy*, Kindle Single (Amazon Digital Services, May 16, 2011), loc. 46.
[141] Jon Meacham, "The World After Bin Laden" in *Beyond Bin Laden: America and the Future of Terror* edited by Jon Meacham (New York: Random House, 2011), eBook, Kindle edition, loc. 57, 67.
[142] Karen Hughes, "Justice Finally Has Its Day" in Meacham ed. *Beyond Bin Laden*, loc. 1060.
[143] Peter L. Bergen, *The Osama bin Laden I Know: An Oral History of al Qaeda's Leader* (New York: Free Press, 2006).
[144] Scheuer was the former head of Alec Station, the CIA unit dedicated to bin Laden. Michael Scheuer, *Osama bin Laden* (New York: Oxford, 2012), ix.

"Those who are the targets of terrorism," wrote David Fromkin, "...
start with a major advantage...that success or failure depends on them
alone. Terrorism wins only if you respond to it in the way that terrorists want you to; which means that its fate is in your hands and not
in theirs. If you choose not to respond at all, or else to respond in a
way different from that which they desire, they will fail to achieve their
objectives."[145] Complicating Victor Davis Hanson's distinction between
understanding and defeating the enemy, Fromkin's work suggests that
the targets of terrorism have an interest in understanding the strategies,
interests, and aims of those who would hurt them. Seeing the conflict
in purely moral or existential terms is redolent of the blindness of tragedy's protagonists and, as such, self-defeating. Coping with – rather than
overcoming – this blindness demands a recognition of the humanity of
those who would hurt America, seeing them as motivated not by evil or
an existential hatred but rather by human needs, desires, and goals. To
recognize the latter is not necessarily to agree or sympathize with their
goals or grievances, simply to accept that the conflict is conflict between
human beings with clashing aims and interests. Although this does not,
by itself constitute politics, it is a precondition for it. The interests served,
moreover, by cultivating a humanist ethic give reasons for action, and
the cultivation of that ethic offers the opportunity for a more complex
picture of those same action-demanding interests. Hanson is therefore
wrong to dichotomize understanding and defeating the enemy not just
because the former might contribute to the latter but also because the
understanding promoted by the humanism he and Honig eschew might
serve to transform – rather than negate – a conflict that has all too often
been misunderstood as an existential "clash of civilizations."[146]

Seeing al Qaeda's motivations as political and not moral, notes
Roxanne Euben, runs counter to the dominant Western "production" of
Islamic fundamentalism.[147] This persistent – and misplaced – trope of an
Islamic hatred of American values was repeatedly invoked before and
after the attacks. Speaking to the nation after launching cruise missile
strikes in Afghanistan and Sudan on August 20, 1998, President Clinton

---

[145] David Fromkin, "The Strategy of Terrorism" in *The U.S. vs. al Qaeda: A History of the
War on Terror* edited by Gideon Rose and Jonathan Tepperman (New York: Foreign
Affairs, 2011), 18. Gerges, *The Rise and Fall*, 76–77.

[146] Samuel P. Huntington, *The Clash of Civilizations and the Remaking of the World Order*
(New York: Simon and Schuster, 1996).

[147] Roxanne Euben, *The Enemy in the Mirror. Islamic Fundamentalism and the Limits of
Modern Rationalism* (Princeton, NJ: Princeton University Press, 1999), 46.

declared of bin Laden and his followers, "The groups associated with him come from diverse places, but share a hatred for democracy, a fanatical glorification of violence and a horrible distortion of their religion to justify the murder of innocents. They have made the United States their adversary precisely because of what we stand for and what we stand against."[148] The view was not just confined to politicians. Philosopher John Gray observed, "What seems fairly clear is that, like Sayid Qutb and many radical Islamists, bin Laden reacted strongly against the hedonism and individualism of Western life."[149] This understanding served a willful blindness about al Qaeda's political motivations, one that allowed the West to refuse to engage with the genuine – though not necessarily legitimate – grievances of Islamic fundamentalists.[150] Indeed, the notion that al Qaeda was motivated by an existential hatred of America rather than political grievances was a source of some irritation to the organization itself. Within weeks of the 2001 attacks, Anwar Al-Awlaki, the later-assassinated American-born cleric and, at that point, perhaps, only an al Qaeda sympathizer, declared, "We were told this was an attack on American civilization. We were told this was an attack on American freedom, on the American way of life. This wasn't an attack on any of this. This was an attack on U.S. foreign policy."[151] Similarly, in October 2004,

---

[148] Bergen, *The Osama bin Laden I Know*, 225. It found further expression in George Bush's address to the nation on the day of the planes. "America," he declared, "was targeted for attack because we're the brightest beacon for freedom and opportunity in the world." Bush, "Text of Bush's Address."

[149] John Gray, *Al Qaeda and What It Means to Be Modern* (New York: Free Press, 2005), 78.

[150] The much-vaunted "Letter to the American People" of October 2002 condemning the U.S. for drugs, gambling, and the spread of AIDS is widely considered to be a fake. Peter Bergen, long an acknowledged expert on bin Laden, points out that, unlike previous and subsequent statements, the letter did not appear on an audio- or videotape but was simply posted on a website and as such cannot be verified. Peter Arnett, the CNN correspondent who, in 1997, was the first Western journalist to speak with bin Laden, noted that "he did not say anything about Madonna, Hollywood, drugs, sex, or any of the kind of cultural issues you might expect him to be concerned with. It's all about what America is doing in his backyard, as he sees it." Likewise, Michael Scheuer observes that "cultural political considerations have not been part of bin Laden's Jihadist rhetoric; … only others – particularly U.S. and Western political, military, and media leaders – have tried to persuade people that al-Qaeda and its allies are motivated by such factors." Peter L. Bergen, *The Osama bin Laden I Know: An Oral History of al Qaeda's Leader* (New York: Free Press, 2006), xxxii, 182; Scheuer, *Osama bin Laden*, 113.

[151] Al-Awlaki's motivations during this time period are a subject of much speculation. He is known to have had contact with at least one of the hijackers while living in San Diego and later, while living in Virginia, with Major Nidal Malik Hasan, who, on November 5, 2009, killed 13 people and injured 29 more during a shooting rampage at Fort Hood, Texas. While he was presented as the face of moderate Islam in the U.S. in the immediate

in a communication entitled "The Towers of Lebanon," bin Laden asked, "despite Bush's claim that we hate freedom, perhaps he can tell us why we did not attack Sweden?"[152] Given the persistent misrecognition of the organization's goals, some have claimed that al Qaeda's violence is itself a form of mortalist humanism – albeit, perhaps, one absent the tragic ethos embodied by Aeschylus and advocated here – aimed at establishing shared loss as a precursor to political engagement. It is a claim that further suggests the problematic nature of the claim that humanism denies rather than seeks to establish a politics.

Chantal Mouffe argues that terrorist violence is, in part at least, a product of the absence of legitimate channels of protest within a global system dominated by a hegemon.[153] In his book *The Terrorist in Search of Humanity* Fasil Devji suggests that this violence is concerned with conveying the shared humanity that the Western production of fundamentalism denies. "In statement after statement," he writes, "al Qaeda's soldiers describe their attacks as a 'language,' in fact as the only one that America or the West understands. In other words, these men define violence as a mode of conversation and persuasion, the common language they share with their enemies."[154] Indeed, the constant invocation of U.S. actions in killing civilians – especially at Hiroshima and Nagasaki – was frequently employed by al Qaeda to justify its actions.[155] It is, Devji continues, "clear from Osama bin Laden's statements that he considers acts of terror necessary so that the West might experience the equivalent of Muslim suffering. But far from being a form of revenge, such equivalence is meant to permit both sets of victims to identify with and indeed speak to each other."[156] Indeed, Khalid Sheik Mohammed, the real architect of the 2001 attacks, offered perhaps the most eloquent recent expression of the mortalist humanist position, observing, "your blood is not made out of gold and ours is made out of

aftermath of the 2001 attacks, it is highly likely that he had long been under FBI surveillance. See Jeremy Scahill, *Dirty Wars: The World Is a Battlefield* (New York: Nation Books, 2013); J. M. Berger, *Jihad Joe: Americans Who Go to War in the Name of Islam* (Washington, DC: Potomac Books: 2011), 133.

[152] Osama bin Laden, "The Towers of Lebanon" in *Messages to the World: The Statements of Osama bin Laden* edited by Bruce Lawrence, translated by James Howarth (New York: Verso, 2005), 238.

[153] Chantal Mouffe, *On the Political* (London: Routledge, 2011), 81.

[154] Faisal Devji, *The Terrorist in Search of Humanity: Militant Islam and Global Politics* (New York: Columbia University Press, 2009), 42.

[155] Terry McDermott and Josh Meyer, *The Hunt for KSM: Inside the Pursuit and Takedown of the Real 9/11 Mastermind, Khalid Sheik Mohammed* (New York: Little and Brown, 2012), 112–113, 279–280.

[156] Devji, *Terrorist in Search of Humanity*, 42.

water. We are all human beings."[157] It is a humanism motivated by, not opposed to, politics and the political: one in which the antipolitical in both senses identified by Loraux, and the extrapolitical – the violent murder of nearly three thousand civilians on American soil – sought political effects. Although not, perhaps, the most appetizing argument in favor of a mortalist humanism, this understanding of al Qaeda's motivations does seem to weaken the claim that the ethical turn is an attempt to overcome conflict rather than to reframe it in politically productive ways.

As with *The Persians*, the most compelling argument for embracing a mortalist humanism imbued with a tragic ethos is the way in which doing so might be thought to be in the polity's interests. The hubris of America's postplanes mourning practices ensured that country entered a conflict whose causes it did not comprehend against an enemy whom it did not understand.[158] The ways in which the need to defend its

---

[157] McDermott and Meyer, *The Hunt for KSM*, 11.

[158] The literature on America's ignorance of its enemy and its motivations is extensive. Such was the production of radical Islam arising from or encouraged by the dominant mode of mourning employed by the polity after the 2001 attacks, that neither the U.S. government nor its military ever understood or attempted to understand, al Qaeda's internal structure or complex relationship to the Taliban. Prior to 2001, for example, many of the terrorist groups that later came under the umbrella of al Qaeda were in active competition with the organization, and rival groups had made at least two attempts on bin Laden's life. It was the U.S. invasion of Afghanistan that drew these groups into al Qaeda's fold. Alex Strick Van Linschoten and Felix Kuehn, *An Enemy We Created: The Myth of the Taliban–Al Qaeda Merger in Afghanistan* (New York: Oxford University Press, 2012), 100. Similarly, although there is some disagreement about al Qaeda's relationship to the Taliban, arising largely from the Afghans' refusal to hand over bin Laden both prior to and after September 2001, the terms set by the Taliban for bin Laden's presence in their country – that he make no media contact without first consulting them and that he neither sponsor nor commit attacks on the U.S. – suggest that the two organizations were quite separate. This is often explained by pointing to Islamic norms of hospitality, and while this may have played a part in the Taliban's decision, Van Linschoten and Kuehn argue that the matter is somewhat more complex. In April 1996, Mullah Mohammad Omar was proclaimed *Amir ul-Mu'mineen*, leader of the Muslim world. The authors suggest that the title was forced on the ignorant and parochial Omar by Pakistani agents keen to alienate the Taliban from the rest of the Muslim world. As *Amir ul-Mu'mineen*, it would have been impossible for Omar to hand over a fellow Muslim to the Americans. Likewise, the highly predictable and disastrous consequences for Mullah Omar's government of the American response to al Qaeda's attacks indicates the lack of cooperation between bin Laden and his hosts. Indeed, as Ahmed Rashid observed, "The Taliban stressed that they considered themselves Afghan nationalists not global jihadists. At the death of bin Laden, the Taliban statement remained circumspect, refusing to eulogize him or call for revenge attacks." Ahmed Rashid, *Pakistan on the Brink: The Future of America, Pakistan, and Afghanistan* (New York: Viking, 2012), 117. Its hubris led America to ignore this important difference and greatly complicated its actions in the region. Indeed, the Taliban made numerous attempts to reach

interests might move a polity to political action, and the ways in which
those actions might then serve to cultivate a humanist ethic of value in
understanding that enemy and protecting those same interests, is suggested by a battlefield program in Afghanistan adopted by the Pentagon
in November 2008. The Human Terrain System was predicated on the
notion that understanding – rather than demonizing – the enemy would
be of strategic value in the Afghan theater. The American resistance to
this kind of reasoning was, nevertheless, suggested when the program
was scrapped for being too successful. Troops often came to empathize
with and understand the Taliban's motives, even after their fellow soldiers had been killed – seeing them as human beings with motivations
rather than a demonized enemy motivated by hatred – in ways that
the Pentagon found uncomfortable.[159] Although unsuccessful on the
Pentagon's terms, the program serves to indicate the plausibility of the
claim that the pursuit of interests can, indeed, be a source of ethical
understanding. The cancelled Afghan program also suggests, however,
that interests alone are insufficient for the cultivation of the ethic of
mortalist humanism: that individuals and/or nations often act against
their own best interests, even when those interests would appear to be
perfectly transparent. There are, nevertheless, further resources in the
polity that suggest the experience of the Human Terrain System might
possibly be replicated and that cultivating the type of mourning for

a peace agreement with the Afghan government starting as early as 2002, but the U.S.'s
understanding of the Taliban's relationship to al Qaeda led the Americans to ignore
the offer. The pattern was repeated until the U.S. finally agreed to tentative talks with
the Taliban in February 2011. Richard N. Hass, "Rethinking Afghanistan" in *Beyond
Bin Laden*, loc. 886; Editorial, "Peace Talks With the Taliban," *The New York Times*,
October 4, 2012. www.nytimes.com/2012/10/05/opinion/peace-talks-with-the-taliban.
html. Accessed Jun. 20, 2013; and Emma-Graham Harrison, "'We should have talked
to the Taliban' says top British Officer in Afghanistan. Exclusive: General Nick Carter
says west could have struck a deal with Taliban leaders when they were toppled a
decade ago" *The Guardian*, June 28, 2013. www.guardian.co.uk/world/2013/jun/28/
talks-taliban. Accessed Jun. 28, 2013. Nor was this confined only to the U.S. military
or its government. Following Michael Moore and Arundhati Roy, Judith Butler repeats
the tired old saw that bin Laden was trained by the CIA. As all of the major bin Laden
experts have pointed out, bin Laden was an Arab nationalist with no need of American
money who would not even align himself with the Afghan Mujahideen, let alone the
U.S. As such, he would have had nothing to do with the CIA even if the Americans
had placed personnel in the country during the conflict, a claim about which there is
also some debate. See Butler, *Precarious Life*, 10; and Bergen, *The Osama bin Laden
I Knew*, 60–61.

159 Vanessa M. Gezari, *The Tender Soldier: A True Story of War and Sacrifice* (New York:
Simon & Schuster, 2013). See also Jennifer Percy, *Demon Camp. A Soldier's Exorcism*
(New York: Scribner, 2014).

the enemy being outlined here – one concerned with understanding the fallen as human beings with rational goals and motivations – may not be entirely implausible in the American context.

BEYOND THE "OTHER"

In her book on Islamic fundamentalism, Roxanne Euben embodies and identifies a common aspect of the Western intellectual tradition: the attempt to eradicate or diminish "otherness" through the identification of common traits, views, or habits. In an echo of the cultural parallels between Athens and Persia identified by Aeschylus, Euben observes that "'Fundamentalism literally refers to an early twentieth-century Protestant movement that called for religion based on a literal interpretation of the Bible."[160] Thus, she notes, the dominant Western production of radical Islam contains within it a projection of what is considered to be a negative Western characteristic – a certain kind of intolerance – that serves as a structuring element in its own political and religious understandings.[161] Likewise, John Gray draws out the fundamentally modernist bent of a worldview – Islamic fundamentalism – that is often seen as backward, pointing to al Qaeda's embrace of technology, organizational structures, and Leninist political tactics.[162] Indeed, most of the serious scholarship on bin Laden is at pains to identify his rationality and reasonableness: the historian Bernard Lewis called bin Laden's declaration of war on Americans "a magnificent piece of eloquent, at times even poetic Arabic prose,"[163] while Michael Scheuer observed that the document "read like our Declaration of Independence ... It was a frighteningly

---

[160] R. Euben, *Enemy in the Mirror*, loc. 1306.

[161] "For Americans it is useful to think of bin Laden's attitude towards Islam's founding leaders and document as akin to that of their fellow citizens who believe governance must be based on the founders' 'original intent.'" That the latter is a perfectly respectable political position in the United States espoused by, among others, citizens, elected representatives, and high-ranking members of the judiciary suggests the similarities between the West and a more fully contextualized production of Islam. Scheuer, *Osama bin Laden*, 174–175.

[162] Gray, *Al Qaeda*. See also Devji, *The Terrorist in Search of Humanity*, 206. "[T]he way in which the West engages al Qaeda is strikingly different with bin Laden invariably seen as irredeemably alien, rarely if ever addressed by his enemies, and usually described as sharing nothing at all with them. And yet what could be more familiar to political life in the West than the spectacle of a leader being fed bits of information and summaries of important books by his research assistants, the very procedure that allows bin Laden to quote Noam Chomsky or assail capitalism."

[163] Lawrence, *Messages to the World*, xvii.

reasoned argument."¹⁶⁴ More prosaically, others have pointed out that al Qaeda was a shockingly bureaucratic organization. In agreeing to join the organization, an applicant agreed to the group's bylaws, which ran to thirty-two pages in English translation, and detailed annual budgets, salaries, medical and disability benefits and policies, retirement packages, grounds for dismissal, and vacation allowances.¹⁶⁵ "For an organization devoted to revolutionary holy war," observed Peter Bergen, "the pre-9/11 al Qaeda sometimes had the feel of an insurance company."¹⁶⁶ In such circumstances, the title of Euben's book – *The Enemy in the Mirror* – could not, perhaps, be more apropos.

That such efforts to diminish otherness through the identification of common traits is a key part of the Western intellectual tradition does not by itself, of course, mean that the polity contains sufficient resources for the empathetic leap required to mourn bin Laden. There are, however, other potential sources of such insight, most obviously the Judeo-Christian tradition. In an essay following bin Laden's death, Michael Walzer pointed to a Jewish commentary on the *Book of Exodus* that noted how, when the Pharaoh's armies were drowned in the Red Sea and the angels in heaven began to celebrate, God rebuked them, asking how they could celebrate when his creatures were dying.¹⁶⁷ Similarly, in the New Testament, Christ twice demands that his followers love their enemies.¹⁶⁸ While loving bin Laden is not a necessary condition for the commitment to mourn him, both the Old and New Testaments call on exercises in empathy and imagination – akin to those demanded by tragic

¹⁶⁴ Philip Shenon, *The Commission: The Uncensored History of the 9/11 Investigation* (New York: Hachette Book group, 2008).
¹⁶⁵ Peter Bergen, *Manhunt: The Ten Year Search for Bin Laden From 9/11 to Abbottabad* (New York: Crown Publishers, 2012), 55. A February 11, 1999, missive to an unnamed agent from Ayman al-Zawahiri, al Qaeda's number two, asked, among other things: "Why did you buy a new fax for $470? Where are the two old faxes? Did you get permission before buying a new fax under such circumstances?" Alan Cullison, "Inside Al-Qaeda's Hard Drive. Budget squabbles, baby pictures, office rivalries – and the path to 9/11," *The Atlantic*, September 1, 2004. www.theatlantic.com/magazine/archive/2004/09/inside-al-qaeda-s-hard-drive/303428/. Accessed Jul. 9, 2013.
¹⁶⁶ Bergen, *Manhunt*, 55.
¹⁶⁷ Michael Walzer, "Killing Osama," *Dissent*, May 10, 2011. www.dissentmagazine.org/online_articles/symposium-the-killing-of-osama-bin-laden. Accessed May 28, 2013.
¹⁶⁸ Matthew 5:44; Luke 6:27. "Unlike the rhetoric used in the War on Terror, which is determined to punish Islamic militants for crimes committed, that used in al Qaeda's jihad would forgive U.S. President Bush and Britain's former Prime Minister Blair for crimes as great if only they were to repent. However preposterous, al Qaeda's rhetoric is more Christian than that of its Western enemies." Devji, *The Terrorist in Search of Humanity*, 32.

mourning – that are aimed at cultivating the values that mortalist humanism demands of its audience. Likewise, just as the protagonists of the *Iliad* expressed respect for one another – the Greeks recognizing that the gods might ultimately favor the Trojans – Lincoln's much-revered "Second Inaugural" recognized that the "Almighty has His own purposes" and, out of this acknowledgment of shared human finitude, came a generosity to the enemy that would serve to make politics possible and to "achieve and cherish a just and lasting peace among ourselves and with all nations."[169] The revulsion, furthermore, expressed by at least some members of the polity over the mistreatment of the bodies of enemy soldiers in Afghanistan suggests the existence of a contemporary equivalent to the Homeric horror at the mistreatment of bodies that might be mobilized to political and strategic ends. It also underlines the inextricable connection between interests and ethic: expressions of distaste for the sacrilegious act are frequently combined with a concern about how it might affect the treatment of American troops or attempts to capture Islamic hearts and minds.[170] Indeed, unconsciously echoing Peter Euben's account of Socrates' conflation of the moral, the political, and the strategic, Senator John McCain captured the complexity of these issues when, in calling for an end to American practices of torture during the War on Terror, he declared, "It's not about them, it's about us."[171]

This same mutually reinforcing combination of ethic and interests might also be thought to be present in other American attempts to place its enemies among Loraux's "race of mortals." Jess Goodell, a Marine veteran whose job was to collect, identify, and repatriate the remains of U.S. soldiers and military contractors in Iraq, notes the difficulty she and her colleagues experienced in separating American body tissue from that of locals, particularly in the case of suicide bombings. Even when the distinction was clear, moreover, she observes, it was frequently impossible to tell the difference between innocent Iraqi civilians and the perpetrators of the attacks. Consequently, every body at the site was recovered, and those non-American bodies not claimed by family members were buried in graves facing Mecca following the

---

[169] Abraham Lincoln, "Second Inaugural Address." www.bartleby.com/124/pres32.html. Accessed Apr. 23, 2015.

[170] Graham Browley and Matthew Rosenberg, "Video Inflames a Delicate Moment for the U.S. in Afghanistan," *The New York Times*, January 12, 2012. www.nytimes.com/2012/01/13/world/asia/video-said-to-show-marines-urinating-on-taliban-corpses.html?pagewanted=all&_r=0. Accessed May 13, 2014.

[171] Jane Mayer, *The Dark Side: The Inside Story of How the War on Terror Turned into a War on American Ideals* (New York: Anchor, 2009), 329.

recital of Islamic prayers for the dead. When her unit became aware
that it was Iraqi custom for an elder to meet and take tea with the
relatives of the deceased, it built a room and purchased a tea set precisely for that purpose, with an officer sitting with the family coming
to search for or reclaim a body.[172] Although far from the tragic rituals enacted by the Greeks for the fallen Persians, these moments of
respect – also embodied in the Islamic rituals offered for the body
of Osama bin Laden – suggest the possibility of an American tragic
mourning for the fallen enemy.[173]

MOURNING BEYOND ORIENTALISM

Some time after bin Laden's death, a daughter of the terrorist leader
would recall that on the night of the raid, she heard her father's head
banging on each step as the Navy Seals retreated with his body.[174] As
with Aeschylus' account of the Persian women and parents left bereft by
the Battle of Salamis, such a detail might serve to temper the U.S. jubi-
lation over the death of the head of al Qaeda, especially when, it has
been argued, such tempering might be shown to benefit the American
polity. As with Aeschylus' attitude towards the Persians, this is not to
claim that the U.S. should regret bin Laden's demise, simply to embrace
the ambivalence expressed in certain parts of the polity about the celebration of his death and to employ more fully the resources within the
nation that might make further such ambivalence possible. As Aeschylus
demonstrates, pride in victory is not inappropriate, but it should be tempered by the recognition of the costs to others lest it become the hubristic
triumphalism that befell Xerxes. It is a perspective that it is of benefit
to the polity not only in terms of its foreign relations but also in terms
of its domestic interactions, with democracy understood as an ongoing
project. Such a perspective promises much not only for the functioning of
a highly polarized American polity but also for those Muslim Americans

---

[172] Jess Goodell with John Hearn, *Shade It Black: Death and After in Iraq* (Philadelphia:
Casemate, 2011), 76–8.

[173] Journalist John Hersey's articles for *The New Yorker* – later published in book
form – following the U.S. bombing of Hiroshima similarly detailed Japanese suffering in an entirely empathetic and nontriumphalist fashion. John Hersey, *Hiroshima*
(New York: Vintage, 1989).

[174] Mark Bowden, "The Hunt for 'Geronimo,'" *Vanity Fair*, November 2012. www
.vanityfair.com/politics/2012/11/inside-osama-bin-laden-assassination-plot. Accessed
Jul. 22, 2013.

subject to suspicion, discrimination, and abuse in the years since the 2001 attacks.[175]

In America, the most famous image of the Islamic world's response to the 2001 attacks was of West Bank Palestinians celebrating the attacks, handing out candy so that their children might connect it with the perceived sweetness of the damage done to the U.S.[176] In Iraq, Saddam Hussein's government issued a statement declaring, "The American cowboys are reaping the fruit of their crimes against humanity."[177] In Egypt, according to Fouad Ajami, "there was an unmistakable sense of glee and little sorrow among upper-class Egyptians for the distant power – only satisfaction that America had gotten its comeuppance."[178] More generally, he suggests, "in thwarted, resentful societies there was satisfaction ... that the American bull-run and the triumphalism that had awed the world had been battered, that there was soot and ruin in New York's streets."[179] Such words and pictures confirmed and perpetuated the dominant Western production of an Islamic fundamentalism motivated by a hatred of the West, a claim that created its own feedback loop of *mênis*. "The unspoken imputation of such rhetoric," observed Rashid, "was that if *they* hated *us*, then Americans should hate Muslims back and retaliate not just against the terrorists but against Islam in general."[180] There is no sense in which the tragic pedagogy advocated here seeks to deny this perspective, to suggest, that is, that the Islamic world is without hatred or malice towards the U.S., nor does it suggest that the U.S. should not seek to defend itself against those who would do it harm. It merely aims to generate an awareness of the necessarily partial nature of this viewpoint, seeking to cultivate an ethic conducive to political engagement by highlighting the polity's interests in so doing. The question of what such an approach might look like is, fittingly enough, answered by a fuller picture of the Islamic world's response to al Qaeda's murderous attacks.

"The immediate response in the secular Arab press," observed Michael Scott Doran, "... fell broadly into three categories. A minority denounced

---

[175] See, for example, Martha C. Nussbaum, *The New Religious Intolerance: Overcoming the Politics of Fear in an Anxious Age* (Cambridge, MA: Belknap Press, 2012); and Peter Morey and Amina Yaqin, *Framing Muslims: Stereotyping and Representation After 9/11* (Cambridge, MA: Harvard University Press, 2011).

[176] See, for example, www.youtube.com/watch?v=HRAoNKQok6E. Accessed Jul. 1, 2013.

[177] Seth G. Jones, *Hunting in the Shadows: The Pursuit of Al Qa'ida Since 9/11* (New York: Norton Books, 2012), 72.

[178] Fouad Ajami, "The Sentry's Solitude" in *The U.S. vs. al Qaeda*, 59.

[179] Ibid., 66.

[180] Rashid, *Descent into Chaos*, lv.

the attacks forcefully and unconditionally, another minority attributed
them to the Israelis or to American extremists like Timothy McVeigh, and
a significant majority responded with a version of 'Yes, but' – yes, the terrorist attacks against you were wrong, but you must understand that your
own policies in the Middle East have for years sown the seeds of this kind
of violence."[181] Beyond this nuanced response, there were some explicit
expressions of sympathy. Yusuf al-Qaradawi, an Egyptian firebrand
cleric with a wide following on satellite TV, issued fatwas condemning
the attacks as contrary to Islam, further demanding that the perpetrators be caught and punished.[182] The Taliban condemned the attacks.[183]
Libya's Muammar Gaddafi denounced the carnage as "horrifying."[184]
Tehran's *Iran News* described the attacks as an "atrocity" and condemned
the slaughter.[185] It might be argued, of course, that such responses were
strategic rather than genuinely felt expressions of sorrow, especially at a
time when the U.S. government had announced an indiscriminate war
on a nebulous enemy. Certainly, the double-edged declaration by Iran's
President Mohammad Khatami that "My deep sympathy goes out to the
American nation. Terrorism is condemned and the world public should
identify its roots and its dimensions and should take fundamental steps
to eliminate it" could be thought to apply as much to the U.S. as to al
Qaeda.[186] Nevertheless, the argument presented here suggests that the
divide between ethic and interest in the cultivation of a tragic mourning
is far less clear than has previously been suggested. There were, moreover,
several non-state-centered responses to the attacks that were indicative
of a genuine concern for the fallen enemy. In North Tehran, for example, thousands of people spontaneously took to the streets, replacing their
usual cries of "death to America," with the chant "death to terrorists,"
while Iranian soccer fans observed a minute of silence in memory of the
victims of the attacks before an international match with Bahrain.[187] The
American reluctance to understand such a complex position is suggested
by the experience of the Iranian president, who, on a visit to New York

---

[181] Doran, "Somebody Else's Civil War" in *The U.S. vs. al Qaeda*, 85. See also Burke, *The
9/11 Wars*, 29.
[182] Philip Gordon, "Can the War on Terror Be Won?" *Foreign Affairs*, November/December,
2007, 62.
[183] Van Linschoten and Kuehn, *An Enemy We Created*, 218.
[184] Jones, *Hunting in the Shadows*, 72.
[185] David Crist, *The Twilight War: The Secret History of America's Thirty-Year Conflict
with Iran* (New York: Penguin Books, 2012).
[186] Ibid., 427–428.
[187] Ibid., 428.

City for the November 2001 meeting of the United Nations, expressed a desire to visit Ground Zero to light a candle. He was forbidden from doing so. "A visit by the president of a terrorist nation would not only insult the memory of those killed," a senior Bush administration official observed, "it threatened to undermine the monolithic nature of the war on terrorism, which lumped Iran, Iraq, and Syria all into the same nefarious category."[188]

It is in the "yes, but" identified by Michael Scott Doran, that the tragic ambivalence of the mode of mourning being advocated here can most clearly be seen, that which condemns but also contextualizes, recognizing that both sides in any conflict belong to Loraux's "race of mortals." In bin Laden's case, it might, then, be apropos to consider the possibility of a national memorial service on May 1, 2021, on the tenth anniversary of his death: a service in which the nation both celebrated its victory and sought to offer a more nuanced picture of the man whom they had killed, offering a "yes, but" that addressed both the costs of the nation's victory, and the motivations of the Saudi and his followers that necessitated it. The Iranian president's experience in New York City suggests, nevertheless, the difficulties the nation might face in any attempt to consider mourning for our enemy when we would not even permit our perceived enemy to mourn for us. Such hostility may arise, in part, from the influence of the nationalist, romantic, and/or neo-Homeric modes of mourning that dominate American public responses to loss. In these terms, mourning bin Laden might be misunderstood as an act of veneration rather than clear-eyed evaluation. Nevertheless, just as Aeschylus allows his audience at the end of *The Persians* to see Xerxes stripped of the mythological power with which he had been imbued by his previous successes, mourning bin Laden might permit Americans to understand that the bogeyman they had created was, by the end of his life, an isolated, ineffectual figure with no ability to threaten the nation or affect international politics, a truly tragic figure whose moment of greatest success proved to be his undoing. Such an understanding might then serve to undercut the triumphalism of May 1, 2011, not just as a means of disciplining the polity's excesses but also as a way of offering a fuller understanding of the causes and consequences of the challenges that face a nation enmeshed in a world complicated by its previous actions. As Pericles observed to the Athenians during the war against Sparta: "Your empire is now like a tyranny: it may have been wrong to take it; it is certainly dangerous to let it go."[189]

[188] Ibid., 432–433.
[189] Thucydides, *The History of the Peloponnesian War* translated by Rex Warner (New York: Penguin, 1972), 161.

On May 15, 2014, President Obama dedicated the memorial museum at the site of the September 2001 attacks in Lower Manhattan. A manifestation of the *álaston pénthos* that marked the nation's response to the deaths of thousands of its residents and citizens, the museum contained an inadvertent nod toward the nineteen men on four airplanes whose actions most immediately precipitated the demand for memorialization. A sixty-foot-long inscription on the wall separating visitors from those remains kept on site declares, "No day shall erase you from the memory of time."¹⁹⁰ The quote – from Virgil's *Aeneid* – refers to a pair of Trojan soldiers who slaughtered numerous enemies in what the classicist Helen Morales called a "suicide mission." Interviewed by *The New York Times* about the appropriateness of the inscription, Morales observed:

> Virgil's line memorializing them is ironic. So my first reaction is that the quotation is shockingly inappropriate for the U.S. victims of the ... attack. But my second reaction is that this may be a productive irony. Which is to say that the quotation makes us remember the suicidal killers ... as well as their victims. Remember with horror, anger, disbelief, to be sure, but remember them nonetheless.¹⁹¹

In this, perhaps, Morales captures the ethos of a potential American mourning for its enemies. Not so much in her suggestion that the nation should remember in horror, anger, and disbelief – though these *emotions* might provide *reasons* America should seek to remember a fallen enemy – but rather more in her willingness to embrace a second look and the duality of the perspective that permits it. America should mourn its enemies, it suggests, because both they and we must die.

---

¹⁹⁰ I am grateful to Andrew Poe for drawing this point to my attention.
¹⁹¹ David W. Dunlap, "Scholarly Perspectives on Inscription at 9/11 Memorial Museum,"
     The New York Times, April 2, 2014. cityroom.blogs.nytimes.com/2014/04/02/scholarly-
     perspectives-on-inscription-at-the-911-memorial-museum/.

4

Homecoming and Reconstitution: Nostalgia, Mourning, and Military Return

Whether they know it or not, they certainly act as if their motto were: let the dead bury the living.

— *Friedrich Nietzsche, Untimely Meditations*

"The nation of the tragic mysteries," observed Friedrich Nietzsche of democratic Athens, "fought the war with Persia, and a people who had conducted such a campaign had the need of the restorative of tragedy."[1] This understanding of Greek tragedy as a ritual of mourning for a polity almost perpetually at war has a strong pedigree.[2] Simon Goldhill, J. J. Winkler, and Nicole Loraux, among others, identify a connection between the rituals of the funeral oration and those of Athens' springtime theatrical festival, the Great Dionysia. They further note that the playwrights were often veterans of Athens' wars and that the audiences for the plays were predominantly made up of citizen-soldiers seated by military unit.[3] As Loraux observes of Aeschylus' *The Persians*, "Many of its spectators

---

[1] Friedrich Nietzsche, *The Birth of Tragedy & the Genealogy of Morals*, translated by Francis Golffing (New York: Anchor Books, 1956), 124.

[2] It is estimated that the average Athenian citizen spent well over half of his adult life in combat. Robert Emmet Meagher, *Herakles Gone Mad: Rethinking Heroism in an Age of Endless War* (Northampton, MA: Olive Branch Press, 2006), 46.

[3] Simon Goldhill, *Love, Sex, & Tragedy: How the Ancient World Shapes Our Lives* (Chicago: University of Chicago Press, 2004), 224; J. J. Winkler, "The Ephebes' Song: Tragoidia and Polis," *Representations*, 11 (Summer) 1985: 32–33; and Nicole Loraux, *Mothers in Mourning* translated by Corinne Pache (Ithaca, NY: Cornell University Press, 1998). Both Aeschylus and Sophocles are known to have experienced combat. See Lawrence A. Trittle, *From Melos to My Lai: War and Survival* (New York: Routledge, 2000), 11; and Meagher, *Herakles Gone Mad*, xi, 47.

at the initial performance were the warriors who eight years earlier had defeated the Persians and caused horrible losses that Xerxes laments in the play."[4] Drawing on a reading of Aristotle, Jonathan Shay – a Boston psychiatrist who specializes in the treatment of war veterans – further suggests that the rituals of mourning embedded in the Great Dionysia were also rituals of homecoming for Athens' warrior-citizens. Building on the claim that the theater was a key source of civic education, Shay argues that it was also a major source of *re*education for the citizen-soldiers whom war often rendered unfit for democratic politics.[5] At the heart of this democratic reeducation was, Shay observes, a commitment to a form of mourning predicated on the notion that "to forget the dead dishonors the living veteran."[6]

America's dominant form of mourning for its contemporary wars is, it will be argued, *nostalgic*: concerned with the restoration of an imagined past untouched by the casualties of the conflicts that necessitated its rituals of loss. Such nostalgic mourning shares much with the previously identified nationalist and romantic responses to loss, not least of which is its commitment to unity and consensus. Nevertheless, the term "nostalgic" is employed here not simply because it draws on the Greek word *nostos* – meaning homecoming – but also because it suggests a concern with temporality that is less present in its alternatives: a longing for the past that denies time and change in the present. The effects of this denial of time and change on politics and the political are, it will be argued, twofold. First, it cultivates an understanding of democracy as a fixed set of procedures that interpolates different groups into the polity in exactly the same way. As such, it stands in contrast to an understanding of democracy as an ongoing practice whose activities and identity are continually being remade even as it maintains certain core functions. The second effect is to commit such mourning to a politics of recognition. In this, nostalgic mourning focuses attention on issues of honor and respect that are important to veterans while nevertheless undermining their needs and demands in ways that do damage not only to returnees but also to the democratic polity of which they seek to be a part. For, as Shay observes,

---

[4] Nicole Loraux, *The Mourning Voice: An Essay on Greek Tragedy* translated by Elizabeth Trapnell Rawlings (Ithaca, NY: Cornell University Press, 2002), xi.

[5] Jonathan Shay, "The Birth of Tragedy – Out of the Needs of Democracy," *Didaskalia: Ancient Theater Today*, 2(2), April, 1995. www.didaskalia.net/issues/vol2no2/shay.html. Accessed Apr. 24, 2015.

[6] Jonathan Shay, *Odysseus in America: Combat Trauma and the Trials of Homecoming* (New York: Scribner, 2002). 80. In this, Shay's work further suggests that the stories a polity tells about its dead help to shape the lives and politics of its living.

in the aftermath of combat, both "the veteran and the community collude in the belief that [the veteran] is 'no longer one of us.' "[7]

In order to suggest the ways in which tragedy might ultimately offer a more democratically productive set of responses to wartime losses – in the sense of promoting an agonistic account of democracy as an always ongoing process of political becoming – the chapter begins by setting out an understanding of the nostalgic drawn from the work of Svetlana Boym. Identifying her distinction between *restorative* and *reflective* nostalgia – one complacent, the other critical – it suggests that nostalgic mourning is predicated solely on the former. The chapter then turns to identifying a distinction between two forms of democratic interpolation: recognition and acknowledgment. While the former is, it is suggested, connected to a set of nostalgic responses to loss and thus to a politics of unity and consensus, the latter offers an agonistic understanding of democratic politics, one more likely to emerge from a tragic form of mourning. Employing this distinction between nostalgic and tragic mourning, the chapter then identifies the dominance of the former in America's response to its wartime losses. Demonstrating what Boym calls the "contagious nature" of nostalgia, it argues that nostalgic mourning also leads the polity to mourn its *living* returnees by recognizing them with the same narratives of heroism, service, and sacrifice with which it recognizes its military dead. Outlining the ways in which such nostalgic mourning cultivates a social and political death for many military veterans, it then details the damage that such mourning does – not only to returnees but also to the democratic polity that would recognize their homecoming without acknowledging their experiences.[8] Having identified the problems posed by nostalgic mourning to returning veterans and the democratic polity, the chapter turns to recent attempts to revive tragedy as a contemporary ritual of mourning and return. Noting that a number of organizations have offered readings and performances of Greek tragedy for audiences of military veterans, their families, and civilians that seek to provoke reflection on and dialogue about veterans' experiences of war, the chapter nevertheless identifies a nostalgic urge underpinning even these attempts at tragic return. Pointing to the language of "restoration" that is explicit not only in these projects but also in the work that provides much of their intellectual justification, such attempts are, it is argued, more nostalgic

---

[7] Ibid., 152.
[8] The term "social death" is borrowed from Orlando Patterson. Orlando Patterson, *Slavery and Social Death: A Comparative Study* (Cambridge, MA: Harvard University Press, 1985).

than tragic, committed to consensus, unity, and the return of both the polity and the veteran to their antebellum states. As such, it is suggested, these projects deny both time and change in a way that ultimately rein-scribes on the polity – and its veterans – the very problems they seek to address.

Having established the problems of both nostalgic responses to loss and return and recent attempts to employ tragedy as a tool for addressing the same, the chapter offers a reading of Aeschylus's *Eumenides* by way of a possible corrective. This reading seeks to demonstrate how a more thoroughgoing engagement with tragedy than that offered by Shay and others might provide a model for a mutually meaningful and democrati-cally productive exchange between the polity and its returning veterans, one predicated on and generative of a politics of acknowledgment. Taking on the claim that *The Oresteia* has the happiest ending in Greek tragedy and Patchen Markell's somewhat darker reading of the play's conclusion, *Eumenides*, it is argued, is a play without an end, one whose challenge to its democratic audience continues to reverberate in modernity. In this, it is suggested, the play posits an understanding of mourning and return as an always ongoing project of agonistic reconstitution. A thoroughly tragic approach to mourning, it is argued, embodies the hopeful – in the sense suggested by W.E.B. Du Bois in the earlier chapter on African American responses to loss – possibility of a form of homecoming that places the responsibility for return on an ongoing engagement between the polity and the veteran rather than, as is currently the case, the veteran alone. The chapter concludes by outlining what such a thoroughly tragic and hopeful approach to mourning and return might look like in the contemporary polity and by identifying the resources available for con-structing the necessary set of institutions. As such, it offers a model for homecoming as reconstitution that is itself a reconstitution of the polity's existing commemorative practices.

IN SEARCH OF LOST TIME

Despite its Greek root in the word *nostos*, the concept of nostalgia origi-nated in seventeenth-century Europe. Coined by a Swiss doctor, Johannes Hofer in 1688, it was defined as "the sad mood originating from the desire to return to one's native land."[9] It was, said Hofer, a single-minded obsession that led its victims to confuse the past with the present and

---

[9] Svetlana Boym, *The Future of Nostalgia* (New York: Basic Books, 2008), 3.

the real with the imaginary. The concept was, moreover, associated with the military from the very beginning: among those first diagnosed were, Boym notes, Swiss soldiers fighting abroad. Imbued with a romantic commitment to the ideal and predicated on a confused temporality, nostalgia evinces a relationship with the dead and embodies the singular perspective of tragedy's protagonists. Indeed, Boym identifies a considerable overlap between the blindness of nationalism and that of the nostalgic. "It is the promise to rebuild the ideal home," she argues, "that lies at the core of many powerful ideologies of today, tempting us to relinquish critical thinking for emotional bonding. The danger of nostalgia is that it tends to confuse the actual home and the imaginary one. In extreme cases it can create a phantom homeland, for the sake of which one is ready to die or kill."[10] Boym suggests, furthermore, that while individuals might suffer from nostalgia, it is ultimately a social condition, one whose origins are historical not psychological. It serves, she argues, to mediate between personal and collective memory.[11] Drawing on Michael Kammen's observation that nostalgia "is essentially history without guilt," Boym further argues that it is predicated on a false understanding of the past.[12] Indeed, echoing Frederick Douglass, she notes the ways in which commemorations seek to obscure memory in favor of idealized history.[13] As a matter of state policy, she argues, "the stronger the loss, the more it is overcompensated with commemorations, the starker the distance from the past, and the more it is prone to idealizations."[14] Nostalgia is politically problematic, she suggests, "because it does not help us deal with the future."[15] As such, it is a particular threat to democracy, a political system predicated – as Walt Whitman repeatedly observes – on a commitment to the same. Indeed, Boym reminds us that nostalgia was originally understood to be a disease of democracy, one that posed a threat to politics and the public well-being.[16]

Nostalgia is, then, a backward-looking worldview that shares much with nationalism and the romantic, one that seeks unity and consensus through an agreement on an idealized account of the past and a denial of the temporal. As such, nostalgic mourning should be understood as

[10] Ibid., xvi. "Unreflected nostalgia," she concludes, "breeds monsters."
[11] Ibid., xvi, 7.
[12] Ibid., xiv, 15.
[13] It is telling, perhaps, that doctors believed that the U.S. did not succumb to nostalgia until the Civil War. Ibid., 6.
[14] Ibid., 17.
[15] Ibid., 351.
[16] Ibid., 5.

a response to loss that seeks unity and consensus by denying change in the face of death. Like nationalist responses to loss, nostalgic public mourning defines itself in opposition to "the other," offering "a pre-modern conception of good and evil ... a Manichean battle of good and evil and the inevitable scapegoating of the mythical enemy."[17] On this account, writes Boym identifying nostalgia's frequently conspiratorial tone, "home" is "forever under siege, requiring defense against the plotting enemy."[18] Critics might, nevertheless, point to the use of Greek tragedy and nineteenth-century models of mourning in this study and suggest that it too is guilty of the nostalgia it would identify in others. In response, it might be noted that this analysis seeks to employ the past as a way of thinking about both the present and future and that, as such, it eschews nostalgic desire in favor of critical engagement with the current and coming polities. Boym, moreover, identifies two forms of nostalgia – the *restorative* and the *reflective* – and considers only the former to be democratically problematic. Restorative nostalgia, she observes, "stresses nostos and attempts a transhistorical reconstruction of the lost home" and "does not think of itself as nostalgia, but rather as truth and tradition," both of which it seeks to protect. The reflective, by contrast, "dwells on the ambivalences of human longing and belonging and does not shy away from the contradictions of modernity" and, while restorative nostalgia seeks to defend "the truth," "reflective nostalgia calls it into doubt."[19] Reflective nostalgia, Boym continues, "is a deep form of mourning that performs a labor of grief both through pondering pain and through play that points to the future."[20] As such, reflective nostalgia might be thought to overlap significantly with the tragic.

If the two modes of mourning – the nostalgic and the tragic – being employed here are associated with two understandings of democratic politics, democracy as consensus and democracy as agonism, it might also be noted that each is associated with a different mode of democratic interpolation: recognition and acknowledgment. Identifying the ways in which these interpolations relate to the nostalgic and the tragic and thus to different modes of mourning provides a framework for thinking about how the polity's response to its veterans – both living and dead – might serve to shape its present and future democratic outcomes.

[17] Ibid., 43.
[18] Ibid.
[19] Ibid., xviii.
[20] Ibid., 56.

NOSTALGIC RECOGNITION, TRAGIC ACKNOWLEDGMENT

In *Bound by Recognition*, Patchen Markell offers a critique of contemporary theories of democratic politics that predicate their claims to and understanding of justice and democracy on a politics of recognition.[21] As formulated by Charles Taylor and others, a politics of recognition concerns itself with the ways in which political identities are understood and incorporated into the polity.[22] In contrast to theories of liberal individualism that see the rationally choosing agent as the primary source of political identity, proponents of the politics of recognition note the ways in which such agents are always already embedded within particular group identities: this tribe, that language community, this ethnicity, that sexual orientation, and so on. As such, they argue, social justice and democracy require, first, that agents be *recognized* and understood as members of these groups and, second, that they be permitted to make their political claims *as* members of these collectives rather than as the atomistic individuals of liberal theory. Markell's critique is not, to be sure, that of those who would dismiss "identity politics" in the name of some larger social whole, not least because those who would make such a claim are also engaged in a politics of recognition, simply calling for recognition of the identity of that social whole rather than a particular group.[23] Moreover, Markell notes that a politics of recognition can actually be of real benefit to marginalized groups. Nevertheless, he suggests, such benefits are Janus faced:

[T]he pursuit of recognition [is] at best an equivocal instrument of emancipation, replete with double binds. Movements organized around demands for recognition may indeed produce concrete gains for members of subordinated groups. Yet in characterizing injustice as misrecognition of identity, and embracing equal recognition as an ideal, they may simultaneously make it more difficult to comprehend and confront unjust social and political relations at their root. In some cases, even apparently successful exchanges of recognition may reinforce existing injustices, or help to create new ones.[24]

[21] Patchen Markell, *Bound by Recognition* (Princeton, NJ: Princeton University Press, 2003).
[22] Charles Taylor, "The Politics of Recognition" in Charles Taylor and Amy Gutmann eds. *Multiculturalism and "The Politics of Recognition"* (Princeton, NJ: Princeton University Press, 1992), 25–74. There are, as Markell notes, several different formulations of the politics of recognition. Nevertheless, all seem to share – in one way or another – the qualities that Markell finds problematic. As such, their nuances need not be elaborated here.
[23] Markell, *Bound by Recognition*, 6.
[24] Ibid., 5.

While rejecting the notion of the autonomous liberal agent whose
identity is formed prior to society and accepting the importance of group
identity, Markell argues that the politics of recognition is at once too
ambitious and not ambitious enough. It is too ambitious because it seems
to imply that were marginalized groups to be properly recognized for
who they are, then political conflict could be overcome: it suggests a *telos*
of reconciliation and agreement that – consciously or unconsciously –
eschews politics in favor of consensus.[25] Such commitment to consensus,
it has been argued, damages those who do not – or cannot – conform to
it, marking them out as deviant or "other." It is insufficiently ambitious,
Markell argues, because it assumes a preexisting identity that is formed
prior to politics rather than one that is continually being shaped and
reshaped by the exigencies of its conflicts.

Markell contrasts this problematic politics of recognition with a "politics of acknowledgement." Predicated on an Arendtian understanding of
the unpredictability of action, Markell notes that identity formation is
always ongoing. As such, he suggests, the problem with the politics of
recognition is that it takes what is temporary and mistakes it for what is
permanent. "Invoking 'identity,'" he writes, "as a *fait accompli* precisely
in the course of the ongoing and risky interactions through which we
become who we are...at once acknowledges and refuses to acknowledge
our basic condition of intersubjective vulnerability."[26] As such, injustice
does not require malice on the part of state or society actors, simply
that certain groups be seen only through the lens by which they demand
and/or are granted recognition. The politics of acknowledgment seeks
to address this problem by stressing the essential temporality of identity,
refusing to make or receive claims predicated on fixed understandings of
particular persons or social groups, what William Connolly has called a

[25] The extent to which a politics of recognition corresponds to an understanding of democracy as consensus is, nevertheless, a matter of some debate. James Tully has, for example,
argued for a politics of recognition as an ongoing activity rather than a consensus to
be achieved. Of Tully's claims, Markell observes, "These qualifications are useful, but
they do not go far enough, for they leave the notion of successful recognition in place
as a regulative idea, a constantly receding horizon toward which our politics nevertheless ought to strive, interminably." Markell, *Bound by Recognition*, 16. See James Tully,
"Struggles Over Recognition and Distribution," *Constellations*, 7(4), 2000: 469–480.
Markell does, however, note that the understanding of the politics of recognition as corresponding to consensus and acknowledgment to agonism may, at times, be overdrawn.
Patchen Markell, "Contesting Consensus: Rereading Habermas on the Public Sphere,"
Constellations, 3(3), 1997: 377–400.
[26] Markell, *Bound by Recognition*, 14.

politics of becoming.[27] Such a politics requires, Markell writes, "that no one be reduced to any characterization of his or her identity for the sake of someone else's achievement of a sense of sovereignty or invulnerability, regardless of whether that characterization is negative or positive, hateful or friendly."[28]

The politics of recognition might, then, be thought to correspond to the nostalgic. Indeed, Terence Cave asserts that recognition is "par excellence the vehicle of nostalgia. It invests in securities, moral, legal, social, political; it parades before us the ghosts of all we ever wanted and always failed quite to grasp and hold."[29] Its commitment to a fixed understanding of identity that is – more often than not – understood to be historical in origin and whose importance is seen to have been overlooked is not simply backward looking; it is also a profound denial of time and change. As such, it contrasts sharply with a politics of acknowledgment predicated on an understanding of political identity as an always incomplete and ongoing process. Such a politics recognizes the limitations on its understanding and seeks not fixedness but rather a strategy for engaging and coping with change, what is here being called tragedy as response. It is a mode of political interpolation that corresponds to, cultivates, and is predicated on an understanding of democratic agonism.

Markell's account of the distinction between recognition and acknowledgment might, then, be thought to provide a useful framework for thinking about the politics of mourning and return, not least because both depend crucially on the way in which the identity of the deceased and/or the returned is understood or conceived. Such an analysis might, nevertheless, flounder on Markell's understanding of his work as being concerned with the ethos of the would-be acknowledger – "something about the self"[30] – rather than with a politics *per se*. Indeed, Joan Cocks denies that "what Markell calls the 'politics of acknowledgment' really counts as something as grand as a *politics*. It seems to be much more modestly a condition of practical wisdom: a foreswearing by the individual of imperial temptations and an embrace or risk and irresolution in human

[27] William E. Connolly, *A World of Becoming* (Durham, NC: Duke University Press, 2011). This does not, it should be noted, necessitate a constant process of destabilization on the part of the acknowledger or the acknowledged, simply a reconceptualization of the ongoing relationship of identity to time and action. See Markell, *Bound by Recognition*, 23.
[28] Indeed, he notes, "...positive images can be instruments of subordination too." Markell, *Bound by Recognition*, 7.
[29] Ibid., 39.
[30] Ibid., 35, 6, 36, 112.

affairs."[31] There are, however, at least two reasons it might be considered legitimate to employ Markell's work to consider matters external to the agent. The first is that Cocks has already done so with the author's imprimatur, employing Markell's theories to consider identity issues in American politics.[32] The second, that Markell does allow that acknowledgment has "implications for the shape of social and political relations among persons" and observes that "if" there is a politics to the idea of acknowledgment, among other things, it involves "articulating different political imaginaries."[33] Seeking to reorient the polity's relationship to its practices of mourning and its returning veterans might constitute just that.

The claim that nostalgic mourning is predicated on and generative of a politics of recognition that poses problems for American democracy and, as such, is in need of reimagining, would seem to be borne out by the nature of the polity's engagement with its military dead. The latter is suggested by its response to the death of its most famous postplanes enlistee.

AGE SHALL NOT WEARY THEM

On May 3, 2004, at a nationally televised memorial service for the Army Ranger and former Arizona Cardinal Pat Tillman, Navy SEAL Steve White recounted the story of his friend's death in Afghanistan. "He dismounted his troops," said White, "taking the fight to the enemy, uphill, to seize the tactical high ground...Pat sacrificed himself so that his brothers could live."[34] At the time, White was unaware that this story was false. Tillman had been the victim of "friendly fire": a possibly deliberate fratricide whose exact details remain unclear despite several official inquiries.[35] White's story was provided to him by military officials who, it later emerged, suspected fratricide at the time of the memorial and rushed through Purple Heart and Silver Star commendations for Tillman to embellish the official narrative of his death.[36] Though taking

---

[31] Joan Cocks, "Sovereignty, Identity, and Insecurity: A Commentary on Patchen Markell's 'Bound by Recognition,'" *Polity*, 38(1), 2006, 14.

[32] Ibid. Patchen Markell, "Ontology, Recognition, and Politics: A Reply," *Polity*, 38(1), 2006, 32.

[33] Markell, ""Ontology, Recognition, and Politics," 37, 39.

[34] Mary Tillman with Narda Zacchino, *Boots on the Ground by Dusk: My Tribute to Pat Tillman* (New York: Modern Times, 2008), 166.

[35] Mike Fish, "An American Tragedy. Part One: Pat Tillman's Uncertain Death," ESPN.com, sports.espn.go.com/espn/eticket/story?page=tillmanpart1. Accessed May 5, 2015.

[36] Mike Fish, "An American Tragedy. Part Two: Playing With Friendly Fire," ESPN.com, sports.espn.go.com/espn/eticket/story?page=tillmanpart2. Accessed May 5, 2015.

place on a larger scale than most, the commemoration of Tillman's death embraced all the nostalgic tropes with which the American polity recognizes its war dead.[37] The story of Tillman's death was not only predicated on the sort of false history central to the nostalgic, it was also free of complexities and contradictions: there was no attempt to capture the confusion of war or the tensions that made fratricide – deliberate or otherwise – possible. Likewise, the memorial was marked by a commitment to a singular narrative of God, country, and sacrifice at the expense of Tillman's atheism and his belief that war in Iraq – where he had previously served – was illegal. Indeed, it also ran counter to Tillman's stated reluctance to become a poster boy for such narratives. "I don't want them to parade me through the streets," he is said to have told a friend about his possible postmortem return.[38] The commitment to consensus at the heart of the memorial was suggested by the response to critical comments made by one of Tillman's brothers. "Pat's a fucking champion and always will be," Robert Tillman angrily declared at the memorial. "But just make no mistake, he'd want me to say this, he's not with God; he's fucking dead."[39] Lisa Olson of the *New York Daily News* was one of several journalists and commentators who expressed distaste for the younger Tillman's breach of decorum, labeling him "slightly crazy" and noting that a "war veteran standing not too far from the stage bristled" at his comments.[40] Indeed, that Robert was not the only Tillman made deviant by the national consensus on military mourning further illustrates the power of nostalgic narratives to undermine the democratic by excluding minority viewpoints. The *manner* in which the whole Tillman family was demonized serves, moreover, to reveal much about the problematic relationship between the language of heroism and the politics of recognition.

[37] Thereby echoing Boym's suggestion that the greater the perceived loss, the greater the commemoration.
[38] Jon Krakauer, *Where Men Win Glory: The Odyssey of Pat Tillman* (New York: Doubleday, 2009), 295.
[39] Tillman, *Boots on the Ground*, 174.
[40] Lisa Olson, "Tillman Tribute Reflects the Man," *New York Daily News*, 05/04/2004, 76. The generalizability of this claim about the public response to attempts to disrupt the nostalgic narrative of heroism is to be found in the experience of MSNBC anchor Chris Hayes. On Memorial Day, 2012, Hayes attempted to parse, albeit delicately, the use of the term "heroes" to refer to America's war dead. The response was swift and vitriolic, and Hayes was later forced to apologize. Andre Tartar, "MSNBC's Chris Hayes 'Uncomfortable' With the Word *Hero*, Conservative Bloggers Uncomfortable With Him," nymag.com/daily/intelligencer/2012/05/chris-hayes-uncomfortable-with-word-hero.html. Accessed May 12, 2015.

Given the myriad of inconsistencies plaguing the official versions of Tillman's death, his family repeatedly sought further investigation. Many saw their persistence as deviance. Indeed, an exasperated Ralph Kauzlarich, the lieutenant colonel who conducted the military's initial inquiry, declared that the family's inability to accept the official narrative was the result of their lack of Christian faith.[41] His remarks were revealing not only of the social and political marginalization engendered by the nostalgic but also of the conception of the heroic that underpins and is fueled by it. For the Greeks, the word most often associated with heroes was *deinos*, meaning terrible, strange, and wondrous. The heroes of Greek tragedy both repel and attract their audiences, telling a story that many would prefer not to hear but that is nevertheless compelling, both painful *and* alluring.[42] Like Thucydides' Pericles, these heroes offer lessons they themselves can never learn. The Christian understanding is, by contrast, predicated on a conception of the heroic as an embodiment of goodness. The lessons offered by these heroes are didactic not interpretive. Thus, when the war dead are recognized through a Christian heroic lens, it is a way of denying the complexities and contradictions of their deaths and, indeed, the implications of these deaths for the polity that sent them to war. The nostalgic denial of temporality that underpins such narratives is suggested by the treatment of the deceased, both before and after their return to the United States.

In *Operation Homecoming*, a collection of wartime narratives collated by the National Endowment for the Arts, Colonel Marc M. Sager recounts his experience of visiting Dover Air Force Base in Delaware, where the remains of the military dead from the wars in Iraq and Afghanistan were prepared for their return to the U.S.[43] "Every time they referred to a deceased soldier, sailor, airman, or Marine," observes Sager of the morgue staff, "it was always 'the fallen hero.' At first this seemed to me like one of the politically sanitized phrases that many of us have used in various settings over the years, but as the visit continued, it became

---

[41] "When you die, I mean, there is supposedly a better life, right? Well, if you are an atheist and you don't believe in anything, if you die, what is there to go to? Nothing. You are worm dirt. So for their son to die for nothing, and now he is no more – that is pretty hard to get your head around that. So I don't know how an atheist thinks. I can only imagine that that would be pretty tough." Fish, "An American Tragedy: Part One."

[42] Meagher, *Herakles Gone Mad*, 35.

[43] Colonel Marc M. Sager, "Dover. Personal Narrative" in *Operation Homecoming: Iraq, Afghanistan, and the Home Front, in the Words of U.S. Troops and Their Families* edited by Andrew Carroll, Updated edition (Chicago: University of Chicago Press, 2008), 369–372.

clear to me that this was the phrase everyone used, and that it was the most appropriate."[44] He further recalls that "Everything that can be done to make the remains look 'normal' is done ... expert makeup personnel restore the faces to look as natural as possible."[45] Finally, detailing the extraordinary efforts that were made to dress the remains in the appropriate military uniforms, complete with rank insignia and medal ribbons, Sager observes, "Every person I met at the mortuary exuded pride in what they did and their role in ensuring the families got back their loved one in the best manner possible, appropriate and in keeping with the sacrifice they performed for this country."[46] The commitment to making the remains look "natural" and "normal" is, of course, deeply nostalgic, a denial not only of the passing of time but also of the causes of their deaths. In this it is redolent of the nineteenth-century commitment to the "Good Death," which similarly sought to deny the realities of human mortality.[47] Indeed, while such cosmetic treatment of the bodies seeks to deny time and change in the private mourning of the household, the public treatment of bodies goes further, denying death by hiding the deceased from both linguistic and physical view.

The terms "hero," and "the fallen" are euphemisms that aim to obscure the violence of military death.[48] They further seek to deny the

[44] Ibid., 370.
[45] Sager, "Dover," 371.
[46] Sager, "Dover," 372. Likewise, Jess Goodell, a Marine veteran whose job in Iraq was to collect, identify, and repatriate the remains of U.S. soldiers and military contractors, notes the existence of similar ceremonies for the dead prior to their return to the U.S. Jess Goodell with John Hearn, *Shade It Black: Death and After in Iraq* (Philadelphia: Casemate, 2011), 39.
[47] As such, it further recalls some of the Civil War photographs of Alexander Gardener, most obviously his "Sharpshooter in Repose" – in which a deceased Confederate soldier was posed as if sleeping – an image that stood in stark contrast to the more gruesome images of war offered by his mentor Matthew Brady in his 1862 exhibit, "The Dead of Antietam." Both Gary Laderman and Mark Schantz point to the ways in which these images helped mask the issues left unresolved by the Civil War, thereby cultivating the nostalgia that served to undermine the black freedoms the war had promised. See Gary Laderman, *The Sacred Remains: American Attitudes Toward Death, 1799–1883* (New Haven, CT: Yale University Press, 1996), 148–151; and Mark. S. Schantz, *Awaiting the Heavenly Country: The Civil War and America's Culture of Death* (Ithaca, NY: Cornell University Press, 2008), 163–206. That the romance of the nineteenth-century "Good Death" remains a powerful engine for nostalgia in the contemporary polity is, Boym suggests, evidenced by the continuing popularity of Civil War reenactments in which obsessive detail is paid to the details of uniforms, guns, and other accouterments, but none to the experience of death and/or racial politics. Boym, *The Future of Nostalgia*, 37.
[48] See also the term "sleeping" repeatedly employed by Robert Poole to refer to those interred at Arlington National Cemetery. Robert M. Poole, *On Hallowed Ground: The Story of Arlington National Cemetery* (New York: Walker and Company, 2009).

political rupture that might occur should those deaths be acknowledged with more complex narratives of loss. Such linguistic obfuscations find their physical counterpart in the way in which the war dead are concealed from the public. Prior to 2009, for example, photographers were prohibited from taking pictures of the caskets containing the repatriated remains of U.S. service personnel killed overseas. Likewise, the 2007 decision by the Pentagon to end its practice of returning bodies to families in the holds of commercial flights – a practice that demanded that passengers remain on the plane until the casket had been removed – opting instead to charter private jets, served, according to Major Steve Beck, as "a further detachment of the populace [in] not seeing their fallen service member come home."[49] Given, moreover, that when the ban on photographing coffins of the war dead was lifted in 2009, the polity was not deluged with such images suggests that concealing the bodies is not only a state policy aimed at shoring up its sovereignty by "protecting" civil society from the costs and consequences of war, but also a product of willful blindness on the part of the citizenry.[50]

In their predication, then, on a fixed, singular, and historically false narrative of service and sacrifice, their denial of time and change, and their commitment to consensus and unity at the expense of complexity, the rituals of mourning with which the democratic polity currently recognizes its war dead are deeply nostalgic. By championing a Christian heroic, these rituals prevent the polity from seeking a full accounting not only of military deaths but also of the policies and processes that led to the wars that produced them. They further deny the conflict at the heart of politics and make deviant those who lie outside the consensus: the dead, in Nietzsche's words, bury the living. The politically problematic implications of nostalgic mourning are, moreover, exacerbated by its treatment of living returnees who are recognized – and thus mourned – with exactly the same narratives as the war dead. Identifying the ways in which the living returnee is recognized by the polity and the problems that this poses for both suggests the

---

[49] Jim Sheeler, *Final Salute: A Story of Unfinished Lives* (New York: Penguin Press, 2008), 146–147. Sheeler's book, detailing the procedures for informing next of kin of military deaths, contains Todd Heisler's chilling Pulitzer Prize–winning photograph of the casket containing the body of Iraq veteran Lieutenant James Cathey being unloaded from a commercial flight while passengers look on from the plane's windows. See www.pulitzer .org/archives/5586. Accessed May 7, 2015.

[50] Such photography is now permitted with the consent of the deceased's family. Judith Bumiller, "Defense Chief Lifts Ban on Pictures of Coffins," *The New York Times*, February 26, 2009. www.nytimes.com/2009/02/27/washington/27coffins.html?fta=y. Accessed May 13, 2015.

reasons some contemporary thinkers and activists have sought to embrace the tragic as a solution to the issues of democratic military return.

THE WALKING DEAD

The history of America's relationship with and treatment of its returning military veterans is – despite rhetoric to the contrary – an inglorious one. At least as far back as the Civil War, the alienated and wandering veteran has been a mainstay of American life and culture. The word "hobo" is, for example, said to be a contraction of the term "hoe boys" used to refer to groups of itinerant Civil War veterans who roamed the countryside in search of work and shelter.[51] The problem has not gone away: about one third of all adult homeless men are veterans, and, according to a 2010 survey, on average, 131,000 find themselves on the street or in charity sanctuaries on any given night.[52] Women too now find themselves part of the equation, making up 11 percent of homeless veterans of the recent wars in Iraq and Afghanistan.[53] These veterans are, moreover, slipping into poverty and homelessness more quickly than veterans of previous wars, taking an average of 18 months to hit rock bottom compared to five years for prior groups of returnees.[54] Likewise, soldiers deployed overseas are more likely to be unemployed than other similarly situated and skilled citizens, and nearly one in ten prison inmates has served in the military.[55] Even those who enter the formal systems of veteran care are likely to face long delays for benefits and treatment. Indeed, while a 2007 *Washington Post* exposé revealed the deplorable conditions faced by veterans at the Walter Reed Army Medical Center in Washington, DC, it is not clear that the conditions for veterans have significantly improved in the period since.[56] This neglect of military veterans is, perhaps, directly

---

[51] Shay, *Odysseus in America*, 155.

[52] "Homeless on Veterans Day," *The New York Times*, 11/11/2009. www.nytimes.com/2009/11/11/opinion/11wed4.html?_r=1. Accessed May 15, 2015.

[53] Helen Benedict, *The Lonely Soldier: The Private War of Women Serving in Iraq* (Boston, MA: Beacon Press, 2009), 213–214.

[54] "Homeless on Veterans Day."

[55] R. Jason Faberman and Taft Foster, "Unemployment among veterans during the Great Recession," *Economic Perspectives*, 37:1, 2013: 1–13; Matthew Wolfe, "From PTSD to Prison: Why Veterans Become Criminals," *The Daily Beast*, July 28, 2013. www.thedailybeast.com/articles/2013/07/28/from-ptsd-to-prison-why-veterans-become-criminals.html. Accessed May 13, 2015.

[56] Michael D. Shear and Dave Phillips, "Progress Is Slow at V.A. Hospitals in Wake of Crisis," *The New York Times*, March 13, 2015. www.nytimes.com/2015/03/14/us/obama-va-hospital-phoenix.html?ref=topics. Accessed May 13, 2015.

connected to the ways in which the polity seeks to recognize their service – by situating them within the same narratives of heroism and sacrifice with which it recognizes its war dead – creating a social death that silences their voices and marginalizes their existence. The polity's rituals of mourning and return hide its veterans in plain sight in ways that not only deny their experiences but also the acknowledgment that might promote a more effective exchange between veteran and polity and, with it, a more meaningful and democratically productive form of homecoming for both.

Demonstrating, perhaps, the validity of Terence Cave's claims about nostalgia, the predominant form of collective return for America's veterans has long been the parade. The rationale for this mode of return is suggested by the Iraq and Afghanistan Veterans of America (IAVA) who, in 2012, called on President Obama to designate a national day of homecoming for veterans of America's war in Iraq with parades in several major cities. "Parades," it argued, "have been a means to welcome home returning troops since America's founding…[and]…are a key way Americans have marked the closure of war." Indeed, Paul Rieckhoff, the IAVA's founder and executive director, noted the success of a "Welcome Home for Heroes" parade that had taken place in St. Louis a few weeks earlier.[57] Although the Pentagon denied the request on the grounds that there were still troops fighting in Afghanistan, it nevertheless affirmed its commitment to a homecoming parade at the cessation of the conflict.[58] The use of the word "closure" in the IAVA's request is revealing. The term has become a commonplace in American public discourse following such traumatic events as the Oklahoma City bombing, the 2001 terrorist attacks, or the aftermath of Hurricane Katrina. Derived from popular literature on psychology, it is, nevertheless, widely derided by psychiatric professionals, not least because it suggests that dealing with trauma is simply a matter of denying the catastrophic, often by returning to a prior state.[59] Parades are thus a nostalgic form of commemoration not just in the sense of being concerned with homecoming

---

[57] Paul Rieckhoff, "Mr. President: Americans want to Welcome Home the Troops, Too," February 16, 2012. www.huffingtonpost.com/paul-rieckhoff/mr-president-americans-wa_b_1280892.html. Accessed May 4, 2015.

[58] This view also supported by the Veterans of Foreign Wars. Oliver Knox, "Veterans Group Presses Obama on 'Welcome Home' for Iraq Troops." news.yahoo.com/blogs/ticket/veterans-group-presses-obama-welcome-home-iraq-troops-171846457.html. Accessed Sept. 28, 2012.

[59] See Jenny Edkins, *Trauma and the Memory of Politics* (Cambridge: Cambridge University Press, 2003), 11–12; and Edward T. Linenthal, *The Unfinished Bombing: Oklahoma City in American Memory* (Oxford: Oxford University, 2001), 9.

but also in the sense of seeking to restore the polity to its antebellum state, "closing" the experience of war and conflict in ways that deny the temporal.

The polity's belief in the power of the parade as a meaningful form of homecoming for its military is further suggested by the popularity of the *post hoc* welcome home celebrations for veterans of the war in Vietnam.[60] Indeed, the popular understanding of the latter's homecoming has done much to shape the nostalgic politics of recognition embodied by the current responses to returnees. As *New York Times* journalist William Deresiewicz observed in 2011, the parades arranged for and demanded by contemporary veterans "play on a justified collective desire to avoid repeating the mistakes of the Vietnam era, when hatred of the conflict spilled over into hostility toward the people who were fighting it."[61] Although there is now some debate about the nature of the homecoming experienced by America's Vietnam veterans, the popular memory of that return – in which veterans were spat on and vilified for their role in an unpopular and cruelly orchestrated conflict – serves to shape the experience of the current returnees in the Janus-faced fashion identified by Markell.[62] While the service of contemporary veterans is publicly

---

[60] In August 2009, at Fort Campbell, Kentucky, the 101st Airborne Division and the Army were welcomed home from Vietnam. Upward of 1,500 veterans were fêted in a series of ceremonies recognizing both their service and the nation's alleged failures during the period of their initial return. Addressing the veterans, Major General John F. Campbell observed, "We realize that many of you did not receive the honorable homecoming you deserved as American heroes…We wanted to make sure that another day doesn't go by when you did not have a proper welcome home." Kristin M. Hall, "Fort Campbell welcomes home Vietnam vets." Associated Press, August 16, 2009. archive.armytimes.com/article/20090816/NEWS/908160302/Fort-Campbell-welcomes-home-Vietnam-vets. *Accessed* May 4, 2015. Despite rhetoric to the contrary, this was not the first occasion upon which such a corrective rewelcome had been offered to veterans of America's seemingly most-reviled war. As Eric T. Dean observes, "something of a national obsession to 'welcome home' the Vietnam vet developed in the late 1970s." On May 7, 1985, for example, 25,000 veterans marched in a ticker-tape parade in New York City that was attended by more than a million people, while in June 1986, 200,000 veterans participated in a "Welcome Home" celebration in Chicago – featuring Playboy bunnies in military uniform – which was overseen by General William Westmoreland, commander of American military operations in Vietnam between 1964 and 1968; and in May 1987, another 200,000 veterans paraded in a similar celebration in Houston, Texas. Smaller ceremonies also took place in Modesto, California; Anderson, Indiana; Northfield, Vermont; and Kalamazoo, Michigan. Eric T. Dean, *Shook Over Hell: Post Traumatic Stress, Vietnam, and the Civil War* (Cambridge, MA: Harvard University Press, 1997), 19–20.

[61] William Deresiewicz, "An Empty Regard," *The New York Times*, August 20, 2011. www.nytimes.com/2011/08/21/opinion/sunday/americas-sentimental-regard-for-the-military.html?pagewanted=all. Accessed Apr. 30, 2015.

[62] The sociologist Jerry Lembcke argues that the widely repeated claim that civilians spat on veterans returning from Vietnam is apocryphal. He uses this as a synecdoche for

valorized, the narratives of heroism and service by which they are recognized nevertheless fail to capture the complexity of their experiences. As such, the politics of recognition proves socially, politically, and psychologically injurious to both veterans and their polity.

For many veterans of America's most recent conflicts, the quintessential moment of recognition occurs at an airport, bus terminal, or train station, when a member of the public approaches the uniformed soldier, grasps his – or, less often, her[63] – hand and declares "Thank you for your service."[64] This moment of recognition finds its complement in the "Support Our Troops" car decals that became ubiquitous following the outbreak of the war in Iraq. Writing for many veterans – in language redolent of Markell's work on recognition – veteran Jess Goodell declares of being thanked for her service, "And there we were in a bind. So as it happened, the civilians we were most anxious around, and therefore tended to most avoid, were exactly the good citizens who thought they were helping us."[65] Similarly, she writes of the "Support our Troops" bumper sticker,

I knew that these people on their way to work or home or dinner had no idea what it was they were supporting. They did not have a clue as to what war was

a more general set of claims in which he seeks to debunk popular narratives about America's allegedly negative response to Vietnam returnees. Jerry Lembcke, *The Spitting Image: Myth, Memory, and the Legacy of Vietnam* (New York: New York University Press, 1998). Likewise, James Wright cites a 1971 Harris Poll that revealed 94 percent of respondents agreed that Vietnam veterans deserved the same "warm reception" as those in other wars. James Edward Wright, *Those Who Have Borne the Battle: A History of America's Wars and Those Who Fought Them* (New York: Public Affairs, 2012), 202. Paradoxically, perhaps, Karl Marlantes suggests that while reports of spitting were exaggerated, he himself was spat upon. Karl Marlantes, *What It's Like to Go to War* (New York: Atlantic Monthly Press, 2011), 177–178. Lawrence Trittle, on the other hand, recounts several firsthand accounts of veterans being spat on and questions Lembcke's claims that such incidents did not occur simply because they were not reported in the press. Trittle, *From Melos to My Lai*, 197.

[63] Nowhere, perhaps, is the double bind of recognition better illustrated than in the experience of women veterans, in part, perhaps, because of the ways in which the most recent conflicts blurred and ultimately erased the lines between combat and noncombat roles. Mickiela Montoya, a female veteran of the Iraq war observes, "We don't get the same respect, we have to fight for it. I don't even tell people about seeing death and being shot at anymore 'cos they don't believe me. They assume that all I did was office work." Helen Benedict, *The Lonely Soldier: The Private War of Women Serving in Iraq* (Boston, MA: Beacon Press, 2009), 198. Women frequently have to fight for the very recognition for their service that so often proves debilitating to them and other returnees.

[64] Elizabeth Samet, "On War Guilt, and 'Thank You for Your Service,'" August 2, 2011. www.bloomberg.com/news/articles/2011-08-02/war-guilt-and-thank-you-for-your-service-commentary-by-elizabeth-samet. Accessed Apr. 3, 2015.

[65] Goodell, *Shade It Black*, 140.

like, what it made people see, and what it made them do to each other. I felt as though I didn't deserve their support, or anyone's, for what I had done. No one should ever support the activities in which I had participated. No one should ever support the people who do such things.[66]

Hers is a familiar complaint. Joshua Casteel, a former U.S. military interrogator at Abu Ghraib, observed of his own experience of returning to civilian life,

[P]eople wanted to hear stories that either reaffirmed their patriotic notions or reaffirmed that the person they love was doing something worthwhile. They didn't want to hear how their loved ones were harassing taxi drivers and devastating a country. They don't want to hear how soldiers came back and committed suicide. They don't want to hear that. But that is what it's like.[67]

It is not surprising, then, that many veterans have sought to escape the narratives of "heroism" and "service" by which they are most often recognized. In a 2014 article in *The Washington Post*, Benjamin Summers, a U.S. Army captain, declared, "Not every service member is a hero. The quicker we realize that, the quicker we start creating a political environment that can foster genuine debate and answer the difficult policy problems we face." Indeed, Summers explicitly identified the ways in which such language often obscures questions of veterans' postwar treatment and well-being.[68] He was not alone in this concern. In a 2013 article in the *Atlantic Monthly*, Iraq veteran Alex Horton suggested that the polity could help veterans by "taking them off the pedestal":

The word hero is tossed around and abused to the point of banality. The good intentions of civilians are rarely in question, but detached admiration has always been a stand-in for the impulse to do "something" for veterans. So civilians clap at football games. They applaud returning troops in airports in outward appreciation, satisfied with their magnanimous deeds. Then – for many of them – it's back to more tangible concerns, like the fragile economy.[69]

---

[66] Ibid., 139.

[67] Aaron Glantz, *The War Comes Home: Washington's Battle Against America's Veterans* (Berkeley: University of California Press, 2009), 11.

[68] Benjamin Summers, "Hero worship is getting in the way of good policy," *The Washington Post*, June 20, 2014. www.washingtonpost.com/opinions/hero-worship-of-the-military-presents-an-obstacle-to-good-policy/2014/06/20/053d932a-foed-11e3-bf76-447a5df6411f_story.html. Accessed Apr. 30, 2015.

[69] Alex Horton, "Help Veterans by Taking Them Off the Pedestal," *The Atlantic Monthly*, November 10, 2013. www.theatlantic.com/national/archive/2013/11/help-veterans-by-taking-them-off-the-pedestal/281316/. Accessed Apr. 30, 2015. See also David Masciotra, "You don't protect my freedom: Our childish insistence on calling soldiers heroes deadens democracy," *salon.com*, November 9, 2011. The suggestion that civilian engagement with veterans is largely that of clapping at football games was revealed to be all the

That this narrative of heroism merely serves to recognize rather than to acknowledge veterans is suggested by Rory Fanning, a former Army Ranger, who noted. "We use the term hero in part because it makes us feel good and in part because it shuts soldiers up (which, believe me, makes the rest of us feel better)."[70]

Given Fanning's observation about the silencing of veterans, it is, perhaps, not too hyperbolic to suggest that democracy prefers its returnees to be dead. For a political system that is ideologically committed to consensus, a dead hero is preferable to a live returnee. Whereas the former are subject to being spoken about and for, the latter may pose considerable problems by refusing to be situated within or to conform to the established narratives of military service and sacrifice with which the polity would recognize their experiences. As classicist and Vietnam veteran Lawrence Trittle observes, some returnees "pose an embarrassment to history or other forms of memory as the nature of their experiences may not coincide with the general view of the past or its recollection."[71] Indeed, many of the problems experienced by veterans on their return arise from their inability to align their experiences with the dominant identity by which the polity would recognize them. "Parades and family reunions," writes Robert Emmet Meagher, "... rarely acknowledge the horror of what has been endured and inflicted by returning veterans; they mostly evade those demons and, instead, cheerily celebrate the returnees as heroes, one and all, when all too often this is the very last thing these men and women feel themselves to be."[72] This silencing of the veteran takes many forms, many of them redolent of the mechanisms by which actual military deaths are hidden from public view.

In the first instance, the polity's reluctance to hear about their returnees' experiences of war serves to shape the public discourse in ways that disadvantage the veteran. In the asymmetric warfare between the

---

more insidious in 2015 when the Department of Defense admitted that it had spent upward of $10 million since 2012 to sports franchises in the MLS, NBA, NFL, and NHL to honor local veterans at sporting events. Dave Hogg, "The military paid pro sports teams $10.4 million for patriotic displays, troop tributes," SBNation, November 4, 2015. www.sbnation.com/2015/11/4/9670302/nfl-paid-patriotism-troops-mcain-flake-report-million. Accessed Mar. 9, 2016. www.salon.com/2014/11/09/you_dont_protect_my_freedom_our_childish_insistence_on_calling_soldiers_heroes_deadens_real_democracy/ . Accessed Apr. 30, 2015.

[70] Rory Fanning, "Stop thanking me for my service," *salon.com*, October 28, 2014. www.salon.com/2014/10/28/the_decadence_and_depravity_of_thanking_our_troops_partner/. Accessed Apr. 30, 2015.

[71] Trittle, *Melos to My Lai*, 107.

[72] Meagher, *Herakles*, 4.

narratives of war and return offered by the polity and narratives offered by returnees, the former will always win: they are more easily told and there are more people to tell them. This is, in part, a product of an ever-widening civilian–military divide. Douglas Kriner and Francis Shen argue that combat soldiers in the U.S. are drawn from an increasingly smaller pool; likewise, both Nancy Sherman and James Wright note that far fewer politicians have had military experience than in previous eras. Sherman adds, furthermore, that there is a dwindling number of ROTC units on college campuses.[73] The result is civilian ignorance of military experiences and concerns. Indeed, a 2008 Pew Research Center Survey showed that only 28 percent of Americans knew that more than 4,000 U.S. military personnel had, at that point, died in America's then-ongoing wars.[74] The divide is, moreover, deliberately constructed. Just as the bodies of the dead are hidden from public view, the bodies of the injured are similarly concealed. In a form of what might be called the "Good Social Death," wounded service personnel are flown into the United States at night and are forbidden from flying on commercial jets if they have visible injuries.[75] Injured minds are also hidden from public view. Indeed, the medicalization of combat trauma is, perhaps, the most significant way in which the polity seeks a return to its antebellum state and/or denies the temporality that would disrupt its nostalgic commitment to unity and consensus.

Although the term "posttraumatic stress disorder" was not included in the American Psychiatric Association Manual until 1980, it was but a belated recognition of a set of symptoms common to victims of trauma – including depression, anxiety, guilt, sleeplessness, and suicidal thoughts – variously called "shell shock," "railway spine," and "soldier's heart," whose diagnosis stretched back to well before the American Civil War.[76] The implication that those who exhibit such symptoms are suffering from a "disorder," as opposed to an appropriate response to the traumas of

---

[73] Douglas L. Kriner and Francis X. Shen, *The Casualty Gap: The Causes and Consequences of American Wartime Inequalities* (Oxford: Oxford University Press, 2010); Wright *Those Who Have Borne*, 269; Nancy Sherman, *Stoic Warriors: The Ancient Philosophy Behind the Military Mind* (Oxford; Oxford University Press, 2005), 21.

[74] Glantz, *The War Comes Home*, 176. Most thought it was half to three quarters of that number.

[75] Elizabeth D. Samet, *Soldier's Heart: Reading Literature Through Peace and War at West Point* (New York: Farrar, Straus and Giroux, 2007), 240. Kathy Dobie, "Denial in the Corps" *The Nation* January 31, 2008. www.thenation.com/article/denial-corps?page=full. Accessed May 14, 2015.

[76] Edkins, *Trauma and the Memory of Politics*, 42.

war, suggests the ways in which those who do not fit into the dominant nostalgic narrative of heroism are not only marginalized but also stigmatized. Indeed, many military personnel often refuse to seek psychological counseling because of the associated shame and the fear that doing so will damage their careers.[77] "When medical treatment is provided," writes Jenny Edkins, "survivors become patients whose aim is recovery. Their anger, shame, and guilt, are now turned into nothing more than symptoms of an unfortunate disorder. We no longer need to take what they say seriously. Their memories no longer exist."[78] As such, nostalgic history is able to eclipse their personal experiences. Once medicalized, moreover, combat trauma becomes a private rather than a public concern, one in which hospitals and prisons frequently become the receptacles of wartime injury.[79] Indeed, an inability to overcome such symptoms can easily be seen as a personal failing rather than a legitimate consequence of war.[80]

"War," observed veteran and author Phil Klay, "is too strange to be processed alone."[81] Historically, return was a communal experience for warrior societies: both the Greek Dionysia and Native American war dances were postbattle rituals of cleansing and purification.[82] The medicalization of contemporary combat trauma serves, however, to individuate such experiences, hiding them from public view in much the same way as the return of individual bodies to individual families masks the enormity of the polity's losses. This suggests the fundamentally veteran-centric nature of the nostalgic mode of mourning and return and, indeed, the profoundly incoherent

---

[77] Sara Corbett, "The Permanent Scars of Iraq," *The New York Times*, February 15, 2004. www.nytimes.com/2004/02/15/magazine/15VETS.html?pagewanted=all. Accessed May 14, 2015.

[78] Edkins, *Trauma and the Memory of Politics*, 55.

[79] Jonathan Shay, *Achilles in Vietnam: Combat Trauma and the Undoing of Character* (New York: Simon and Schuster, 2010), 194.

[80] This is suggested by Eric T. Dean assertion that "[t]he continuing anger and bitterness emanating from some Vietnam veterans suggests, essentially, an inability to ever forget or put the war into any sort of realistic perspective." Dean, *Shook Over Hell*, 190. Likewise, by conservative radio host Michael Savage's diatribe against mental illness, depression, and sufferers of PTSD, in which he suggested that the failure of Americans to take responsibility for their experiences was the cause of the military's inability to defeat ISIS. David Ferguson, "Conservative loon Michael Savage attacks veterans with PTSD: Boo-hoo-hoo!" rawstory.com, October 21, 2014. www.rawstory.com/2014/10/conservative-loon-michael-savage-attacks-veterans-with-ptsd-boo-hoo-hoo/. Accessed May 19, 2015.

[81] Dave Phillips, "Coming home to damaging stereotypes," *The New York Times*, February 15, 2015. www.nytimes.com/2015/02/06/us/a-veteran-works-to-break-the-broken-hero-stereotype.html?_r=1. Accessed May 15, 2015.

[82] See Jonathan Lear, *Radical Hope: Ethics in the Face of Cultural Devastation* (Cambridge, MA: Harvard University Press, 2006), 153–154; and Kupfer, "Like Wandering Ghosts," 9.

politics of recognition at their core. On the one hand, veterans are to be recognized as heroes, separate from and elevated above the citizenry; on the other, medicalization demands that the veteran be returned more or less as he or she was prior to the conflict, restored to the very society over which they have been elevated. Revealing the restorative and nostalgic impulse at the heart of such medicalization, Rabbi Arnold Resnicoff – a senior chaplain during the war in Bosnia – declared, "We don't want our people just to come home physically; we want them to come back close to the human beings before they went in."[83] This commitment to restoration is, moreover, partly a product of a nostalgic understanding of a previous military return, one that serves to further undermine those veterans who are held up to this prior example and found wanting.

It should, perhaps, be a truth universally acknowledged that as far as damage to veterans is concerned, Tom Brokaw has a great deal for which to answer. As Thomas Childers observes, Brokaw's book *The Greatest Generation* – and its lucrative spin-offs – have become "our public memory of [World War II] and its aftermath, a quasi-official transcript of events that glides sentimentally over what for many veterans was a deeply trouble reentry into a civilian world that, like themselves, had undergone dramatic change."[84] Brokaw writes,

When the war was over, the men and women who had been involved, in uniform and in civilian capacities, joined in joyous and short-lived celebrations, then immediately began the task of rebuilding their lives ... battle-scarred and exhausted, but oh so happy to be home. The war had taught them what mattered most in their lives and they wanted now to settle down and live.[85]

As Childers notes, however, such a narrative – itself perhaps monumentalized in the quasi-fascist National World War II Memorial in Washington, DC[86] – obscures considerable civilian anxiety of the returning veterans, and indeed, the multitude of problems faced by the veterans themselves. For, despite Brokaw's nostalgic narratives, there was a genuine fear of returnees among the civilian population. This was expressed in newspaper stories headlined "Will your boy be a killer when he returns home?" and in the suggestion that veterans should spend time in

---

[83] Nancy Sherman, *Stoic Warriors: The Ancient Philosophy Behind the Military Mind* (New York: Oxford University Press, 2005), 119.
[84] Thomas Childers, *Soldier from the War Returning: The Greatest Generation's Troubled Homecoming from World War II* (Boston: Houghton, Mifflin, Harcourt, 2009), 4.
[85] Ibid.
[86] See Kirk Savage, *Monument Wars: Washington, D.C., the National Mall, and the Transformation of the Memorial Landscape* (Berkeley: University of California Press, 2009).

reorientation camps before they were permitted back into society.[87] The much-vaunted postwar benefits, including the G.I. Bill, were, moreover, frequently resented by the civilian population: a 1946 article in the *Saturday Evening Post* declared the Bill to be "a tempting invitation to the shirker, the goldbricker, and the occasional crook."[88] Brokaw's work also ignores the struggles that many veterans faced when they attempted to organize politically. In some cases they were forced to resort to protest and hunger strikes to gain a voice in the democratic process, and when they did so, they were accused of communist agitation by the House Un-American Activities Committee.[89] It is little wonder, then, that a 1947 poll found that one third of all veterans felt estranged from nonmilitary life and another that 20 percent of veterans felt "completely hostile to civilians."[90] In this, perhaps, these veterans were not only socially but also politically deceased. Further suggesting the contagious nature of nostalgia, the false history of post–World War II return serves to make deviant those in the contemporary era who are incapable of returning in the idealized fashion of "the Greatest Generation." As such, this denial of conflict at the heart of Brokaw's narrative serves to perpetuate the same conflicts – and thus the same social and political problems – for America's most recent returnees, those whom some have tried to label the "New Greatest Generation."[91]

Just as many World War II returnees found themselves frozen out of politics and society by a public fear of veterans, many contemporary

---

[87] So pervasive is this narrative that even Edward Tick, a therapist who works with veterans and notes the frequency of inadequate responses to the needs of returnees in American history, asserts, "The World War II veterans' welcome home is the exception, the only time in U.S. history when vets were thanked and honored and given decent benefits." David Kupfer, "Like Wandering Ghosts. Edward Tick on How the U.S. Fails its Returning Soldiers," *The Sun*, 390 (June, 2008): 6. See also David R. B. Ross, *Preparing for Ulysses: Politics and Veterans During World War II* (New York: Columbia University Press, 1969). Childers, *Soldier from the War Returning*, 6.

[88] Childers, *Soldier from the War Returning*, 217. Similarly, the paper also asked "Are we making a bum out of G.I. Joe?" Ibid., 8.

[89] In what became known as "The Battle of Athens," frustrated Ohioan veterans who formed their own political party to fight county elections were physically assaulted, intimidated, and arrested by sheriff's deputies working for the incumbent. When the ballot boxes were confiscated by the deputies, veterans stormed the National Guard Armory, seized weapons and ammunition, and marched on the local jail, where a gun battle ensued. Having secured a fair count of the ballots, the veterans prevailed and became a rallying point for other veterans across the country, who threatened "another Athens" when their voices went unacknowledged. Ibid., 213–215.

[90] Ibid., 8.

[91] David Eisler, "Beyond the Bad News. The Dangers of a Sensationalist Portrayal of Veterans," *The New York Times*, August 5, 2013. atwar.blogs.nytimes.com/2013/08/05/the-dangers-of-a-sensationalist-portrayal-of-veterans/. Accessed May 20, 2015.

returnees find themselves similarly ostracized. In popular culture, fear of the veteran has been a persistent trope, with John Frankenheimer's 1962 *The Manchurian Candidate* being the classic of the genre, a film that was remade by Jonathan Demme in 2004 to address a new generation of returnees, and, more recently, channeled by the Showtime television drama *Homeland*.[92] Socially, many veterans find it hard to secure employment, in part because many employers doubt the applicability of their skills to peacetime activities, but also because of a more generalized fear that the trauma that veterans have suffered overseas will make them unreliable employees. In 2011, the unemployment rate for veterans aged 20–24 was more than double that for nonveterans of the same age, a fact that also helps to explain, perhaps, their high rate of homelessness.[93] This alienation from an uncomprehending polity that is unwilling or unable to acknowledge rather than simply recognize their experiences of war, finds its most disturbing manifestation in the suicide rate among military veterans. In February 2008 the head of the Veterans' Administration noted that among those veterans within the system, there were approximately 1,000 suicide attempts per month,[94] while a July 2010 Pentagon report noted that the army suicide rate had risen above the suicide rate of the general population for the first time since the Vietnam War.[95] These figures, disturbing as they are, nevertheless fail to capture the extent of the problem, ignoring the "hidden suicides" of those who take their lives or engage in risky activity that leads to their deaths in the months and years after their military service.[96] An additional human cost of such trauma is, moreover, the violence that is often inflicted on military families by untreated veterans. On average, according to the Pentagon, a child or spouse dies each week at the hands of a relative in the military.[97]

[92] And, perhaps, by Don Draper – who literally comes back from the Korean War as a different person – in AMC's *Mad Men*.

[93] Shaila Dewan, "As Wars End, Young Veterans Return to Scant Jobs," *The New York Times*, December 17, 2011. www.nytimes.com/2011/12/18/business/for-youngest-veterans-the-bleakest-of-job-prospects.html?_r=1. Accessed May 15, 2015.

[94] Editorial, "The Suffering of Soldiers," *The New York Times*, 5/11/08. www.nytimes.com/2008/05/11/opinion/11sun2.html. Accessed May 15, 2015.

[95] Army, *Health Promotion, Risk Reduction, Suicide Prevention. Report 2010*. usarmy. vo.llnwd.net/e1/HPRRSP/HP-RR-SPReport2010_v00.pdf. Accessed May 15, 2015. The statistic suggests the value of Sophocles' *Ajax* to contemporary discussions of return.

[96] See Aaron Glantz, "After Service, Veteran Deaths Surge," *The New York Times*, 10/16/10. www.nytimes.com/2010/10/17/us/17bcvets.html. Accessed May 15, 2015.

[97] Similarly suggesting the value of Euripides' *Herakles* to contemporary discussions of return. Meagher, *Herakles Gone Mad*, 48. In 2002, for example, three Special Forces soldiers returned to Fort Bragg, North Carolina, from Afghanistan and, in a six-week period, killed their wives before taking their own lives. Corbett, "Permanent Scars."

In much the same way that political disagreement was seen as radical deviance by the House Un-American Activities Committee (HUAC) after World War II, a 2009 intelligence report issued by the Department of Homeland Security identified the potential dangers of "Disgruntled Military Veterans" who, "disillusioned, or suffering from the psychological effects of war," might use their skills to "boost the capabilities of extremists – including lone wolves or small terrorist cells – to carry out violence."[98] As Jonathan Shay suggests, however, the political problems posed by the alienation of veterans from democracy runs much deeper than a simple hostility to their possible radicalism or perceived deviance; it impacts the entire system by fundamentally undermining veterans' capacity to take part in it. "The painful paradox," of democracy, he writes, "is that fighting for one's country can render one unfit to be its citizen."[99] In addition to facing a population that recognizes their service but fears its consequences, veterans, Shay notes, often find the mechanics of democracy deeply problematic. Many, for example, fear crowds. Democracy, Shay further notes, "embodies the apparent contradiction of safe struggle," the process by which disagreements can be negotiated.[100] Nevertheless, for some veterans, experience of combat means that disagreements can only be experienced conflictually. As such, many find themselves unable to engage in the peaceful – if sometimes heated – negotiations and exchanges that democracy requires. This inability to engage in democratic negotiation is, Shay suggests, further hampered by the absence of trust between the veteran and the polity. In the first instance, the veteran who has been misled into war or who has experienced the polity's inability to hear his or her stories of combat has little reason to believe that he or she can trust his or her fellow citizens to negotiate in good faith, a problem, that is no doubt exacerbated by the increasing civilian/military divide. In the second, the polity's frequently displayed but linguistically disavowed fear of the veteran undermines trust on both sides. Excluded from public assembly and peaceful verbal exchange, many veterans find themselves ostracized from the political system altogether. It is an exclusion that has consequences not only for the veteran but also for his or her polity. When those with most experience of war are systematically excluded from the

---

[98] Department of Homeland Security *(U//FOUO) Rightwing Extremism: Current Economic and Political Climate Fueling Resurgence in Radicalization and Recruitment*, 7. fas.org/irp/eprint/rightwing.pdf. Accessed May 15, 2015.

[99] Jonathan Shay, *Achilles in Vietnam: Combat Trauma and the Undoing of Character* (New York: Athenaeum, 1994), xx.

[100] Ibid., 180.

process by which such life-and-death decisions are made, it is to the clear
detriment of the political community. Those closest to the sunk costs argument of war – the claim that the dead shall not have died in vain – are,
Shay notes, least likely to support it.[101] Thus, Shay argues, the failures of
the current rituals of return fundamentally undermine democratic politics. "Unhealed combat trauma," he writes, "… destroys the unnoticed
substructure of democracy, the cognitive and social capacities that enable
a group of people to freely construct a cohesive narrative of their own
future."[102] It is a problem that, Shay suggests, is further exacerbated by the
linguistic problems engendered by military conflict.

"Although there are as many ways to describe war as there are writers,"
observes James Tatum, "one thing all agree on is its indescribability."[103] The
inadequacy of language for describing war is a perennial theme of its literature. As one Northern veteran of the Civil War observed, "[t]he half of it can
never be told – language is all too tame to convey the horror and meaning of
it all," while Kate Cumming, a Confederate nurse, noted of her time on the
wards of a Southern hospital, "[n]othing I had ever heard or read have given
me the faintest idea of the horrors witnessed here. I do not think that words
are in our vocabulary expressive enough to present to the mind the realities
of that sad scene."[104] It is, perhaps, for this reason that many veterans feel
most comfortable with other veterans who have undergone similar experiences.[105] Some returnees, and especially those who feel they have been led
into war under false circumstances, come to distrust language – the medium
of democracy – because of the euphemisms they have been forced to employ
and the very indescribability of what they have experienced. The experience
of Steve White, Pat Tillman's friend and eulogist, is suggestive. Testifying
before the Congressional committee investigating the circumstances of
Tillman's death, White stated that discovering the falsity of his memorial
story about Tillman was not only a source of considerable distress to him, it
fundamentally undermined his trust in the military.[106]

Nostalgic rituals of mourning and return, then, that merely recognize
rather than acknowledge the veteran further estrange him or her from

[101] Ibid., 158.
[102] Ibid., 181.
[103] James Tatum, *The Mourner's Song: War and Remembrance from the Iliad to Vietnam* (Chicago: University of Chicago Press, 2003), 51.
[104] Dean, *Shook Over Hell*, 57, 78.
[105] See, for example, Dan Barry, "Veteran Tries to Get Back to Who He Was," *The New York Times*, 5/26/2008. www.nytimes.com/2008/05/26/us/26land.html. Accessed May 15, 2015; and Sheeler, *Final Salute*, 44, 58.
[106] www.youtube.com/watch?v=Og_m48LWkR8. Accessed May 15, 2015.

the polity and reinforce the notion that homecoming is an individual problem for the returnee rather than a collective problem for the polity. Indeed, even Nancy Sherman and James Wright, authors who are deeply sympathetic to returnees, inadvertently reinforce the veteran–polity divide even as they seek to address it. "As a public that sends its citizen soldiers to war," writes Sherman, "it is our duty to understand better, and help heal *their* inner wars."[107] Likewise, on Wright's account, veteran trauma is understood to be largely attitudinal, with society's role being that of a psychological cheerleader. "These young men and women," he writes of veterans suffering from combat trauma, "need to be reminded and encouraged to reach beyond their condition." They require, he suggests, job counseling "that will encourage them to dream for more and enable them to reach these dreams." Indeed, he concludes that current programs are deficient because "[w]hat is missing is encouragement to aspire and to participate and confidence to know this can be done."[108] On this account, as on many others, it is the veteran's job to return to an "unchanged" polity rather than a changed polity's job to rise to meet a veteran whose experiences should be acknowledged rather than denied. As Markell writes, a politics of acknowledgement "demands that each of us bear our share of the burden and risk involved in the uncertain, open-ended, sometimes maddeningly and sometimes joyously surprising activity of living and interacting with other people."[109] As such, recent attempts to embrace tragic theater as a ritual of mourning and return are perhaps to be welcomed in that they seek a collective response to the problems that military homecoming poses for democratic politics. Nevertheless, their ongoing limitations are suggested by their nostalgic commitment to restoration and to a politics of recognition.

TRAGEDY AS RESTORATION

"There are two holidays honoring veterans in this country," observed Edward Tick, a counselor who works with military returnees, "but we have betrayed their sacred meaning. A lot of veterans are angry that Veterans Day, which was originally called 'Armistice Day,' has become an excuse for patriotic displays. We have a parade and shoot off fireworks,

[107] Nancy Sherman, *The Untold War: Inside the Hearts, Minds, and Souls of Our Soldiers* (New York: W. W. Norton, 2010), 48. Author emphasis.
[108] Wright, *Those Who Have Borne The Battle*, 272–273. Wright's claims are all the more remarkable given his otherwise sympathetic account of the history of the problems faced by veterans upon their return to civilian life.
[109] Markell, *Bound by Recognition*, 7.

which scare the hell out of many veterans. A better way to honor them would be to listen to their stories."[110] At the heart of recent attempts to employ Greek tragedy as a mode of mourning and a ritual of return for America's veterans is the suggestion that the theater offers a two-fold opportunity to achieve Tick's goal. First, as a number of critics have suggested, plays such as *Herakles*, *Philoctetes*, and *Ajax* are plays about veterans written by and for veterans: these are their stories. More significantly, it is suggested that such readings and performances provide an opportunity and prompt for veterans to talk about their experiences in a communal setting, thereby addressing one of their most pressing problems: their individuation and thus their isolation.[111] Indeed, Shay calls for "a modern equivalent of Athenian tragedy." "Combat veterans and American citizenry," he writes, "should meet together face to face in daylight and listen and watch and weep, just as citizen-soldiers of Ancient Athens did at the theater at the foot of the Acropolis."[112] Projects such as Bryan Dorries's Theater of War and Peter Meineck's Ancient Greeks/ Modern Lives attempt to put some flesh on the bones of Shay's approach. They offer performances and staged readings of Greek tragedy for military personnel, veterans, their families, mental health professionals, and, more recently, civilians.[113] While many of those who have attended such events regard their experiences as beneficial, the language employed by Shay and others when talking about these projects suggests that they have yet to overcome the Janus-faced nature of the politics of recognition identified by Markell. Indeed, for all its talk of communality, this approach remains largely veteran centric in outlook.[114]

Recounting his experience of attending an April 2009 Theater of War production in New York City, veteran and classicist Peter Meineck

---

[110] Kupfer, "Like Wandering Ghosts," 6.

[111] For an account of the role that literature might play in cultivating productive democratic discussion, see Simon Stow, *Republic of Readers? The Literary Turn in Political Thought and Analysis* (Albany: State University of New York Press, 2007).

[112] Shay, *Achilles in Vietnam*, 194.

[113] In an email correspondence with the author, Lee Sunday Evans of *Outside the Wire*, the parent organization of *Theater of War*, notes that there are now two types of performances, those for military personnel, veterans, and their families, and those open to a wider audience. Since the project was founded in 2008, it has been embraced by the Pentagon, which provided a grant of $3.7 million in 2009 for the project to visit military bases across the U.S. Likewise, Peter Meineck's organization has been funded by the National Endowment for the Humanities.

[114] Patrick Healy, "The Anguish of War for Today's Soldiers, Explored by Sophocles," *The New York Times*, November 11, 2009. www.nytimes.com/2009/11/12/theater/12greeks.html?pagewanted=all&_r=0. Accessed May 19, 2015.

observed, "One of the most frequent comments heard at the ... event was that veterans were seeking 'restoration': though they had physically returned home, they were spiritually still fighting their wars and dealing with disconcerting feelings such as survivor guilt, isolation, frustration, anger, and despair."[115] This language of restoration is telling and finds its echo in Shay's work, most notably in *Odysseus in America*, where he devotes an entire section to a discussion of the ways in which the communal therapy offered by tragedy can help restore veterans, both to themselves and to their communities.[116] Such language suggests the belief that veterans can and should be returned to the identity that they possessed before the war. It is an approach that seems to embrace the politics of recognition by positing a fixed identity as the goal of the therapeutic process, suggesting the sort of "closure" embodied by the *telos* of reconciliation and agreement central to the nostalgic modes of mourning and return. Indeed, the understanding of tragedy that underpins this approach – with its commitment to the restoration of an idealized understanding of a prior condition – seems far more nostalgic than tragic.

"[W]hat the American public always wants," William Dean Howells is said to have observed in a comment capturing the cultural pervasiveness of the nostalgic, "is a tragedy with a happy ending."[117] Markell's account of what he calls Hegel's "reconciliatory voice" best captures what appears to be the understanding of tragedy underpinning recent attempts to employ Greek theater as a ritual of mourning and return. This voice, observes Markell, "promises us that at the end of this journey lies the prospect of a homecoming, of finally arriving at a state in which contradiction, division, suffering, and other manifestations of negativity have not necessarily eliminated, but at least *redeemed* as moments of an intelligible, internally articulated whole."[118] The nostalgic and restorative impulse suggested by the understanding of tragedy underpinning Shay's work suggests the veteran-centric nature of his approach. By positing a preexisting identity of citizenship as the model for successful return, he

---

[115] Peter Meineck, "'These Are Men Whose Minds the Dead Have Ravished'": *Theater of War/the Philoctetes Project,*" *arion*, 17(1), 2009: 176–177.

[116] Shay, *Odysseus in America*, 147–201.

[117] David W. Blight, *Beyond the Battlefield: Race, Memory and the American Civil War* (Amherst: University of Massachusetts Press, 2002), 123.

[118] Markell, *Bound by Recognition*, 93. See also J. G. Finlayson, "Conflict and Reconciliation in Hegel's Theory of the Tragic," *Journal of the History of Philosophy*, 37(3), 1999: 493–520; Mark W. Roche, "The Greatness and Limits of Hegel's Theory of Tragedy" in *A Companion to Tragedy* edited by Rebecca W. Bushnell (Malden, MA: Blackwell Publishers, 2005), 51–67.

seems to underplay the potential role for the broader political community in his account of homecoming. Shay does suggest the ways in which the polity should "strive to be a trustworthy audience for victims of abuse of power" and to offer a respectful listening constituted by a "readiness to be changed by the narrator," but his aim is, nevertheless, to restore the veteran to the polity rather than to acknowledge fundamental change in either.[119] As with the work of Wright and Sherman, few demands are made of the broader citizenry. Nor, indeed, is very much attention paid to the ways in which the political identity of the polity may have been changed by war. Instead of offering an understanding of the polity as being formed by its pre-, intra-, and postwar experiences, Shay and others largely ignore the social and political context of such reform. As such, the restorative impulse blocks the power of tragedy to engage with and shape the political community in ways more conducive to a democratically productive mode of mourning and military return.

The problem with these attempts to employ tragedy to address the problem of return faced by veterans is, then, that while they call for the communalization of grief, that communalization is limited and predicated on the belief that it will return veterans to the identity of an antebellum citizen of an antebellum polity. They reinscribe on the polity the nostalgic language of restoration and the politics of recognition, serving to make the veteran a problem to be solved rather than a meaningful contributor to democratic life and politics. It is only by abandoning the nostalgic – and its concomitant politics of recognition – that tragedy might be more productively employed as a ritual of mourning and return for both the veteran and polity alike.

TRAGEDY AS RECONSTITUTION

Given that, as James Finlayson and Patchen Markell both note, Hegel predicated his reconciliationist theory of tragedy on Aeschylus' *Oresteia* rather than – as is more commonly supposed – *Antigone*, trying to establish the *Oresteia* as the basis for a politics of acknowledgment, and, as such, an understanding of tragedy as ongoing process of reconstitution might seem to be something of a mistake.[120] Nevertheless, despite Markell's reading of the play-cycle as a drama of recognition, there are strong reasons for regarding the play as a model for a thoroughly tragic

---

[119] Shay, *Achilles in Vietnam*, 193, 189.
[120] Finlayson, "Conflict and Reconciliation," 512; Markell, *Bound by Recognition*, 96.

form of mourning and military return, one that denies the nostalgic, not least by acknowledging the ways in which both the veteran and the polity have been changed by war. Such a claim, nevertheless, requires an account of how it understands the potentially politically loaded term "reconstitution."

At one end of a potential spectrum of meaning, the verb "to reconstitute" might be understood to mean something akin to "refound" or "to begin again anew." At the other, it might be thought to suggest a restoration to a prior state. Here, however, it is being used to suggest a combination of continuity and change. One of the definitions offered by the *OED* is "to change membership of (an official body)," capturing the way in which an ongoing commitment to reconstitution might be thought to maintain a political continuity, perhaps by regularly replacing its elected officials or by enfranchising new groups. A nostalgic reading of such reconstitution would, of course, see only consistency in this understanding – a process of incorporation rather than change – but here reconstitution should be understood in a manner suggested by Bonnie Honig's work on democratic theory. A politics of becoming, she writes, "recognizes that each new inclusion comes with disturbance and possibly transformation for those people and rights that are already in, as well as for the antecedent rules that aspire to govern or subsume all new cases and events."[121] Indeed, Honig's work is particularly useful in the context of military return, for it suggests the ways in which the alienation of the veteran might pave the way for the reconstitution of the polity. "[L]egitimation theorists," she writes, "worry that alienation can be a source of civic cynicism and withdrawal. It can. But it can also be a source of civic activism, unrest, and protest. The positive side of 'alienation' is that it marks a gap in legitimation, a space that is held open for future refounding, augmentation, and amendment."[122] Such refoundings, augmentations, and amendments – what is here being labeled "reconstitution" – should not, of course, be seen as *tabula rasa* beginnings but rather as parts of an ongoing project of politics in which even apparently radical breaks – such as that achieved by Lincoln at Gettysburg – are constructed out of existing materials. Just as, perhaps, one might reconstitute a house over time, possibly by changing its design or layout and/or building an addition, it would still maintain its core purpose as a dwelling place. This is how the

---

[121] Bonnie Honig, *Emergency Politics: Paradox, Law, Democracy* (Princeton, NJ: Princeton University Press, 2009), 49.

[122] Honig's *Democracy and the Foreigner* (Princeton, NJ: Princeton University Press, 2003) 31.

claim that contemporary tragic mourning and return might be conceived as a form of ongoing democratic reconstitution should be understood. It is an understanding that promises to help address the political and social limitations of the nostalgic.

At the heart of Aeschylus' *Oresteia* is a series of revenge killings and returns that culminate with Orestes' trial for killing his mother and her lover. For many, the culmination of that trial – the jury is deadlocked on Orestes' guilt or innocence, and only the intervention of the goddess Athena sets him free – is the epitome of the reconciliationist reading of tragedy offered by Hegel. W. B. Stanford calls it the happiest and most optimistic ending in all of Greek tragedy; likewise, Richard Seaford sees it as a closing that binds the polity together.[123] Markell, on the other hand, offers a darker reading of the play's conclusion that nevertheless corresponds to the Hegelian account of tragedy as reconciliation. Following the slaying of his mother, Orestes is pursued by the Furies, a group of female spirits – the near personification of the trauma that he has experienced – who terrorize him even as he sleeps. With the Furies outraged by the outcome of the trial, Markell argues that the "last scenes of the *Oresteia* in which Athena persuades the Furies to become a part of the city constitute a classic instance of political recognition."[124] Athena, he suggests, recognizes the Furies and offers them a secure if circumscribed place within the city as a way of nullifying their threat to the community. For Markell, that Athena's act is one of recognition rather than acknowledgment is suggested by the manipulative words with which she persuades the Furies to become part of the city – echoing, perhaps, the misleading language that proves so damaging to veterans – and the threat of Zeus's thunderbolt – for which we might read the disciplinary power of a state that medicalizes its veterans – upon which the only apparently new social compact is predicated. Although Markell does not say so directly, for him, this act of recognition seems to be a way of returning to the status quo prior to the unleashing of the Furies. They are domesticated by recognition, and the polity is restored.

While sharing much with Markell's reading, including his – albeit less precisely used – language of recognition, James Finlayson offers a way to think about the play that suggests an understanding of the social and

---

[123] W. B. Stanford, *Greek Tragedy and the Emotions: An Introductory Study* (London: Routledge & Kegan Paul, 1983), 163; Richard Seaford, "Historicizing Tragic Ambivalence – the Vote of Athena" in *History, Tragedy, Theory: Dialogues on Athenian drama* edited by Barbara Goff (Austin: University of Texas Press, 1995), 202–222.

[124] Markell, *Bound by Recognition*, 191.

political life that it engenders as an ongoing process. It is a reading indicative of the ways in which an understanding of tragedy as reconstitution might underpin a more democratically productive engagement with the genre as a ritual of mourning and return. Finlayson writes:

> Only the exercise of Athena's considerable powers of persuasion manages to effect a reconciliation. It is as if Aeschylus is telling us that justice, reason, and lawfulness are not established facts that need merely to be recognized for what they are by an act of theoretical contemplation but ongoing practical tasks within the new social order, and reconciliation between the different ethical powers, between citizens and their new institutions is not a state already attained but an ongoing process.[125]

Between, then, Markell's dark reading of the *Oresteia*'s conclusion and W. B. Stanford's optimistic one, lies the suggestion that the conclusion offered by the trilogy is neither positive nor negative but rather no conclusion at all.

A number of scholars, including Rush Rehm and Elizabeth Markovits, have drawn critical attention to the final procession of the cycle in which the Furies, now reconstituted as Eumenides, leave the theater and enter the city.[126] "[T]he *Oresteia*," writes Rehm, "moves temporally toward its audience as it moves spatially toward the Athens of the Acropolis, the Areopagus, and the Theater of Dionysus."[127] It is a moment of meta-theatricality – what Paul Woodruff calls "transgressive theater"[128] – that suggests the reconstitutive possibilities of tragedy. The Furies become incorporated as Eumenides – metics – who now play a circumscribed role in the city.[129] Such an inclusion, as Honig reminds us, always creates new tensions to be negotiated as part of an always ongoing process.[130] Indeed, the Eumenides are, in the words of Pat Easterling, "equally potent as invisible forces, they in some way represent the past and the implications of what you (or your family, or your city) have done in the past: you

---

[125] Finlayson, "Conflict and Reconciliation," 516.
[126] Their transformation embodies both the continuity and change here being suggested by the term "reconstitution."
[127] Elizabeth Markovits, "Birthrights: Freedom, Responsibility, and Democratic Comportment in Aeschylus' *Oresteia*," *American Political Science Review*, 103(3), 2009: 430, 427–441; Rush Rehm, *The Play of Space: Spatial Transformation in Greek Tragedy* (Princeton, NJ: Princeton University Press, 2002), 92.
[128] Paul Woodruff, *The Necessity of Theater: The Art of Watching and Being Watched* (Oxford: Oxford University, 2008), 115.
[129] See Demetra Kasimis, "The Tragedy of Blood-based Membership. Secrecy and the Politics of Immigration in Euripides' *Ion*," *Political Theory*, 41(2), 2013: 231–256.
[130] Their status as metics further suggests the value of Honig's *Democracy and the Foreigner* for thinking about these issues.

never know when they may catch up with you, where the blow will come from: they will continue to have the job of punishing those who do wrong." [131]

Much has been written about the pedagogical aspects of Greek tragedy, and, as Markovits notes, "the *Oresteia* was not just an analysis of the ways judgment should work in a democratic setting; rather it called on the spectators to judge themselves." [132] Here the entry of the reformed Furies into the city suggests the ways in which that which was depicted on stage – the incorporation of traumatic memories into public life – should be enacted in the polity. Peter Meineck, moreover, argues that the *Oresteia* was written at a time of Athenian civic renewal, with the evidence of the costs of war present in the buildings destroyed by the Persians; indeed, he argues that the pledges that the Furies and Athena make to one another are "apt pledges for a people who have been struggling to rebuild their city and help to further reinforce the *Oresteia*'s status as a work that advocates political, social, and urban renewal." [133] Such a project is, however, always ongoing, and thus, with the entry of the newly reformed Furies into the city, a cycle of plays that is fundamentally concerned with returns serves to return politics to its audience, demanding that they acknowledge – rather than simply recognize – the complexities with those with whom they must engage and the ways in which that engagement will continue to change both them and their fellow citizens. [134] It is a politically productive reading that overcomes what Simon Goldhill calls "the desire for a single simple message from the *Oresteia*," that which "distorts any understanding of its democratic *paideusis*." [135]

[131] Pat Easterling, 2008. "Theatrical Furies: Thoughts on *Eumenides*" in *Performance, Iconography, Reception. Studies in Honour of Oliver Taplin* edited by Martin Reverman and Peter Wilson (Oxford: Oxford University Press, 2008), 233. See also Jean-Pierre Vernant and Pierre Vidal-Naquet, *Myth and Tragedy in Ancient Greece* (New York: Zone Books, 1988), 141. Of *The Oresteia*, they write, "The trilogy ends with a nocturnal procession 'by the light of dazzling torches'...whose brilliance this time, is not deceptive but sheds light upon a reconciled universe – though this does not mean, of course, a universe free from all tensions."

[132] Markovits, "Birthrights," 478. For an extended discussion of the way in which Greek tragedy called on its audiences to judge themselves by modeling that judging on stage, see Simon Goldhill, *Sophocles and the Language of Tragedy* (Oxford: Oxford University Press, 2006).

[133] Peter Meineck, "Opsis: The Visuality of Greek Drama," Ph.D. Thesis, University of Nottingham, 2011, 241.

[134] Helen Bacon, "The Furies' Homecoming," *Classical Philology*, 96(1), 2001: 48–59.

[135] Simon Goldhill, "Civic Ideology and the Politics of Aeschylean Tragedy, Once Again," *The Journal of Hellenic Studies*, 120(2000): 48.

Against this background, it might be argued that *The Oresteia* provides
a more compelling model of tragedy as a ritual of return than either
Ajax or *Philoctetes*, the plays employed by the Theater of War, or even
Euripides' *Herakles*, favored by the Ancient Greeks/Modern Lives series,
not least because these plays are focused on the struggles of individuals rather than the community as a whole. More than this, however, the
understanding of tragedy as a source of reconstitution rather than restoration offers a better model for any attempt to employ tragedy as a
ritual of homecoming for veterans. Whereas the restoration model pushes
returnees into inherently contradictory preexisting categories of heroism
and of citizenship – identities that, in Markell's terms, secure others' sovereignty at the expense of the recognized – and toward a polity unwilling to reflect on the ways in which war has changed both its politics
and its veterans, the reconstitution model not only seeks no such fixed
identity, it is also prepared to acknowledge the manner in which veteran
and polity may have been changed by war. Moving beyond the veteran-
centric notion of return embodied in the rituals of restorative nostalgia,
the reconstitutive calls on the polity to engage with the veteran. Here
again, Aeschylus is instructive.

When Athena encounters Orestes and the Furies at her shrine, the goddess initially dwells on their deviance – "like no one born of the sown seed
/ no goddess watched by the gods / no mortal either / not to judge by your
look at least / your features…"[136] – excluding them from the possibility
of community. Initially it is, as *per* Markell, a moment of recognition: the
Furies are seen in purely one-dimensional terms. Athena, however, quickly
reverses herself. She calls on the traditions of her community to acknowledge the Furies in a way that moves beyond mere appearance. "Wait, I call
my neighbors into question / They've done nothing wrong. It offends the
rights / it violates tradition."[137] It is this moment of acknowledgment that
makes politics – embodied in the subsequent trial and quest for justice –
possible. Having been acknowledged and heard by Athena – "Two sides
are here, and only half is heard" – the Furies are, even as outsiders, able
to become a part of the democratic activity of the city. "We respect you,"
the leader observes. "You show us respect."[138] This respect – which moves
beyond mere recognition – proves crucial when the result of Orestes' trial
goes against the Furies. It is this respect that allows Athena to dissipate

[136] Aeschylus, *The Oresteia: Agamemnon; The Libation Bearers; The Eumenides* translated
    by Robert Fagles (New York: Penguin Group, 1984), 249.
[137] Ibid.
[138] Ibid., 249, 251.

their anger, not least by offering them a further acknowledgment of their experiences. "I will bear with your anger," she declares. "You are older / The years have taught you more, much more than I can know."[139] Thus, Aeschylus demonstrates the value of acknowledgement to those excluded from consensus. It is acknowledgment – both as something about the self and as a basis for engagement with others – that makes politics possible. Indeed, although neither Athena nor the Furies are human, their relationship might once again suggest the importance of humanism – itself, perhaps, a form of acknowledgment – as a precursor to politics and the political.[140]

Although the Furies are not the product of war, they might be considered the product of the kind of trauma that war generates in citizen-soldiers: war is, after all, not the only cause of PTSD.[141] The polity that emerges from Orestes' trial – that which is returned to the Athenians by the theatrical procession out of the theater – is by no means perfect, nor does it aspire to be. Rather, it makes the Furies a part of the city in a way that acknowledges their continuing role within it: they do not vote, but their presence will affect all future decisions. The Furies, as the embodiment of trauma, have been tamed but not neutered, and the polity continues to acknowledge their voice and presence in future decisions. As such, perhaps, it is possible to see the ways in which Markell, while aspiring to a politics of acknowledgment, may undermine his own argument with his account of the *Oresteia*'s conclusion. Markell's complaint about Athena's persuasive words and the threat of Zeus's thunderbolt as elements of the reconstituted city suggests a nostalgic quest for purity: a return to a city that is an ideal speech situation rather than a much messier politics in which the agonism he seeks can function as a structuring aspiration rather than as an essential reality. As Markovits notes of the reconstitution of the polity in *The Oresteia*, "This occurs not by erasing the past and starting with a clean slate, but by acknowledging [the history] and forging a new path in light of it."[142] It is a politics, that

---

[139] Ibid., 269.

[140] Although they are, of course, portrayed by humans.

[141] See Judith Herman, *Trauma and Recovery. The Aftermath of Violence from Domestic Abuse to Political Terror* (New York: Basic Books, 1992). It is, moreover, possible to see *The Oresteia* as a response to the horrors of war with Persia, in particular the impact of the Athenians' evacuation of the city during the second invasion. Although the Athenians managed to avoid the terrors of the actual invasion, the fear that prompted the evacuation and the potential consequences of their being caught no doubt generated a kind of trauma that may have found theatrical embodiment in the Furies. This is not to suggests, of course, that returning veterans or traumatized citizens should *themselves* be understood as Furies.

[142] Markovits, "Birthrights," 437.

is, not of nostalgic restoration but rather of tragic reconstitution, one
that acknowledges the past while looking toward the future. In such a
politics, the threat of the Furies remains, but it is a threat to be acknowledged and negotiated rather than denied. The benefits of this politics of
acknowledgment to veterans are, moreover, not simply that they might
avoid being bound by recognition as "heroes" but also by any possible
recognition as "victims."

The Vietnam veteran, observed Eric Dean, has become the "most
romanticized war hero in American history."[143] The dominant image of
these veterans is, perhaps, captured in John Rambo, the troubled drifter
depicted by Sylvester Stallone in the movie *First Blood* and its many
sequels.[144] Such stereotyping, many have noted, serves to marginalize
the veteran still further, undermining his or her employment prospects
or personal relationships by propagating the myth that, when pushed, he
or she will slip into a murderous rage that threatens the citizenry. "If we
fetishize trauma as incommunicable," writes Phil Klay, "then survivors
are trapped – unable to feel truly known by their nonmilitary friends
and family."[145] Here again, *The Oresteia* might prove instructive. "In
the course of the trilogy," writes Helen Bacon, "the Furies advance from
being outcasts, inhabitants of outer darkness, working unseen by gods
and mortals, to being legitimized members of the cosmic community,
part of the *consciousness* of mortals and gods."[146] It is an understanding
of the play that gestures toward recent work in the field of posttraumatic
growth (PTG): the notion that trauma can teach persons or polities valuable lessons, an echo, perhaps, of the Aeschylean maxim that wisdom
comes through suffering. The posttraumatic growth literature holds that
"[p]eople are capable of finding pathways to reverse the destructive-
ness of trauma and turn it to their advantage."[147] A number of veterans
of America's most recent wars have suggested the same.[148] "As anyone

[143] Dean, *Shook Over Hell*, 8.
[144] For a typically illuminating discussion of the movie *First Blood*, see Steven Johnston,
American Dionysia: Violence, Tragedy, and Democratic Politics (New York: Cambridge
University Press, 2015).
[145] Phil Klay, "Role for Civilians. After War, a Failure of the Imagination," *The New York
Times*, February 8, 2014. www.nytimes.com/2014/02/09/opinion/sunday/after-war-a-
failure-of-the-imagination.html?_r=0. Accessed May 20, 2015.
[146] Bacon, "The Furies' Homecoming," 57.
[147] Stephen Joseph, *What Doesn't Kill Us: The New Psychology of Posttraumatic Growth*
(New York: Basic Books, 2011), xvi.
[148] Most recent at the time of writing.

who has spent time in the world of soldiers and veterans knows, serving in war and enduring its hardships," writes returnee David Eisler, "have made many veterans stronger."[149] As such, he suggests, veterans have something to offer the polity beyond their prior service and heroic identity. One of the dangers of this kind of claim is, nevertheless, that it becomes a further form of recognition and thus another stick with which to beat those who fail to demonstrate the qualities that are understood to constitute such growth. Indeed, the work of Victor Frankl – as the intellectual forebear of posttraumatic growth theory – might suggest that condemning the perceived failures of others is an inevitable consequence of its claims. Certainly the manner in which Frankl dismisses those who proved incapable of surviving the Nazi work camps appears to foreshadow claims about the failures of veterans to integrate more fully into society.[150] Indeed, Frankl's work also suggests the ways in which this work on PTG might be generative of a further narrative of redemption: a romantic response to loss and return that holds any and all suffering to be worthwhile. Once again, however, the turn to Aeschylus provides the necessary resources for embracing the possibilities of PTG and military return without buying into its potentially redemptive narratives. "There is," as Simon Goldhill notes, "in the Aeschylean tragic, always a recognition of the dark webs of involvement beneath even a shining triumph."[151]

A thoroughly tragic approach to America's rituals of mourning and return, one that moves beyond the language of recognition and restoration toward acknowledgment and reconstitution might, then, serve to address – or at least provide a starting point for addressing – the problems faced by veterans of America's most recent wars, wars that are themselves, in part at least, products of the polity's problematic responses to the planes. Such a claim necessarily poses the question of what such rituals of mourning and return might look like in the contemporary polity. Here, paradoxically perhaps, Steven Johnston's work on memorials and patriotism proves particularly useful.

---

[149] Eisler, "Beyond the Bad News." See also Dave Philips, "A Veteran Works to Break the 'Broken Hero' Stereotype," *The New York Times*, February 6, 2015. www.nytimes.com/2015/02/06/us/a-veteran-works-to-break-the-broken-hero-stereotype.html. Accessed May 20, 2015.

[150] Victor Frankl, *Man's Search for Meaning* translated by Ilse Lasch (Boston: Beacon Press, 1992).

[151] Goldhill, "Civic Ideology," 54.

IF YOU LOVE THIS LAND OF THE FREE, BRING 'EM HOME

In the *Odyssey*, Odysseus famously lashes himself to the mast to avoid the seductive song of the Sirens. Although the song of the Sirens is filled with erotic overtones, its allure resides in its offer of understanding:

> We know all the pains that the Greeks and Trojans once endured
> on the spreading plain of Troy when the gods willed it so –
> all that comes to pass on the fertile earth, we know it all!

It is a powerful force. Odysseus declares, "the heart inside me throbbed to listen longer / I signaled the crew with frowns to set me free."[152] On Jonathan Shay's reading, Odysseus is a combat veteran whose quest for home is both literal and metaphorical. He exhibits many of the qualities most often demonstrated by contemporary combat veterans. The pirate raid on Ismarus indicates an inability to leave what Shay calls "the combat mode"; the recklessness of his unnecessary engagement with the Cyclops suggests the restlessness and boredom that comes from leaving a war zone;[153] his descent into the Underworld, the guilt associated with the recollection of fallen comrades; and most tragically, perhaps, his failure to recognize his home upon his return echoes the experience of numerous veterans alienated from family and all that was once comforting.[154] For Shay, the appeal of the Siren song reflects the desire of the veteran to be heard or, in Markell's language, to be acknowledged. Nevertheless, America's contemporary rituals make such acknowledgment highly unlikely.

American national holidays have, as John Schaar noted, become little more than extended opportunities for consumption.[155] Days set aside for the commemoration of veterans and the war dead are, furthermore, frequently meaningless and perfunctory for many veterans, or, worse still, a source of great distress. For this reason, Edward Tick suggests, "[i]nstead of having a parade and going shopping, we could use our veterans'

---

[152] Homer, *The Odyssey* translated by Robert Fagles (London: Penguin Books, 1996), 277.

[153] Recently, a number of veterans from the wars in Iraq and Afghanistan have returned to other theaters of war. Dave Phillips and Thomas James Brennan, "Unsettled at Home, Veterans Volunteer to Fight Isis," *The New York Times*, March 12, 2015. www.nytimes.com/2015/03/12/us/disenchanted-by-civilian-life-veterans-volunteer-to-fight-isis.html?hp&action=click&pgtype=Homepage&module=first-column-region&region=top-news&WT.nav=top-news. Accessed May 26, 2015.

[154] Shay, *Odysseus in America*, 20, 45, 76, 120.

[155] John H. Schaar, "The Case for Patriotism" in *Legitimacy in the Modern State* (New Brunswick, NJ: Transaction Books, 1981), 289.

holidays as an occasion for storytelling. Open the churches and temples
and synagogues and mosques and community centers and libraries across
the country, and invite the veterans to tell their stories."[156] Such a ritual
of homecoming would, of course, place considerable demands on the
polity, especially one that has shown a remarkable reluctance to hear the
voices of its veterans. This is, in part, perhaps, because the polity has not
been trained to hear their stories; there is nothing akin to the traditions
that Athena draws on to acknowledge the Furies, or, indeed, to the Great
Dionysia so important to Athens. While Shay calls on the polity to "be a
trustworthy audience for victims of abuse of power" and to offer a respectful listening constituted by a "readiness to be changed by the narrator" –
an echo, perhaps, of what Connolly calls a "presumptive generosity" – it
is not necessarily clear how these goals might be achieved.[157] Johnston
offers a possible solution.

In his 2009 essay "American Dionysia" and his subsequent book of the
same name, Johnston calls for three new national holidays and for the
reinvention – or reconstitution – of Independence Day. On the latter, he
calls for the erection of giant screens on the National Mall in Washington,
DC, and the showing of Westerns, specifically those of John Ford, which,
Johnston argues, are examples of the contemporary tragic.[158] There are,
perhaps, some problems with this argument, not least among which is
that the citizenry are – initially, at least – unlikely to be as gifted view-
ers and readers as Johnston.[159] Nevertheless, as a thought experiment,
Johnston's work suggests the untapped possibilities of national holidays
and some form of the patriotic. Johnston is, of course, a staunch critic of
patriotism, which, he argues, "feeds on death." As such, he suggests, any
attempt to theorize "healthy forms of patriotism" is doomed to failure.[160]
Here, however, it has been argued that both the Great Dionysia and

[156] Kupfer, "Like Wandering Ghosts," 6. For the importance of listening to democracy, see
Susan Bickford, *The Dissonance of Democracy: Listening, Conflict, and Citizenship*
(Ithaca, NY: Cornell University Press, 1996).
[157] Shay, *Achilles in Vietnam*, 193, 189.
[158] Steven Johnston, "American Dionysia," *Contemporary Political Theory*, 8(3), 2009:
255–275.
[159] For many, such a day out might constitute little more than an opportunity for popcorn,
hotdogs, and John Wayne. This approach would, perhaps, be insufficient on its own;
indeed, it would seem to rely on a preexisting tragic sensibility for its full effect. Such
an ethos does not emerge without extensive training in a tragic tradition: the *depiction* of the tragic is not enough. For an extended discussion of this argument, see Stow,
Republic of Readers? especially 121–135.
[160] Steven Johnston, *The Truth About Patriotism* (Durham, NC: Duke University Press,
2007), 162–163.

the Gettysburg Address embody a possibility that Johnston denies: the Dionysian, or tragically patriotic, with the combination of nationalistic celebration and searing critique helping constitute the "jarring pleasure of oxymoron" by which the Greeks made sense of the world.[161] Unexpectedly, perhaps, there are moments when Johnston seems to agree. In his account of a contemporary Dionysia, Johnston acknowledges that, for the Greeks, "Patriotic celebration and affirmation framed the tragic theater that followed. While not negating the critical nature of the plays, the patriotic trappings of the Dionysia provided a safe, secure, affective environment in which they could be delivered."[162] Despite himself, then, there are moments when Johnston appears to believe that patriotism has a significant role to play in the cultivation of the tragic. Indeed, it is telling that Johnston's contemporary Dionysia is located on the National Mall, echoing the democratically productive juxtaposition of patriotism and critique he identifies in Greek theater. This attempt to read Johnston against himself is not, of course, an effort to refute his arguments, simply to identify and make useful a tension in his thought. Indeed, the democratic possibilities of this tension are further suggested by his discussion of the Vietnam Veterans' Memorial in Washington, DC, itself a site of mourning and return for both the polity and its veterans.

Although the design of the Vietnam Veterans' Memorial was widely condemned at the time of its construction – labeled a "black gash of shame" and a "degrading ditch" by its detractors[163] – "the Wall" has proven to be one of the nation's more productive monuments. Indeed, noting the role that the memorial has played in the treatment and recovery of veterans – providing a space for the recreation and reexperiencing of trauma – Jonathan Shay argues that its therapeutic effect has also expanded outward to the broader political community.[164] Likewise, Johnston offers a reading of the Wall and the monument complex in which it is situated that appears to work against his own negative reading of the patriotic. "Rather than privilege consensus – the lowest common denominator of commemorative politics," he writes, "– civic space can work to actualize democratic commitments."[165] The Vietnam Veterans'

[161] Nicole Loraux, *The Mourning Voice: An Essay on Greek Tragedy* translated by Corinne Pache (Ithaca, NY: Cornell; University Press, 2002), 65.
[162] Johnston, *American Dionysia*, 42.
[163] Marita Sturken, "The Aesthetics of Absence: Rebuilding Ground Zero," *American Ethnologist*, 31(3), 2004: 122.
[164] Shay, *Odysseus in America*, 201.
[165] Johnston, *The Truth About Patriotism*, 117.

Memorial complex, with the Wall, a statue of the three soldiers, the Women's Memorial, and the plaque for those who lost their lives after the war, embodies just such a space. "It is," writes Johnston, "a memorial with four aspects. No single approach to the war could satisfy the war parties involved. Thus the memorial site is inherently dynamic, variable, at odds with itself. While the design competition mandated that the Vietnam Veterans' Memorial 'make no political statement about the war,' the site has been political since its inception."[166] The monument complex is, then, a sacred space of tragic, oxymoronic juxtaposition, embedded in and made possible by the patriotic setting of the National Mall.[167] It suggests, *contra* Kateb and Johnston, that patriotism, sacred space, and public mourning are not in themselves problematic but rather *how* we love our country, *what* we do in her scared space, and *how* we mourn her losses; that far from sapping the polity of its democratic energies, these activities can be and historically have been democratically productive.[168] It is out of such dynamics that a more meaningful and reconstitutive mode of mourning and return might emerge.

Thus, it might be argued, a tragic mode of mourning and return demands a reconstituted Veterans' Day, one in which the patriotic celebrations of service and sacrifice also permit veterans to tell their stories to a polity that has hitherto been unwilling to listen. Only then, perhaps, would the dominant narratives of service and sacrifice take on more meaning, pointing to exactly what is demanded by service and what has been sacrificed. As such, a reconstituted Veterans' Day might move beyond the banal politics of recognition and consensus to the more substantive politics of acknowledgment and agonism. Likewise, the parades and homecoming ceremonies that are currently central to the polity's rituals of return might be similarly reconstituted to include not only the able bodied and the visibly uninjured but also the wounded, the maimed, and the caskets of the dead. Employing the patriotism of the current rituals and juxtaposing it with the costs of those same narratives in full view of the public might alert the polity to the tragedy of its condition, one in

---

[166] Ibid., 149. Johnston's account of the Grant Memorial in Washington, DC, further suggest the power of official commemoration to undermine itself. Ibid., 135.

[167] Typically, this complexity is threatened by a proposed "education center" that threatens to impose a master narrative on the memorials. C. J. Lin, "Ground is broken for education center at Vietnam Veterans' Memorial," *Stripes*, November 28, 2012. www.stripes .com/news/us/ground-is-broken-for-education-center-at-vietnam-veterans-memorial-1.198691. Accessed May 22, 2015.

[168] George Kateb, *Patriotism and Other Mistakes* (New Haven, CT: Yale University Press, 2006).

which every gain comes with a loss, every victory or even defeat with a
cost. Finally, the polity might reconfigure its practices of memorialization.
Acknowledging the complex experiences of World War II returnees, the
journalist and filmmaker Sebastian Junger notes that

Every year on the anniversary of D-Day, for example, we acknowledge the heroism and sacrifice of those who stormed the beaches of Normandy. But for a full
and honest understanding of that war, we must also remember the firebombing
of Dresden, Frankfurt and Hamburg that killed as many as 100,000 Germans, as
well as both conventional and nuclear strikes against Japan that killed hundreds
of thousands more.

To achieve this more complex narrative and thus to offer its military veterans a more meaningful mode of mourning and return, Junger suggests
the construction of a monument more in keeping with the complexity of
their experiences, one that would also work for the citizens of the polity
to which they sought a homecoming.

[I]magine those men coming back after World War II to a country that has
collectively taken responsibility for the decision to firebomb German cities.
(Firebombing inflicted mass civilian casualties and nearly wiped out cities.) This
would be no admission of wrongdoing – many wars, like Afghanistan and World
War II, were triggered by attacks against us. It would simply be a way to commemorate the loss of life, as one might after a terrible earthquake or a flood.
Imagine how much better the bomber crews of World War II might have handled
their confusion and grief if the entire country had been struggling with those
same feelings. Imagine how much better they might have fared if there had been a
monument for them to visit that commemorated all the people they were ordered
to kill.[169]

Building on Junger's argument and on Aeschylus' even more radical suggestion about the possibility of mourning the enemy, America's national
memorials to its post-2001 wars might seek to commemorate not only
the civilian casualties of America's wars but also those of the militants
and insurgents it killed in those conflicts. Such an approach to memorialization, located on the National Mall, might help to cultivate the tragic
ethos that the polity requires to reconstitute itself after loss.

   It is, then, not only veterans who might benefit from such a set of rituals but also the polity itself. Heidegger famously defined tragedy as a state
of homelessness.[170] Writing in 2003, Donald Pease identified a paradox

---

[169] Sebastian Junger, "Why Would Anyone Miss War?" *The New York Times*, July, 16,
2011. www.nytimes.com/2011/07/17/opinion/sunday/17junger.html. Accessed May 26,
2015.
[170] See Neal Curtis, "Tragedy and Politics," *Philosophy & Social Criticism* 33(7), 2007:
860–879.

at the heart of America's postplanes obsession with the "Homeland." Historically, he observed, "the Homeland named the space that emerged when the people were dissociated from their way of life." "The metaphor of the Homeland," he continued, "thereafter evoked the image of a vulnerable population that had become internally estranged from its 'country of origin' and dependent on the protection of the state."[171] The effect of the establishment of the Department of Homeland Security was, he suggests, to protect and maintain the state of homelessness that has afflicted the polity since 2001. Pease might have added, moreover, that this sense of homelessness also helped maintain the nostalgic dream of home, one in which it was America's love of freedom, not her foreign policies, that provoked radical Islamists to murder nearly 3,000 of her citizens. Indeed, even more problematically, perhaps, given the history of a nation formed by a sense of Puritan – and, later, secularized – mission, are the theological-political implications of the quest for restoration. Underpinning this notion of Homeland is the long-standing trope of American innocence in a world of sin: of the possibility of a return to a mythical previous state. The suggestion that America might return to the favor of God, to a state of prelapsarian innocence, inevitably bolsters not only the nostalgic but also the nationalistic and the romantic, all three of which serve to situate the polity's wartime experiences and the personal and political costs thereof into a master narrative in which any price is worth paying in order to bring that destiny into being. Moreover, this commitment to innocence and nostalgia robs the polity of any capacity for sustained critical reflection on the causes of any conflict by reassuring the nation of both its victim status and the evil embodied by its enemies. As with Odysseus, the allure of homecoming, real or imagined, permits all kinds of atrocities, atrocities that, in the case of the polity at least, make this dreamed-of homecoming impossible. For this reason, America requires a tragic response to its tragic condition, one that might eschew the romantic hope of restoration in favor of a tragic resilience.

A central problem for all of these suggestions about the democratic possibilities of tragic mourning is, nevertheless, that the contemporary age is larger, far less homogenous, and more geographically dispersed than the model – largely drawn from the Ancient world – on which they are based. Although many of the possibilities that have so far been outlined rest on suggestions about reconstituted national holidays

[171] Donald Pease, "The Global Homeland State: Bush's Biopolitical Settlement," *boundary*, 2, 2003L 8.

and/or the revival of older traditions, most if not all are predicated on a commitment to collective rituals in an atomistic age. Returning to Thucydides suggests, however, the possibility of a text-based tragic mourning, one that promises to cultivate an *ethos* in its reader-citizens appropriate to the kinds of democratically productive responses to loss even in a time of political and social estrangement. It is an approach that might be thought to offer a tragic hope for America's collective future.

5

Mourning as Democratic Resilience: Going on Together in the Face of Loss

Why be afraid? Chance governs human life, and we can never know what is to come. Live day by day, as best you can.

— *Sophocles, Oedipus Tyrannus*

In the aftermath of the planes, America became a security state committed to the "never again."[1] Even those for whom American democracy had always been something of a myth were forced to concede that this increased commitment to security further undermined what they perceived to be the nation's already tenuous claims to democratic values: that torture, domestic surveillance, an off-shore gulag, the summary execution of U.S. citizens, and a weakened commitment to *habeas corpus* all served to create what one critic called a "neofascist state."[2] Given that terrorism as a political strategy relies for its effects on the response of its victim, the

---

[1] Following the 2001 terrorist attacks, argues Louise Comfort, "The tolerance for risk in U.S. society dropped to near zero, as reflected by two major policy changes: the passage of the U.S.A. Patriot Act and the establishment of a cabinet-level Department of Homeland Security." Louise Comfort, "Risk, Security, and Disaster Management," *Annual Review of Political Science*, 8, 2005: 341. See also Juliette Kayyem, "Never Say Never Again," *Foreign Policy*, 10 (9): 2012. www.foreignpolicy.com/articles/2012/09/10/never_say_never_again?page%25C2BCfull#.UFIslAvZ-RY.twitter. Accessed Oct 17, 2012. For a compelling counterargument to such claims about America's postplanes commitment to security, see Elisabeth R. Anker, *Orgies of Feeling: Melodrama and the Politics of Feeling* (Durham, NC: Duke University Press, 2014). Examining melodrama as a political genre, Anker argues that after the planes, Americans – mistakenly – turned to the state to protect their freedom.

[2] Cornel West and Christa Buschendorf, *Black Prophetic Fire* (Boston: Beacon Press 2014). Kindle Edition, Loc. 2461. See also Noam Chomsky, *9/11: Was There an Alternative?* Second edition (New York: Seven Stories Press, 2011); and Noam Chomsky, *Interventions* (San Francisco: City light Books, 2013).

irony of this hubristic commitment to security at the expense of all other
values – save, perhaps, revenge – was that it served to make America less
secure. In the short term, the initial reaction to the 2001 attacks gave
encouragement to those who would harm the nation, showing how easily and at what little cost the life of a superpower could be disrupted.[3] In
the longer term, the very measures taken in the name of increased security and the simplistic understanding of terrorism that underpinned them
served to perpetuate the latter's causes. Although largely forgotten by the
American public, the abuses at Abu Ghraib, the ongoing detention without trial of the prisoners at Guantanamo Bay, the terror inflicted by drone
warfare, and the continuing destruction and violence being wrought on
and in Iraq, Afghanistan, and Syria remain potent recruiting tools in the
Arab world.[4] Such, perhaps, is the tragic condition: that those actions
taken to forestall terrorism served to exacerbate its effects. Stephen Flynn
notes, for example, that following the attempted bombing of Northwest
Airlines flight 253 on Christmas Day 2009, "congressional leaders on
both the left and the right declared it better to overreact than underreact
to the risk of terrorism. This rare bipartisan consensus was unfortunately
entirely wrong."[5] Indeed, he argued, "U.S. officials should avoid making
the kind of statements…to the effect that terrorists have to be right only
once, whereas U.S. officials have to be right 100 percent of the time.
Such declarations might demonstrate firm resolve, but they set an impossible standard; no security regime is foolproof."[6] The self-perpetuating

---

[3] Rejecting the claim that their 2010 attempt – tellingly titled Operation Hemorrhage –
to destroy two cargo planes over the United States with bombs disguised as printer
cartridges had failed, al Qaeda in the Arabian Peninsula noted that they had managed to disrupt international trade and impose billions of dollars in additional security
costs with three months' planning and less than $5,000. Andrew Zolli and Ann Healy,
Resilience: Why Things Bounce Back (New York: Free Press, 2010), 64. Similarly, in
2012, David Sanger calculated that for every dollar that al Qaeda spent on their 2001
attacks on America, America spent $6.6 million dollars in response. David Sanger,
Confront and Conceal: Obama's Secret Wars and Surprising Use of American Power
(New York: Broadway Books, 2012), 418.

[4] Ahmed Rashid is, perhaps, the best chronicler of the counterproductive nature of
America's response to the planes. See Ahmed Rashid, *Descent into Chaos: The U.S. and
the Disaster in Pakistan, Afghanistan, and Central Asia* (New York: Penguin Books,
2009; and Ahmed Rashid, *Pakistan on the Brink* (New York: Penguin Books, 2013). For
an account of drone warfare as terrorism, see Thomas Dumm, "Obama's Catastrophic
Drones," *Contemporary Condition*, November 11, 2013. contemporarycondition.
blogspot.com/2013/11/obamas-catastrophic-drones.html. Accessed Oct. 24, 2014.

[5] Stephen Flynn, "Recalibrating Homeland Security. Mobilizing American Society to
Prepare for Disaster," *Foreign Affairs*, May/June 2011: 136.

[6] Ibid., 132.

nature of the "never again" is suggested by the feedback loop and sub-sequent policy distortions that inevitably emerge from the problematic grief-wrath of *mênis*. "Creating unrealistic expectations," Flynn writes, "guarantees anger, disappointment, and mistrust should a terrorist attack succeed."[7]

In the face of the counterproductive "never again," a number of secu-rity scholars have sought to embrace *resilience*: that which recognizes the always-ongoing possibility of crisis or catastrophe and seeks not prevention but rather preservation through the cultivation of values and resources that might maintain the nation's important institutions in the face of loss.[8] Resilience as a doctrine is multifaceted and polygenetic, emerging from literature in several disciplines including biology, ecol-ogy, and psychology.[9] Its appeal is broad, gaining traction not only in those disciplines but also in a number of others including economics and urban planning.[10] It is, however, not without its critics, with some argu-ing that, in addition to placing an undue burden on the most vulner-able populations by holding them responsible for the precariousness of their condition, resilience cultivates a mere survivability at the expense of

---

[7] Ibid., 133.

[8] Here a crisis might be understood as a turning point, or a crucial moment at which the values of a system are threatened. A catastrophe, on the other hand, might be thought to be an "overturning" of those values. In the words of Linda Ross Meyer, "Catastrophes, then, are not just bad luck, harmful events in the world, expected losses, or injustice. But events that call into question our normative ground and cause radical normative disorientation. They are events that cause us to feel 'unheimlich' – not at home in the world. Everything we took for granted is open to question. Everything we counted on is missing." Linda Ross Meyer, "Catastrophe: Plowing up the Ground of Reason" in Austin Sarat, Lawrence Douglas, and Martha Merrill Umphrey, *Law and Catastrophe* (Palo Alto, CA: Stanford University Press, 2007), 21.

[9] See, for example, Stuart Kauffman, *The Origins of Order: Self-Organization and Selection in Evolution* (Oxford: Oxford University Press, 1993); Lance H. Gunderson, "Ecological Resilience – in Theory and Application," *Annual Review of Ecology and Systematics*, 31, 2000: 425–439; Marten Sheffer, Steven Carpenter, Jonathan A. Foley, Carl Folkes, and Brian Walker, "Catastrophic Shifts in Ecosystems," *Nature*, 413(October) 2001: 591–596; and Judith Herman, *Trauma and Recovery: The Aftermath of Violence from Domestic Abuse to Political Terror* (New York: Basic Books, 1997). Although he himself does not use the term, perhaps the most famous proponent of psychological resilience is Victor Frankl, who considers its role in the survival of work camp prisoners during the Nazi Holocaust. See, Victor E. Frankl, *Man's Search for Meaning* (Boston: Beacon Press, 1992).

[10] See, for example, Lawrence J. Vale and Thomas J. Campanella, eds., *The Resilient City: How Modern Cities Recover from Disaster* (Oxford: Oxford University Press, 2005); Adam Rose, "Economic resilience to natural and man-made disasters: Multidisciplinary origins and contextual dimensions," *Environmental Hazards*, 7(4), 2007: 383–398; and Jon Coaffee, "From Counterterrorism to Resilience," *The European Legacy*, 11(4), 2006: 389–403.

human flourishing. Such claims overlap and intersect with recent debates in democratic theory about "emergency politics" and about the ability of a polity to engage in meaningful, collective political action in the face of Giorgio Agamben's "bare life" and Carl Schmitt's "state of exception."[11]

Noting that few authors concerned with resilience have chosen to pay attention to the democratic costs of the "never again" – largely focusing on its economic impact and/or its implications for American foreign policy – this chapter considers the democratic possibilities of the doctrine, arguing that the values that it seeks to cultivate such as pluralism, ongoing critical reflection, considered deliberation, the flow of power from the state to civil society, and what has been termed a "postheroic" politics are precisely those values most conducive to democratic flourishing. Engaging critically with the literature both for and against the doctrine, it is argued that much of the contemporary criticism of resilience is predicated on a misunderstanding of the theory and/or on the misplaced assumptions of its critics. Noting, nevertheless, that the arguments for resilience are not without their flaws, it rejects the suggestion – made by one of its strongest advocates – that "resilience-thinking can be understood as the first post-liberal or post-modern episteme: the first coherent, positive, alternative to modernist frameworks on the subject and the world."[12] Rather, it points to a much older account of the doctrine offered – *avant la lettre* – by Thucydides in his *History of the Peloponnesian War*. Arguing that Thucydides, not the more recent advocates of the theory, should properly be seen as the intellectual godfather of resilience, it suggests that, when understood as a form of tragic mourning for Athens imbued with hope for the city's future, his work offers a more compelling response both to the contemporary critiques of the resilience and to some of the problems with its current formulations. Tragic mourning, it argues, offers the best hope for an effective and democratically productive strategy of resilience in an age of the "never again."

The chapter proceeds, first, by defining "resilience," a task complicated by the diversity of literatures that use the term and by the lack of rigor with which it is often employed. Second, it sets out the claims of those who would shift the focus of America's security strategy from "never again" to

[11] See Carl Schmitt, *Political Theology: Four Chapters on the Concept of Sovereignty* translated by George Schwab (Chicago: University of Chicago Press, 2006); and Giorgio Agamben, *State of Exception* translated by Kevin Attell (Chicago: University of Chicago Press, 2005).
[12] David Chandler, *Resilience: The Governance of Complexity* (Oxford: Routledge, 2014), Kindle locations 1160–1162.

resilience, identifying the ways in which such a shift might be thought to cultivate practices conducive to democratic life and politics. It further argues that while a central tenant of the turn to resilience in national security is – somewhat paradoxically – the low probability of another major terrorist attack on American soil, the benefits to democracy of adopting a properly formulated understanding of the theory suggest that the doctrine might be embraced even in the absence of such a threat. Outlining the claims of two of resilience's harshest critics and those of one of its strongest advocates, part three identifies the problems, lacunae, and tensions in these accounts. Turning to Thucydides, understood as a precursor to contemporary theories of resilience, part four presents his work as a form of tragic mourning for Athens, one that is predicated – like resilience – on the recognition of the inevitability of crisis and catastrophe. Building on this suggestion, part five shows how such mourning might be understood as a pedagogy of democratic resilience. Taking on the claim that tragedy is politically impotent, it offers an account of the role of hope in the *History*, one that, it is argued, shows how a tragic worldview can be a source of agency and action and thus of democratic reconstitution in the face of potential despair. The book and the chapter conclude by moving beyond the narrower question of resilience to show how, by both depicting and cultivating hope as the source of tragedy's creativity, Thucydides offers his readers a model for a text-based, nonritualized, democratic pedagogy of mourning, one that addresses its audience both as individuals and as citizens of a political collective. It is an approach which, it is argued, is even more appropriate for an age fractured by political, socioeconomic, and cultural divisions than it was for Thucydides' own.

RESILIENCE AS RESTORATION, RESILIENCE AS RECONSTITUTION

"There is," notes David Chandler, "very little consensus on the concept of resilience...How we understand [it] depends a lot on the disciplinary fields in which we work and, to a certain extent, on the era in which we were brought up."[13] Despite, or perhaps precisely because of, this lack of consensus, he continues, "resilience seems to be an increasingly ubiquitous concept."[14] Among those who employ the term for policy purposes, there

---

[13] David Chandler, *Resilience: The Governance of Complexity* (Oxford: Routledge, 2014), Kindle locations 231–241.

[14] Ibid., locations 1138–1140.

is, nevertheless, a considerable degree of overlap among their definitions, most obviously on the idea that resilience identifies the capacity of "a system, enterprise, or a person to maintain its core purpose and integrity in the face of dramatically changed circumstances."[15] Aaron Wildavsky's observation that many activists, scholars, and professionals conceive of resilience as the capacity of a system or person to "bounce back" from adversity suggests a key understanding of the term.[16] For some, it is a form of restoration, a system's capacity to return to its previous state; for others, it is a form of reconstitution, connoting a system's capacity to adapt to changed circumstances while maintaining its core functions. It is, perhaps, the difference between rubber's capacity to rebound and plastic's capacity to mold to different shapes.[17] Both offer an understanding of resilience that fuels, and is fueled by, the literature on posttraumatic growth – itself an echo of the Aeschylean notion of suffering as a form of pedagogy – one that permits an individual and/or a society to emerge from trauma with new understandings, capabilities, and insights.[18]

[15] Zolli and Healy, *Resilience*, location 158–160. In 2012, for example, the International Panel on Climate Change report defined resilience as "the ability of a system and its component parts to anticipate, absorb, accommodate, or recover from the effects of a potentially hazardous event in a timely and efficient manner, including through ensuring the preservation, restoration, or improvement of its essential basic structures and function." IPCC, *Managing the Risks of Extreme Events and Disasters to Advance Climate Change and Adaptation* (New York: Cambridge University Press, 2012), 34. www.ipcc-wg2 .gov/SREX/images/uploads/SREX-All_FINAL.pdf. Accessed Oct. 15, 2014. Likewise, the United Nations defined it as "the capacity of a system, community or society potentially exposed to hazard, to adapt by resisting or changing in order to maintain an acceptable level of functioning and structure." Brad Evans and Julian Reid, *Resilient Life: The Art of Living Dangerously* (Cambridge: Polity Press, 2014), Kindle location 1613–1618.

[16] Aaron Wildavsky, *Searching for Safety* (New Brunswick, NJ: Transaction Books, 1988), 77. This understanding of resilience is noted in almost all the literature on the topic. See, for example, Steven M. Southwick and Dennis S. Charney, *Resilience: The Science of Mastering Life's Greatest Challenges* (New York: Cambridge University Press, 2012), 6; Coaffee, "From Counterterrorism to Resilience," 396; Evans and Reid, *Resilient Life*, Kindle location 150–151, 336–338; and, most obviously, the subtitle – *Why Things Bounce Back* – of the book by Zolli and Healy.

[17] This Nietzschean notion of "plasticity" and its relationship to resilience is central to Wildavsky's definition. See Friedrich Nietzsche, *Untimely Meditations* translated by R. J. Hollingdale (Cambridge: Cambridge University Press, 1983), 62; and also William James, *Habit* (New York: Henry Holt & Co., 1914), 6. Wildavsky and Dennis J. Coyle argue that "[p]lasticity and feedback epitomize resilience by allowing forms and functions to change rapidly in response to emergency needs." It is, as the economist Burton Klein suggests, a dynamic understanding of resilience, somewhat richer than that which simply focuses on restoration. Wildavsky, *Searching for Safety*, 166, 5.

[18] Once again, although he does not himself employ the term "posttraumatic growth" or "PTG," Victor Frankl's *Man's Search for Meaning* is a foundational text in this literature. See also Richard G. Tedeschi, Crystal L. Park, and Lawrence G. Calhoun,

Although resilience aims to shift the focus of crisis and catastrophe planning from prevention to preparedness, prevention nevertheless remains an essential part of its toolkit. It seeks a – decidedly Greek – middle position between prevention and cure, between the proactive and the reactive.[19] It is a balance that, Wildavsky suggests, is achieved by careful thinking about the costs and benefits of both action and inaction, something that, he notes, is missing from purely prevention-based strategies. "Deciding that there is a potential for danger," he writes, "is just the beginning. The next step is to ask, 'compared to what?' "[20] Indeed, he further suggests that "[w]hen people routinely say that prevention is better than amelioration, they neglect the policy costs of premising action on the wrong predictions."[21] In addition to foreshadowing recent critiques of the postplanes obsession with prevention and security, Wildavsky also captures the problems of the preventative approach both for democratic politics and for those caught in the literal and figurative crossfire of America's quest for safety. "Predicting wrongly," he notes, "when these 'guesstimates' are backed up by the force of the state, wreaks havoc upon innocents: lives are disrupted, jobs lost, anxiety increased, and resources diverted from more productive and hence safer uses."[22]

Resilience is, furthermore, something more than *robustness*, a quality for which it is often mistaken. The latter is achieved by building redundancies into complex systems. Andrew Zolli and Ann Marie Healy employ the term *robust-yet-fragile* to suggest the ways in which robustness is a poor solution for systems that seek to steel themselves against unknown future events:

eds., *Posttraumatic Growth: Positive Changes in the Aftermath of Crisis* (Mahwah, NJ: Lawrence Erlbaum Associates Publishers, 1998); Tzipi Weiss and Roni Berger, eds., *Posttraumatic Growth and Culturally Competent Practice: Lessons Learned from Around the Globe* (Hoboken, NJ: Wiley & Son, 2010); For evidence of its similarly Nietzschean foundations, Stephen Joseph, *What Doesn't Kill Us: The New Psychology of Posttraumatic Growth* (New York: Basic Books, 2011).

[19] Coaffee, "From Counterterrorism to Resilience," 397. Indeed, echoing Aristotle, Zolli and Healy suggest that resilience "is often found in having just the right amounts" of the qualities required to maintain system function in the face of the catastrophic. Zolli and Healy, *Resilience*, location 4016–4018.

[20] Wildavsky, *Searching for Safety*, 222.

[21] Ibid., 81.

[22] Ibid., 91. This happens on both a micro and a macro scale. Erik Luna notes an additional 1,500 people were believed to have died in the year following the 2001 attacks because Americans moved from flying, the safest form of travel, to driving, the most dangerous. Erik Luna, "The Bin Laden Exception," *Northwestern University Law Review*, 106(3), 2015, 1495. New securities, as David Chandler notes, create new insecurities. Chandler, *Resilience*, location 371.

[T]he very fact that a robust-yet-fragile system continues to handle commonplace disturbances successfully will often mask an intrinsic fragility at its core, until … a tipping point is catastrophically crossed. In the run-up to such an event, everything appears fine, with the system capably absorbing even severe but anticipated disruptions as it was intended to do. The very fact that the system continues to perform in this way conveys a sense of safety.[23]

The postplanes polity has, perhaps, been marked by just such a misplaced confidence, evidenced by the ubiquity of the suggestion that the security measures implemented in the wake of the 2001 attacks were justified by the relative absence of subsequent successful terrorist attacks on American soil.[24] It is this fallacy, among others, that a number of security scholars have sought to address in their turn to resilience.

DEMOCRACY AND RESILIENCE

At the heart of the move to resilience in national security is the belief that America's response to the planes was grossly disproportionate and eminently counterproductive: what might here be called *hubristic* and *tragic*. It was a reaction that, it has been argued, was both underpinned and inflamed by the polity's nationalistic, romantic, antihumanist, and nostalgic postattack responses to loss, all of which served to perpetuate the belief that both America's safety and/or way of life had been fundamentally undermined. While the legal and civil rights of individuals were among the first victims of the "never again," its negative impact on democratic politics was far deeper and more wide ranging than these more obvious effects alone suggest. Secrecy and security became synonymous in the postplanes era. As a result, the citizenry was disempowered, treated as "hapless targets or potential victims," even though "terrorists' chosen battlegrounds are likely to be occupied by civilians."[25] This commitment

[23] Zolli and Healy, *Resilience*, location 515–519.
[24] James Jay Carfano, Steven P. Bucci, Jessica Zuckerman, "Fifty Terror Plots Foiled Since 9/11: The Homegrown Threat and the Long War on Terror," *The Heritage Foundation*, April 25, 2012. www.heritage.org/research/reports/2012/04/fifty-terror-plots-foiled-since-9-11-the-homegrown-threat-and-the-long-war-on-terrorism. Accessed Oct. 17, 2014.
[25] It is, nevertheless, nonstate actors who have foiled the majority of terrorist attacks in the U.S. since 2001. It was, Flynn notes, a T-shirt vendor who sounded the alarm about the attempted car bombing of Times Square in 2010; passengers on Northwestern Flight 253 who contained the so-called underwear bomber on Christmas Day 2009; and civilian passengers who offered the first significant American resistance to al Qaeda by preventing their plan to crash Flight 93 into the nation's capital. Stephen E. Flynn, "America the Resilient. Defying Terrorism and Mitigating Natural Disasters," *Foreign Affairs*, March/April 2008, 2; 4–5.

to security, notes Juliette Kayyem, was "inherently paternalistic," creating "the mythology that politicians and terrorism experts have been allowed to ride for over a decade ... [that] [t]he government could actually achieve perfect protection. It gave the American people and easy way out, absolving them of responsibility."[26] Much the same might be said for the privatization of war and security, which, as James Risen observes, further insulated America's response to terror from democratic oversight.[27] For this reason, the turn away from the "never again" might, in and of itself, be thought to offer democratic revivification by returning power to the citizenry at the expense of the state. More than this, however, it may be that it is not only the turn *away* from security that promises to revivify democracy but also the turn *to* resilience, for there would appear to be considerable overlap between recent arguments for democratic agonism and those for resilience in national security.

In much the same way that William Connolly and others argue for the importance of democratic pluralism, advocates of resilience in security suggest that a diverse and thriving civil society is essential to ensuring that the nation might sustain itself in the face of a crisis or catastrophe.[28] It is a claim that, as Zolli and Healy point out, is central to the broader resilience literature. Pluralism, they note, "plays an enormous role in resilience and is one of its most important correlates. Whether it's the biodiversity of a coral reef or, in the social context, the cognitive diversity of a group increasing the diversity of a system's constituent parts ensures the widest palette of latent ready responses to disruption."[29] By way of example, they observe that cultivating cognitive diversity was seen as an antidote to the sort of policy-making monomania exhibited by the United States in its post-2001 military operations in Afghanistan. In 2004, they note, the military established Red Team University, a special unit whose job it was to instill agonism into would-be resilient systems by challenging the assumptions underpinning American policy. The hallmarks of this policy-making monomania, were, they argue:

a strong illusion of vulnerability by key decision makers; a belief in the inherent morality of the group; the stereotyping of those who do not agree with the group's perspective; and overly simplistic moral formulations that dissuade deeper rational analysis. Self-appointed thought-guards prevent alternative views from

---

[26] Kayyem, "Never Say 'Never Again.' "
[27] James Risen, *Pay Any Price: Greed, Power, and Endless War* (New York: Houghton Mifflin Harcourt, 2014), Kindle location 81–84.
[28] William Connolly, *Pluralism* (Durham, NC: Duke University Press, 2005).
[29] Zolli and Healy, *Resilience*, location 287–289.

being aired and place significant pressure on dissenters, leading to the illusion of unanimity, even if dissent is rampant below the surface.[30]

This account – tellingly redolent of the broader American response to the planes – suggests the considerable parallels between the commitments underpinning the turn to resilience and the critiques of consensus-based models of democracy offered by theorists of democratic agonism. Certainly those, such as Connolly, who argue for the cultivation of a democratic ethos and the embrace of a bicameral perspective might see much of value in this literature. "What you choose to believe, the mental processes you cultivate, and how you respond to disruption," write Zolli and Healy, "truly shape the whole. Resilience can radiate out from within."[31] Such a cultivation – or "care of the self" – also enables a more complex construction of causality than that offered by the dominant security paradigm, one that might permit a similarly complex construction of the responsibility for actions taken by and in the name of democratic societies. In the wake of catastrophes, observe Zolli and Healy – perfectly capturing the literal demonization of Osama bin Laden – "we end up resorting to simplified, moralistic narratives, featuring cartoon-like villains, to explain why they happened. In reality, such failures are more often the result of the almost imperceptible accretion of a thousand small, highly distributed decisions – each so narrow in scope as to seem innocuous."[32]

In keeping with an understanding of democratic politics as a form of collective action, resilience also embraces what Daniel Innerarity calls a "postheroic" politics.[33] In the wake of the planes, much attention was lavished on the firefighter, the soldier, the police officer, and the EMT at the expense of the ordinary citizen, even though, as Flynn and others have noted, most first responders are generally members of the public.[34]

---

[30] Ibid., location 311–3116.
[31] Ibid., location 4265–4267.
[32] Ibid., location 523–526. In this, perhaps, Osama bin Laden articulated a far more demo-. cratic understanding of responsibility than his enemies. "He is the enemy of ours," he observed of Americans, "whether he fights us directly or merely pays his taxes." Louise Richardson, *What Terrorists Want: Understanding the Enemy, Containing the Threat* (New York: Random House, 2007), Kindle location 307–308.
[33] Daniel Innerarity, *The Future and Its Enemies: In Defense of Political Hope* translated by Sandra Kingery (Palo Alto, CA: Stanford University Press, 2012), 94.
[34] Nevertheless, even when those first responders, such as those citizens on Flight 93, are nonstate actors, the power of the state to embrace them offers a form of transubstantiation in which their actions become heroic acts that embody a national characteristic rather than an attempt to secure their own lives in the face of peril. Flynn, "America the Resilient," 4.

Central to this embrace of the "postheroic" is an emphasis on the quotidian actions of such citizens and on the ongoing practices of civil society – imbued with what Elaine Scarry identifies as important habits of thought central to the longevity of a society's social and political institutions[35] – to surviving and even prospering during a crisis or a catastrophe. It is an understanding of politics that further corresponds to Flynn's suggestion that cultivating self-reliant citizenry is among the most important aspects of a non–prevention-based strategy of national security.[36] Resilience, he notes, seeks to strengthen civil society by empowering the citizenry through training, education, and the free flow of information.[37]

The considerable paradox of the resilience-as-security literature is, nevertheless, that it is predicated on a recognition that the threats to which it is a response are greatly exaggerated. Extremist Islamic terrorism, it has been noted, claims somewhere in the region of 200 to 400 lives per year in non–war zones, approximately the same number of people who drown in bathtubs every year in the United States.[38] Far from undermining the case for resilience, however, the approach's ability to acknowledge the excesses of America's postplanes response points to the importance of complexity of understanding and capacity for critical thought that the doctrine seeks to cultivate in an empowered citizenry. Indeed, seeking to situate terrorism in its proper context not only demonstrates the ways in which resilience overlaps and intersects with a great deal of contemporary democratic theory – demanding and seeking to cultivate a complexity of perspective or *ethos* appropriate to democratic life and politics – it also suggests the ways in which resilience is a perspective that democratic theorists might wish to embrace even in the *absence* of perceived threats.[39] The plausibility of this suggestion crucially depends, however, on how the doctrine is understood. While some might dismiss the posited beneficial relationship between democracy and resilience as – at best, wishful thinking – it may be that those who would embrace the theory do

---

[35] Elaine Scarry, *Thinking in an Emergency* (New York: W. W. Norton & Company, 2009).

[36] Flynn, "Mobilizing American Society," 137.

[37] Flynn, "American the Resilient," 6.

[38] John Mueller and Mark G. Stewart, "The Terrorism Delusion. America's Overwrought Response to September 11," *International Security*, 37(1), 2012: 91.

[39] As Louise Richardson notes, "[w]e will never be able to prevent every attack. But we can control our reactions to those attacks. If we keep terrorist attacks in perspective and recognize that the strongest weapons in our arsenal against terrorism are precisely the hallmarks of democracy that we value, then we can indeed contain the terrorist threat." Richardson, *What Terrorists Want*, locations 235–237.

not go far enough in their formulations of it to capture all of its possible political benefits.

RESILIENCE: THE ROMANTIC AND THE
NOT QUITE TRAGIC

In *Resilient Life: The Art of Living Dangerously*, Brad Evans and Julian Reid set out a wide-ranging critique of resilience as a political, social, psychological, and economic doctrine. Although not focusing directly on the claim that resilience and democracy are or can be mutually reinforcing, much of what they write implicitly or explicitly rejects such arguments. At the heart of their critique is the suggestion that resilience is a doctrine that both expresses and sustains a neoliberal worldview.[40] The commitment to self-reliance that underpins much of the resilience literature is, they argue, a demand for "entrepreneurial practices of self and subjectivity" and an end to government intervention in the market. Resilient people, they write, "do not look to states or other entities to secure and improve their well-being because they have been disciplined into believing in the necessity to secure and improve it for themselves."[41] Indeed, they see the claim – expressed most strongly in the literature on posttraumatic growth – that disaster and/or catastrophe can be opportunities for personal and/or societal development as a stalking horse for neoliberal commitments to individual responsibility and the rejection of public welfare.[42] Their argument that resilience favors the economically powerful at the expense of the poor, especially those populations most vulnerable to certain kinds of catastrophe – such as, for example, the residents of New Orleans's Lower Ninth Ward during Hurricane Katrina[43] – not only suggests that the doctrine makes a mockery of democracy's commitment

[40] They take their definition from David Harvey, who calls it a "theory of political economic practices proposing that human well-being can best be advanced by the maximization of entrepreneurial freedoms within an institutional framework characterized by private property rights, individual liberty, unencumbered markets, and free trade." Evans and Reid, *Resilient Life*, location 1689–1692. See David Harvey, "Neoliberalism as Creative Destruction," *The Annals of the American Academy of Political and Social Science*, 610, 2007: 22–44.

[41] Evans and Reid, *Resilient Life*, location 1720–1723.

[42] Ibid., location 1767–1772.

[43] For a discussion of the connection between neoliberalism, resilience, and mourning, see Simon Stow, "From Upper Canal to Lower Manhattan: Memorialization and the Politics of Loss," *Perspectives on Politics*, 10(3), 2012: 684–698. See also Simon Stow, "Do You Know What It Means, to Miss New Orleans? George W. Bush, the Jazz Funeral, and the Politics of Memory," *Theory & Event*, 11(1) 2008.

to equality, it also points to the ways in which resilience might be a way of segregating society's most vulnerable populations from a meaningful political existence.[44] It is, they argue, a set of policy prescriptions that seek to contain the threat that the poor might pose to the rich.[45] This critique is, moreover, underpinned by a much deeper set of concerns about resilience that are, in equal measure, existential and romantic, concerns that directly challenge claims that resilience might be a source of meaningful democratic politics, human sustenance, and/or individual flourishing.

Resilience, Evans and Reid argue, expresses a nihilistic conception of life that "encourages the subject to accept a will to nothingness" and "turns political ambitions into a neutralizing embrace."[46] By denying the possibility of security, they suggest, resilience also denies the possibility of political agency, teaching citizens "to live in a terrifying yet normal state of affairs that suspends us in petrified awe."[47] Thus, they argue, the

resilient subject is not a political subject who on its own terms conceives of changing the world, its structure and conditions of possibility. The resilient subject is required to accept the dangerousness of the world it lives in as a condition for partaking of that world and accept the necessity of the injunction to change itself in correspondence with threats now presupposed as endemic and unavoidable.[48]

In response to arguments such as Flynn's that reject the notion that a population might be fully insulated against the catastrophic, Evans and Reid observe, "[w]hen policy-makers engage in the discourse of resilience, they do so in terms which aim explicitly at preventing humans from conceiving of danger as a phenomenon from which they might seek freedom and even, in contrast, as that to which they must now expose themselves."[49] It is an understanding that, they suggest, is not only antipolitical but also antihumanist. Indeed, they seek to distinguish themselves from resilience's proponents by articulating a positive – and decidedly romantic – vision of human existence that, they argue, has been suppressed by the recent emergence of resilience in contemporary thought and politics.

Arguing for a "different aesthetic and sensual relationship" to existence than that offered by resilience, Evans and Reid seek to put "political meaning back into the world, such that our relations do not dismiss

---

[44] "There is," they note, "no resilience asked of those who can afford to take flight." Evans and Reid, *Resilient Life*, location 1903.

[45] Ibid., location 756–759.

[46] Ibid., location 847–850.

[47] Ibid., location 268–271; location 500.

[48] Ibid., location 1042–1043.

[49] Ibid., location 1308–1309.

the sense of wonder of experience one enjoys in those poetic moments with fellow humans and the earth which cannot be reduced to the techno-scientific conceit of biopolitical rule." This, they argue, "has everything to do with a willingness to challenge indifferences to the political with more affirmative expressions that demand replacing the vulnerability of catastrophic rule with a poetic confidence in the creation of worlds to come."[50] Although they declare that "all questions about the future are idiotic,"[51] they nevertheless embrace a Whitmanesque concern with democratic futurity, rejecting utopias that, they believe, inevitably descend into totalitarianism in favor of a commitment to a human capacity to shape the future in ways that currently escape resilience's constrained imaginary of mere survivability.[52] As such, they situate themselves in opposition to what they perceive to be the absence of the poetic from contemporary liberalism.[53] While they accept that "it would be ridiculous to dismiss outright the Greek origins of theater as we seek to find alternative intellectual resources,"[54] they nevertheless dismiss as disenabling any worldview predicated on an understanding of tragedy as a part of the human condition.[55] Indeed, they also reject – as a cramping of human existence – the sort of "coping strategies" embodied in an understanding of tragedy as response.[56] Ultimately, they suggest, attempts such as Judith Butler's to employ tragedy and/or mourning for political ends are futile and counterproductive. Power, they argue, does not "feel threatened by those who lament."[57]

[50] Ibid., location 2512–2513. See also locations 2886; 3517; and 3969–3974.
[51] Ibid., location 3026.
[52] This would certainly seem to be the implication of their observation that it "would be wrong to think that we can distinguish between the real and the imaginary" and their call for "a more poetic subjectivity" in democratic life and politics." Ibid., location 3954–3960; and ibid., location 4104.
[53] This is, they argue, an understanding so pervasive that it ensnares even those – such as Judith Butler – who think they are fighting against it. "Whatever we think," they write, "of the veracity of Butler's theory of vulnerability as predicate of life and precondition for subjectivity, it is necessary to note the degree to which this way of thinking about subjectivity is contemporaneous not with an incipient new leftism, but with the dominant episteme and regime of power relations that the Left today has to combat. The ontology of the social underlying Butler's account of vulnerability is deeply liberal." Evans and Reid, *Resilient Life*, location 2298–2304.
[54] Ibid., location 3274–3275. See also their discussion of Sophocles, location 434–441.
[55] See, for example, ibid., location 642–644; and 3065–3068.
[56] Ibid., location 2104.
[57] Ibid., location 3929. Indeed, their assertion that tragedy is something that might be overcome and their call for a political subject "empowered by its hubristic belief in an ability to secure itself from those elements of the world it encounters as hostile" further emphasizes the romanticism of their worldview. Location 2405; 1063. My emphasis.

Although he does not directly address the romanticism of Evans and Reid's critique, David Chandler's response to their work and the elucidation of the broader contours of his argument not only suggest the many ways in which "mere survivability" arguments are often misplaced, they also point to a richness of a perspective that promises more for democratic politics than that only hinted at by the resilience-as-security literature. In contrast to the narrow understanding of resilience set out by Evans and Reid – as little more than a discipline of governance committed to "bouncebackability," neoliberalism, and a constrained democratic imaginary – Chandler offers a capacious account of the doctrine that he calls "resilience-thinking."[58] Labeling his approach "political-ethical," he asserts that resilience is "less a final goal than a mode of thinking and acting in the world."[59] At the heart of this understanding is a rejection of what Chandler calls "a strong subject/object divide." According to "classical" understandings of resilience focusing "on the subject's internal capacity to withstand pressures or stresses which were understood to be externally generated," Chandler offers a "postclassical" or "postliberal" account of the doctrine focused on "resilience through adaptation."[60] On this account, "the subject/object divide is overcome through understanding resilience as an interactive process of relational adaptation. The subject does not survive through its own 'inner' resources; the subject survives and thrives on the basis of its ability to adapt or dynamically relate to its sociological environment."[61] It is an understanding situated somewhere between the claim that human beings can control their fate – the worldview underpinning the "never again" – and the idea, articulated by Evans and Reid, that resilience is about passive survival or mere coping. On this account, writes Chandler, resilience is "an emergent and adaptive process of subject/object interrelations" situated between hubris and resignation.[62] It is here that his work overlaps and intersects with that of William Connolly and other contemporary theorists of democratic agonism.

"Connolly," notes Chandler, "has increasingly articulated the importance of the event in terms of revealing the process of emergent causality, not so much for revealing the public, but in terms of enabling a self-reflexive

---

[58] Chandler, *Resilience*, location 198. Although he does not explicitly align himself with this view, Chandler would seem to be an advocate of the position that "resilience is problematic when used by hegemonic power but that understandings of adaptive complexity can be useful tools of oppositional critique," location 1316.

[59] Ibid., location 443, 413.

[60] Ibid., location 256–264, 272–274.

[61] Ibid., location 275–277.

[62] Ibid., location 279–280. On hubris, see location 803–805, 899–903.

ethic that can act as a guide to a political ethos fitting for engagement with a world of complexity."[63] Although Chandler does not employ the term, much of his argument corresponds to Connolly's concern with "critical responsiveness," an openness to the claims of others that involves a willingness to work on the self.[64] For Connolly, this is a claim about how citizens might interact with those with whom they disagree and one that is predicated on an understanding of the world as a *becoming*: an always-emergent, ongoing entity that is subject to transformation and change.[65] Connolly's claim that "[c]ritical responsiveness is a cardinal virtue of multidimensional pluralism" is thus as central to his political worldview as it is to his understanding of causality, as crucial to his understanding of action as it is to his theory of moral and political responsibility.[66] As such, when Chandler notes that whereas "in classical understandings of resilience security could be strengthened through overcoming vulnerabilities and adaptation, for post-classical understandings, these adaptations would merely produce new and unforeseen consequences: new vulnerabilities. Attempts to achieve security would thereby be understood to be the source of new (and unexpected insecurities),"[67] he captures the way in which both resilience and democracy might be understood as always-ongoing projects concerned with what he calls "governance" in a world of complexity.

Chandler, then, rejects the claim that resilience is necessarily predicated on and generative of a constrained democratic imaginary, not least because Connolly's work suggests that resilience demands continual work on a self whose very becoming is a political act.[68] In a passage cited by Chandler, Connolly writes,

A world of becoming is replete with multiple forces that sometimes intersect to throw something new into the world. So strategic events (including relatively extended periods) periodically arrive when it is pertinent to dwell in an exploratory way in the gap between the disturbance of an emerging situation and those prior investments of habit, passion, faith, identity, progress, and political

[63] Ibid., location 3718–3720.
[64] William J. Connolly, *Pluralism* (Minneapolis: University of Minnesota Press, 2005), 126.
[65] William Connolly, *A World of Becoming* (Durham, NC: Duke University Press, 2011).
[66] William Connolly, *Why I Am Not a Secularist* (Minneapolis: University of Minnesota Press, 1999), 94.
[67] Chandler, *Resilience*, location 369–371. In this, Chandler echoes Honig, who writes, "A politics of becoming...recognizes that each new inclusion comes with disturbance and possibly transformation for those people and rights that are already in, as well as for the antecedent rules that aspire to govern or subsume all new cases and events." *Emergency Politics*, 49.
[68] "Work on the self is the only route to changing the world." Chandler, *Resilience*, location 4686.

priority you bring to it. In the Greek tradition, those who specialized in similar activities were called seers; in religions of the Book they are often called mystics or prophets.[69]

Chandler understands such creativity as an ongoing process situated between past and future, one in which the former is not fully determinative and the latter not entirely open. For this reason, claims about the constrained imaginary of resilience thinking are, perhaps, only trivially true: all imaginaries are necessarily constrained by the circumstances of their construction.[70] Poetry is, as Wallace Stevens famously observed, the imagination pushing back against reality. Greek theater permitted its audience to push back against the tragedy of condition that necessitated it, creating a coping strategy that enabled them to survive, live, and even flourish in the face of the inevitable frustrations and failures of human existence. It is unsurprising, then, that there appear to be considerable parallels between Chandler's account of resilience and tragedy understood as a response to a tragic condition.

Inadvertently echoing Aeschylus's dictum that wisdom comes through suffering, Chandler notes, "failure is a central tenant of resilience-thinking. Using failure productively – that is, seeing failing as an opportunity for growth rather than a final judgment."[71] He likewise pays considerable attention to the Sophoclean theme of blindness and unintended consequences.[72] It is precisely because human beings live in a world of complexity in which actions reverberate in unexpected ways that, Chandler argues, "life is always in excess of power's attempts to control it."[73] Indeed, he seems to capture something of the tragic circumstances of human existence when he writes, "The world of resilience-thinking and complexity is more like a 'condition' which we find ourselves in, than

---

[69] William Connolly, *The Fragility of Things: Self-Organizing Processes, Neoliberal Fantasies, and Democratic Activism* (Durham, NC: Duke University Press, 2013), 134.

[70] To make their argument compelling, Evans and Reid need to show why a commitment to resilience constrains the democratic imaginary *more* than any other possible approach. That they do not is, perhaps, a product of and further evidence for their romantic commitment to self-creation, one that is entirely at odds with any worldview that recognizes the inevitability of constraints on human activity.

[71] Chandler, *Resilience*, location 197–199. "It would appear," Chandler further notes, "that in a world where constituted power is necessarily doomed to fail, all we can do is 'learn to fail better': learn to fail through not attempting anything too ambitious and learn to fail through being continually self-reflective about the intended and unexpected consequences of any policy interventions," location 1341–1343.

[72] Chandler, *Resilience*, location 590.

[73] "Human actors are not," he writes, "aware of the end consequences of the myriad interactions they are involved in every day." Ibid., location 1603.

something produced through political contestation or instrumentality."[74] In a further parallel to tragic understandings of politics, Chandler also conceives of resilience-thinking as an *ethos*. In a world in which there is not always a clear connection between action and outcome, the concept of moral and political responsibility – and, indeed, any understanding of causality – becomes considerably more complex than that allowed by the classical understandings to which Chandler is opposed. A resilience ethic, he notes, "works on the basis of indirect assumptions of responsibility, not on the basis of legal, moral or political responsibility, but on the basis of our relational embeddedness: the understanding of indirect side-effects caused by our associational connectivity in a complex and globalized world."[75] Indeed, not least among Chandler's affinities with the tragic is his belief that "liberal modernist attempts to understand, to shape, to direct and to transform the world for human ends are hubristic and dangerous."[76]

The limits of Chandler's commitment to the tragic are, however, suggested by the tension between his rejection of liberal modernist notions of control and his commitment to the concept of "governance." For, even as he seeks to reject the former, he seems to reintroduce it with the latter. At the heart of this tension is Chandler's decidedly modernist commitment to method. It is a method imbued with postmodernist concerns about complexity, self-reflexivity, and the local, but a method all the same.[77] "Resilience-thinking," he writes, "... argues that governments can

---

[74] Ibid., location 1278–1281.

[75] Ibid., location 2978–2980. It is for this reason, he argues, that agents and states might be thought to bear responsibility for the unintended consequences of their actions. Ibid., location 3104.

[76] Ibid., location 1299–1302. See also location 416, 592, 639, 948, 951, 1196, 1203, 1592, and 1599. Indeed, it might be noted that Chandler repeatedly employs the term *hubris* – variations of it appear at least thirty times in his text – a concept that is drawn from and intimately related to the tragic. When the word "tragedy" does appear in his book, it does so only colloquially, as is also the case for "tragic." He employs, for example, the word "tragedies" to refer to what he calls "extreme events" such as Typhoon Haiyan that hit the Philippines in 2013. Ibid., location 3649, 3766, 3758. Likewise, he suggests, complex life is "beyond the planning, control or comprehension of any individual, no matter how clever they are or what position of power they might occupy." Ibid., 592–593.

[77] Certainly, Chandler's claim "that resilience-thinking can be understood as the first post-liberal or post-modern episteme: the first coherent, positive, alternative to modernist frameworks on the subject and the world" would seem to be called into question by his intermittent reliance on a representationalist theory of truth, his inconsistency about the ontological status of "reality," and the frequent references in his work to an appearance/reality distinction. Ibid., 1160–162. See also Ibid. 1288; 1565–1567; 909; 811, 901, 924, 1202, and 1212; 3489–3497.

intervene to harness this power [life] if they appreciate that this cannot be done through directives and impositions. Complex life is thus transformed from being a limit to governance to being a resource that enables the extension of governance into new realms of 'real' complex life."[78] The problem here is that although Chandler repeatedly talks about "governing" and "governance," he never fully fleshes out his understanding of these terms, and what he does write seems to be underpinned by an aspiration to the sort of control that he would otherwise reject. Thus, he suggests, the "ontology of complexity transforms a neoliberal critique of the rationalist promise of neoliberalism into a positive project of *managing* change."[79] Tellingly here, it is the *change*, not the *self*, that is managed. The latter would suggest something close to the "coping strategy" of tragedy, the former some version of modernist control. Likewise, he suggests, resilience-thinking "provides a *solution* to the problem of governance" and argues that adaptive life of the sort he describes might serve as "the *solution* to complexity" in ways that point to a modernist commitment to overcoming.[80] There seems to be a similar impetus at work in his turn to self-reflexivity and his focus on the local as a resource for management or control, one that neither commitment could reliably deliver.[81] There is, for example, no guarantee that embracing self-reflexivity will actually produce it, nor even that its insight could generate the degree of control over the world that Chandler seems to believe is possible: we can be just as blind about ourselves as we are about others.[82] Similarly, while the insights offered by the local and the marginal may indeed serve as a counterbalance to the more universalized understandings of the world at the heart of modernism, as with the self-reflexive, it is not clear that they

---

[78] Ibid., location 843–845.

[79] Ibid., 1228–1229. My emphasis.

[80] Ibid., 1207, 942. My emphasis.

[81] "Life," writes Chandler, "is the means and ends of governance with practice-based policy-making, self-reflexivity, feedback-loops, reflexive law-making and the inculcation of community capacities and resilience." Ibid., 1591–1592. Similarly, he suggests, the "more surprising the event, the more self-reflexivity is necessary as a response and the more 'reality' is understood to have emerged into view." Ibid., 3501–3502. He suggests, furthermore, that what "distinguishes the critical scholar from the uncritical one is...not a matter of conceptual acumen but an ethos of self-reflexivity." Ibid., 5307–5308.

[82] Certainly this would seem to be the implication of Mark Button's work on second-order blindness: our inability to see our own blindness about our own lack of vision. Mark Button, "Accounting for Blind Spots: From Oedipus to Democratic Epistemology," *Political Theory*, 39(6), 2011: 695–723. This is, of course, further evidence of the ways in which Chandler's work is underpinned by a remarkable – and distinctly modernist – optimism, in this instance, about the transparency of the self.

will do the work that Chandler requires of them. Local views are just as likely to be misleading as universal ones, susceptible to a failure to see the broader contours of an issue in just the same way, perhaps, that top-down understandings can miss the local.

The concerns raised by Chandler's account of resilience-thinking are, however, not only methodological, they are also political. For just as he reinscribes the modernist commitment to control back into his theory, he also reinscribes the commitment to security. A strategy that promises control – albeit control achieved in a very different way – may be just as susceptible to the anger generated by its possible failure as the commitment to the "never again." Chandler's understanding of resilience may, then, be ultimately self-defeating: anger – and/or *mênis* – is not, perhaps, the best route to plasticity or "bouncebackability." It is only by giving up the commitment to control that a polity might develop the resilience necessary to "going on together" in the face of the catastrophic.[83] Such is the promise of the tragic. In *Antigone*, as Simon Goldhill notes, it is precisely those characters who eschew such control and "try to muddle along in a more complex and less extremely colored world" who survive the events of the play.[84] Indeed, turning to the tragic as a resource for resilience not only permits the doctrine to embrace the strengths of Chandler's account – its complex worldview, its cultivation of an *ethos*, its commitment to a care of the self, and its value to democratic thought and practice – while jettisoning his tortured relationship with modernism, it also permits a more effective response to the claims that resilience is a politically impotent, antihumanist doctrine of a mere survivability. Understanding Thucydides' *History* as a form of tragic mourning for Athens offers precisely these possibilities.

NO SECURITY

Writing in 1872, having identified three Socratic maxims connecting virtue to knowledge, Friedrich Nietzsche declared, "In these three basic forms of optimism lies the death of tragedy."[85] In this, writes Walter Kaufmann, Nietzsche rejected the view that if "men would only use

---

[83] Seem Josiah Ober, *Athenian Legacies: Essays on the Politics of Going on Together* (Princeton, NJ: Princeton University Press, 2007).

[84] Simon Goldhill, *Sophocles and the Language of Tragedy* (Oxford: Oxford University Press, 2012), 54.

[85] Friedrich Nietzsche, *The Birth of Tragedy and The Case of Wagner* translated by Walter Kaufmann (New York: Vintage Books, 1967), Kindle Edition, location 1449.

their reason properly ... there would be no need for tragedies."[86] It is the worldview that resilience would reject: the notion that knowledge, be it data, metadata, human intelligence, airport screenings, racial profiling, drone flights, phone taps, battlefield sweeps, e-mail hacks, enhanced interrogation, rendition, and systematic torture might provide the information necessary to making the aspirational "never again" a national security reality. As has been suggested, however, even the most sophisticated of the current formulations of resilience continues to be predicated on a modernist commitment to control, reinscribing on it the modernist optimism that knowledge – albeit differently achieved – might permit those who embrace the doctrine to sustain themselves in the face of the catastrophic. Tragedy as a worldview, by contrast, recognizes that knowledge, no matter how perfect, can never achieve the control that even Chandler's formulation of resilience seeks. It is the lesson that Sophocles' *Oedipus the King*, among other plays, teaches its audience.

The notion that a tragic worldview might be a way of responding to, coping with, and even flourishing in the face of crisis is not, however, an uncontroversial one. Critics such as C. Wright Mills have argued – like Evans and Reid – that tragedy is "a political blind alley," one that negates agency and rejects responsibility.[87] Pointing to the ways in which Thucydides' *History* serves as a tragic form of mourning for Athens imbued with an equally tragic form of hope for the city's future suggests, nevertheless, that these claims are misplaced. Such a reading shows how his text might offer a democratic pedagogy capable of cultivating an ethos, akin to that identified by David Chandler, conducive to political agency and resilience in the face of loss. That it does so by addressing its readers both as individuals *and* as members of a collective further suggests the ways in which Thucydides offers his readers a model of democratically productive tragic mourning that is especially appropriate for a contemporary age marked by political atomism and social estrangement.

Evidence for the claim that the *History* might be understood as a form of mourning for Athens is to be found in the style, structure, and language of the text as well as in its reliance on the tropes of the funeral oration that the work itself depicts. Given the centrality of the funeral oration to Greek life and politics, it is perhaps unsurprising that a number of scholars have noted what Nicole Loraux called "the

---

[86] Walter Kaufmann, *Tragedy and Philosophy* (Princeton, NJ: Princeton University Press, 1968), 165.
[87] For an excellent discussion of this point, see Robert C. Pirro, *The Politics of Tragedy and Democratic Citizenship* (New York: Continuum Books, 2011), 71.

homological relationship ... between the *epitaphios* and the work as a whole." She suggests, furthermore, that "there is not a single word of Pericles that does not find its echo in Thucydides' narrative."[88] Indeed, she continues, the oration serves a double function in the text, both as "a keystone" and as part of "the structure of the work."[89] Likewise, Henry Immerwahr argues that the funeral oration is, "in many ways, analogous to the work itself," noting the many "parallels between the Oration and the work ... such as the refusal to dwell on the past instead of the present."[90] Thucydides was, of course, not alone in demonstrating the influence of the political eulogy on Greek thinkers – both Plato and Aristophanes were forced to wrestle with it in different ways[91] – but it is important to note that, in embracing the genre, Thucydides was not simply reflecting a more general trend. His appropriation of the oration was calculated and deliberate. "The first oddity about the funeral oration contained in book 2," observes Jacqueline de Romily, "is its very presence. *A priori* such a speech had no reason to feature in a history of the war."[92] Its appearance, she suggests, was a conscious narrative and stylistic choice on the part of the author, one that sought to draw on its style, structure, and language. Indeed, that the text in which the oration both appeared and helped to structure should embody so many of the tropes of the genre, including *epainesis*, *parainesis*, and the suggestion that only Athens, the imperial power, could cause its own downfall suggests why many have chosen to categorize Thucydides' work as a form of mourning for the fallen city, as "a *lament* for the eclipse of reasoned moderation in Greek life generally, and in Athenian conduct in particular."[93]

The claim that the *History* is a form of mourning for Athens is, furthermore, bolstered by its embrace of tragedy, itself a genre of loss. Most obviously, perhaps, notes MacLeod, there is the classical theme of reversal. Just as Oedipus goes from being the "best of men" to the "most wretched," Athens starts the war as the most powerful nation in the Greek world and ends it in humiliation, its much-vaunted fleet and democracy in

---

[88] Nicole Loraux, *The Invention of Athens: The Funeral Oration in the Classical City* translated by Alan Sheridan (New York: Zone Books, 2006), 362.

[89] Ibid.

[90] Henry R. Immerwahr, "*Ergon*: History as Monument in Herodotus and Thucydides," *American Journal of Philology*, 81(3), 1960: 285.

[91] Ibid., 332.

[92] Ibid., 512, *n.*82.

[93] David Bedford and Thomas Workman, "The Tragic Reading of Thucydidean Tragedy," *Review of International Studies*, 27, 2001: 52. My emphasis.

ruins.[94] Indeed, embracing the idea that the funeral oration embodied the Athenian self-image at the height of its powers, Stephen Halliwell argues "that the loss (or the unsustainability) of Periclean vision and values was itself, for Thucydides, the city's real tragedy."[95] Likewise, James Boyd White identifies Athenian hubris – understood as excess – as the central theme of the *History*, which, he writes, "has the form and meaning of a tragic drama."[96] That the depiction of such hubris also served as a warning to its readers in the manner of theatrical tragedy is further suggested by the questioning ambivalence at the heart of the text. Loraux notes, for example, that even as the *History* embraces the structure, forms, and language of the funeral oration, it also distances itself from the narcissism of the same, noting, however, that to "distance oneself from something is not, however, to condemn it to oblivion, and the eulogy remains on the horizon of the history."[97] A similar tension exists, she suggests, between the worldviews offered by the oration and that offered by tragedy, indicating, perhaps, the complexity of vision that the latter brought to the worldview of Thucydides' audience, mimicking the Dionysia by simultaneously embracing and rejecting the oration's values, structure, and language.[98] Thus, writes White, the *History* is "ineluctably ambivalent," noting that "irresolution on matters of greatest importance is a structural characteristic of the text as a whole. Again and again it suggests a question, or forces it on the reader, and then offers grounds for conflicting responses."[99] As with Greek tragedy, the text seeks to problematize the values it depicts and the context in which they are depicted, demanding not resolution but rather "an attempt to encompass and make sense of" such ambiguity.[100] Like tragedy, then, the *History* cultivates questioning in its style, structure, and effect.

To claim that Thucydides' text is tragic in both outlook and structure does not, of course, require that Thucydides saw himself as a tragic poet. Certainly, the genre was so pervasive in Greek culture that it is unsurprising that he – among others – should have borrowed from it.

[94] C. MacLeod, "Thucydides and Tragedy" in *Collected Essays* (Oxford: Oxford University Press, 1983), 141–143.
[95] Stephen Halliwell, "Thucydides, Pericles, and Tragedy," *Dioniso*, 1(1), 2002: 77.
[96] James Boyd White, *When Words Lose Their Meaning: Constitutions and Reconstitutions of Language, Character, and Community* (Chicago: University of Chicago Press, 1984), 86–87.
[97] Loraux, *Invention of Athens*, 365–366.
[98] Ibid., 332.
[99] White, *When Words Lose Their Meaning*, 85, 86.
[100] Halliwell, "Thucydides, Pericles, Tragedy," 67.

As Halliwell observes, it is "uncontroversial ... that various ideas and patterns of thought closely associated with tragedy could have been an important background influence ... on any Athenian thinker of this period."[101] MacLeod makes a similar point, noting that as an Athenian, Thucydides "must have absorbed it by attending the Great Dionysia." He further suggests, however, that "Herodotus, another tragic historian, is a much more direct influence ... [on] ... Thucydides' work in its thought, architecture and its phrasing."[102] Regardless of the origin of this influence, the sheer number of scholars drawing parallels between the *History* and Greek tragedy suggests that seeing Thucydides' work as embodying a tragic worldview is not only appropriate, it is unavoidable. Just as MacLeod connects the *History* to Sophocles' *Oedipus*, to Euripides' *Hecuba*, Peter Euben's argument that "Thucydides can and should be read in terms of Greek tragedy" draws similar parallels between the *History* and Aeschylean drama.[103]

Understood as a tragic form of mourning for Athens, then, the *History* offers a worldview that eschews the kinds of control over the world that Evans and Reid, and indeed, in a different way, David Chandler, appear to seek. All three would seem to reject the tragic – either implicitly or explicitly – because of its apparent rejection of political agency, and, in the case of Evans and Reid, because of its alleged inability to generate a meaningful human existence beyond mere survivability. Reading the *History* through its commitment to hope would, nevertheless, appear to suggest that such criticism is misplaced.

HOPE, AGENCY, AND HUMAN FLOURISHING

The myriad of similarities between the *History* and tragedy are not exhausted by its embodiment of a particular worldview or by their similar structure and style. For even as the *History* as a mode of mourning for Athens both depicts and embodies a tragic worldview, it was, like theatrical tragedy, offered as a response to those same condition. Understood in this way, Thucydides' work is not a dispassionate recounting of events in the manner of a contemporary history concerned

---

[101] Ibid., 64.
[102] MacLeod, "Thucydides and Tragedy," Ultimately, however, MacLeod concludes that Homer was the greatest tragic influence on Athenian artists and citizens. 157, 158.
[103] J. Peter Euben, "The Tragedy of Tragedy," *International Relations*, 21(1), 2007: 21. See also J. Peter Euben, *The Tragedy of Political Theory: The Road Not Taken* (Princeton, NJ: Princeton University Press, 1990), 173.

with who, what, why, where, and when but rather a compelling form of political theory concerned with political resilience and reconstitution in the face of loss. "It will," as he famously wrote in the introduction to the *History*,

be enough for me ... if these words of mine are judged useful by those who want to understand clearly the events which happened in the past and which (human nature being what it is) will, at some time or other and in much the same ways, be repeated in the future. My work is not a piece of writing designed to meet the taste of an immediate public, but was done to last forever.[104]

As such, the *History* is, White suggests, "a way of acting in the world," even as it recognizes not only the impossibility of control over that world but also the dangers of even aspiring to it.[105] Thus, when the historian, acknowledging the inevitability of crisis, says that his goal in describing the symptoms of the plague in Athens is to allow it "to be recognized, if it should ever break out again,"[106] he captures the way in which his work is both a description of the world and a resource for action within it. It is, perhaps, for this reason that Euben identifies not only "Thucydides, the intellectual," but also "Thucydides, the activist."[107]

The claim that Thucydides' work might serve as both an analytical resource and a springboard for political action is, of course, precisely the sort of possibility that critics of the tragic worldview and, indeed, of certain forms of resilience, deny. It is the perceived impossibility of agency that leads Evans and Reid, among others, to suggest that tragedy and/or resilience is a doctrine of mere survivability, one that constrains human existence and stifles creativity, artistic or political. Their suggestion that those in power "do not fear those who lament" would, nevertheless, seem to be misplaced. Indeed, Joe Hill's famous dictum – "don't mourn, organize!" – would appear to be somewhat narrowly conceived. In the first instance, the political concerns of tragedy might be considerably broader than that of a particular power struggle within a polity, concerned, rather, with the ongoing existence of that polity. In the second, there have been many political movements driven or sparked by loss, not least among which, it has been noted, was the American civil rights struggle and, more recently, Black Lives Matter.

[104] Thucydides, *History*, 48.
[105] White, *When Words Lose Their Meaning*, 4.
[106] Ibid., 152. The "naturalness" of the disastrous consequences of the plague might, however, be qualified by the recognition that Pericles' policy of bringing those from the surrounding countryside into the city exacerbated its impact on the Athenians.
[107] Euben, *The Tragedy of Political Theory*, 199.

Claims about the lack of agency in the tragic are, then, mistaken, for they misunderstand the centrality of hope to its worldview. Hope is, it might be argued, tragedy's creativity. The importance and role of hope in political agency is suggested by Aeschylus' *Prometheus Bound*. For although his first gift to mankind is less well remembered than his second, Aeschylus recalls that the Titan initially granted humanity ignorance of their own deaths by sewing in them blind hopes about the future.[108] It was, perhaps, an even greater gift than fire, permitting humans to act in the world even though they recognized that their desired goals might never actually come into being. As such, hope could serve as an impetus for action even in the face of possible defeat. Befitting the tragic worldview, however, the hope implicit within it also brings pain with its promise. For hope is, as Nietzsche observed, "the greatest of evils for it lengthens the ordeal of man."[109] In this, hope is qualitatively different from optimism, a decidedly Christian worldview that holds that expected desires – such as the return of Christ – will inevitably occur.[110] Hope – or at least tragic hope – implies no expectation that the thing desired will necessarily come into being or that if it does occur, that the agent will be around to bear witness.[111] In this, such hope embodies an understanding of tragedy as condition, a world in which good intentions are necessarily thwarted, distorted, or worse. It is, nevertheless, Aeschylus suggests, precisely the lack of awareness about how one's actions will turn out that makes such action possible. Drawing on a reading of *Prometheus Bound*, Wendy O'Brien writes,

That these hopes may never come to fruition, that the desires that they entail may never be fulfilled is irrelevant to the exercise of hope. Those who bear witness to hell on earth, those who offer up their testimony and seek to relieve suffering alone do not hope because they believe their hopes will be realized. They hope because they know they will not. And they are unwilling to be satisfied with this. They hope because they are unwilling to accept the inevitability of hopelessness. They reject the hold the past seems to have over the future, not despite all the evidence to the contrary but in light of it. And they pass judgment on the present. Not only do they believe that things can be different, they make the stronger,

---

[108] Simon Critchley, "Abandon (Nearly) All Hope," *The New York Times*, April 19, 2014. opinionator.blogs.nytimes.com/2014/04/19/abandon-nearly-all-hope/?_r=1. Accessed Dec. 15, 2014.

[109] Friedrich Nietzsche, *Human All Too Human: A Book for Free Spirits* translated by Alexander Harvey (Chicago: Charles H. Kerr & Company, 1915), 71.

[110] See, for example, Matthew Avery Sutton, *American Apocalypse: A History of Modern Evangelicalism* (Cambridge, MA: Harvard Belknap Press, 2014).

[111] As was suggested by Martin Luther King in his speech at Mason Temple on the eve of his assassination.

normative claim that things should be different. They will not settle with the way things are. They require something better. And until it can be found, until things can start anew, they will wait. They will hope.[112]

"The purpose of hope is," she writes, "realized in their actions even if their desires are not actualized."[113] Thus, O'Brien suggests, action emerges from an ethos of the sort championed, in different ways, by Chandler, Connolly, and Honig, an ethos diametrically opposed to the sort of optimism that Schopenhauer declared to be "not only a false but pernicious doctrine."[114] Indeed, it is not just that such hope embodies a call to action – "a tragic perspective," writes Honig, "no less than the ancient Greek tragedies themselves, can be seen ... to issue a call to action, responsibility and the creative communalities of festival and ritual – not an excuse to withdraw from them"[115] – but it also imbues the population with a resilience that is unavailable to the optimistic account of human agency that underpins even David Chandler's account of the doctrine. Hope, unlike optimism, recognizes the inevitability of failure and, as such, cultivates resilience rather than a commitment to control. Thucydides' *History*, understood as a form of mourning for Athens imbued with a tragic hope, offers a similar account of agency and creativity in the face of inevitable crises, one that suggests the resilience it seeks to cultivate offers considerably more to its readers than mere survivability.

At first blush, the claim that Thucydides' *History* is imbued with a hope that cultivates resilience and political agency in the face of crisis and catastrophe may, nevertheless, seem counterintuitive if not flat-out wrong. Certainly a number of scholars have pointed to the ways in which hope appears to be a pernicious force in the text, encouraging Athens – and others – to take unwarranted risks. Indeed, many have seen the apparent recklessness that hope engenders as the source of the city's hubris and

---

[112] Wendy O'Brien, "Exercise of Hope" in Andrea M. Stephenson and Janette McDonald, eds., *The Resilience of Hope* (New York: Rodopi, 2010), 34. In this, O'Brien echoes the notion of hope as "a regulative ideal toward which we aspire but which ultimately defies historical fulfillment." Eddie Glaude Jr., *Exodus! Religion, Race, and Nation in Early Nineteenth-Century America* (Chicago: University of Chicago Press, 2000), 112.

[113] O'Brien, "Exercise of Hope," 34.

[114] Joshua Dienstag, *Pessimism: Philosophy, Ethic, Spirit* (Princeton, NJ: Princeton University Press, 2006), 110.

[115] Honig, *Emergency Politics*, 11. Similarly, Mark Roche observes that it is "one-sided to assert, as many contemporary critics do, that tragedy offers us only destruction, uncertainty, and gloom, and that any hidden visions of greatness, harmony, or hope are an anathema to the tragic spirit. Tragedy is too multifaceted and complex for such an either-or reception." Mark Roche, "Introduction to Hegel's Theory of the Tragic," *PhaenEx*, 1(2), Fall 2006: 19.

downfall. In a discussion of the Mytilenian Debate – in which Diodotus
notes that in human affairs, "[h]ope and desire persist throughout and
cause the greatest calamities – one leading and the other following, one
conceiving the enterprise, and the other suggesting that it will be successful"[116] – H. P. Stahl points to the ways in which this theme will be repeated
throughout the text and argues that "irrational hope and ignorance" are
at the root of Athenian decline.[117] Nevertheless, this is, as Joel Schlosser
points out, but one of several forms of hope that Thucydides employs for
analytical and rhetorical purposes in the text. As might be expected of the
Greek worldview, moreover, it was not hope *per se* that was regarded as
problematic but rather the *excess* of it. Certainly this would appear to be
the lesson of the Sicilian expedition in which Athens' hope took the form
of an ultimately destructive overconfidence. As Schlosser notes, however,
although the expedition began with one kind of hope, it ultimately ended
in another. This second kind of hope was more akin to that embodied in
and cultivated by Greek tragedy and, it has been argued, certain forms of
public mourning.[118] It is the hope of agency and resilience against despair.

   In a compelling account of the *History*, Schlosser points to what he
calls "desperate hope, that is…hope as a bulwark against despair," that
which, he suggests, "contrasts…positively with the hopelessness that
comes from resignation."[119] Such hope is, he argues, as evident in Nicias'
response to the failure of the Sicilian expedition as it was in the Melians'
response to the Athenian threats against their city. It is a response that
promises the possibility of agency in the face of despair, albeit the agency
of those who find themselves embedded in humanity's tragic condition.
"Despair," writes Schlosser, "would mean giving up what appears as inevitable; the Melians, in contrast, assert hope as the only means of survival.
As was the case for Nicias, hope here describes an expression of human
longing against seemingly insurmountable odds that might otherwise
condemn the sufferer to resignation." Indeed, he continues, "hope finds a
place in the never-closed crevasses of possibility when despair (and with
it self-annihilation) appears to be the only alternative."[120] It is precisely
such hope that, Schlosser suggests, permits Athens to go on together *as*

[116] Thucydides, *History*, 220.
[117] H. P. Stahl, *Thucydides: Man's Place in History* (Swansea, UK: The Classical Press of
    Wales, 2003), 120–121, 183–184.
[118] Such as that later expressed by W.E.B. Du Bois in mourning his son.
[119] Joel Alden Schlosser, "'Hope, Danger's Comforter': Thucydides, Hope, Politics," *The
    Journal of Politics*, 71(1), 2013: 173.
[120] Ibid., 174.

Athens, a distinction that is particularly pertinent to the claim made by Evans and Reid, among others, that resilience is about mere survivability rather than individual or collective cultural flourishing.[121] In Aristotelian terms, Thucydides is committed not just to living but also to living well. Indeed, tragedy is precisely concerned with just such dualities in a way that nontragic versions of resilience are not.

Thus, while Evans and Reid might be right to claim that certain forms of resilience are devoid of artistic inspiration and a commitment to human flourishing, Greek theater as a form of tragedy as response suggests that their claims about the cultural poverty of a commitment to resilience are wildly overstated. Indeed, it was precisely this cultural form and the worldview it cultivated that permitted Athens to survive in the face of potential devastation. For when Thucydides expresses his admiration of Athens for its endurance of the disaster that was the Sicilian expedition, it is in terms that not only foreshadow later claims about resilience in the face of crisis or catastrophe but also for carrying on *as* Athens.[122] Tellingly, perhaps, a number of scholars invoke the language of "Athenian resilience" to describe the city's survival during the otherwise unmitigated disaster of the Peloponnesian War.[123] If this form of hope is indeed tragedy's creativity in the face of despair, then Schlosser's account of Thucydides' own hopes in writing the text not only provides a further example of that creativity – and of that of tragic mourning more broadly – it also suggests the ways in which Thucydidean mourning offers his readers a pedagogy of democratic resilience in the face of loss.

It is a testament to Thucydides' status as – what William Connolly calls – a seer or a prophet that his claim that his work "was done to last forever" has not been exhausted by the multiple attempts to recover it as

---

[121] In making this claim, Schlosser draws an important distinction between Thucydides' understanding of hope and the more recent account offered by Jonathan Lear about the actions of the Crow Chief Plenty Coups in the face of the cultural devastation of his tribe. Lear, notes Schlosser, "takes it as self-evident that continued survival, no matter the costs, beats annihilation," whereas "the *History* suggests that hope may depend on maintaining certain parts of life despite the threat to one's existence." Schlosser, " 'Hope, Danger's Comforter,' " 177. Jonathan Lear, *Radical Hope: Ethics in the Face of Cultural Devastation* (Cambridge, MA: Harvard University Press, 2006).

[122] And for its continued existence in the face of a long-drawn out war. See Immerwahr, "*Ergon*," 284–285.

[123] Christine Lee, "Thucydides in Wartime: Reflecting on Democracy and its Discontents," *Polis*, 31, 2014: 285; Josiah Ober, *Democracy and Knowledge: Innovation and Learning in Classical Athens* (Princeton, NJ: Princeton University Press, 2010), xiii; and Halliwell, "Thucydides, Pericles, and Tragedy," 73.

a response to crisis in the years since it was written.[124] Indeed, it may be that his text suggests a model for a tragic mode of democratic mourning that is particularly suited to the modern age, an age in which a commitment to individualism over the collective not only threatens the polity's capacity for dealing with loss – "[s]haring the traumatic experience is," writes Judith Herman, "a precondition for the restitution of a sense of a meaningful world"[125] – it also seems to undermine the possibility for action in concert that democratic politics requires. Thucydides, it might be argued, offers a textual – not a ritual – response to loss that cultivates agency and resilience in his readers both as individuals and as members of an imagined community of grief.

TEXTS, READERS, AND THE POSSIBILITY OF COLLECTIVE MOURNING

In the introduction to the *History*, notes Schlosser, Thucydides "clues in his readers…that hope in some form imbues the making and writing the text itself." It is, he continues, "a realistic hope informed both by hope's excesses and by the contingency and unpredictability of human affairs."[126] On this account, Thucydides writes his text as a tragic response to a tragic condition. It is a work imbued with the desire but not necessarily the expectation that by identifying patterns of human behavior that, he believes, will inevitably recur in the future, he might permit his readers to cope with the catastrophes that will accompany them. As with tragic theater, there is no expectation that the depiction of suffering will permit his audience to avoid such crises, simply that his text will seek to cultivate an *ethos* appropriate to coping with and potentially even flourishing in the face of disaster. His hope that his work might prove useful finds its agency in the text's many pedagogical devices. By demanding that his readers do more than simply pass their eyes over the text but rather engage with the hermeneutic demands of a difficult work filled with allusions, paradoxes,

---

[124] See, for example, Katherine Harloe and Neville Morley, eds., *Thucydides and the Modern World, Reception, Reinterpretation and Influence from the Renaissance to the Present* (Cambridge: Cambridge University Press, 2012).

[125] Herman, *Trauma and Recovery*, 70. See also Iraq veteran and National Book Award Winner Phil Klay's observation that "War is too strange to be processed alone." Alexandria Alter, "National Book Award Goes to Phil Klay for His Short Story Collection," *The New York Times*, November 19, 2014. www.nytimes.com/2014/11/20/books/national-book-award-goes-to-phil-klay-for-redeployment.html?_r=0. Accessed Dec. 17, 2014.

[126] Schlosser, "Hope, Danger's Comforter," 178.

oppositional juxtapositions, and mixed narrative forms, Thucydides sought to cultivate in his readers precisely those skills of critical reflection and thoughtful engagement whose very absence, he suggested, had led to Athens' downfall. Like Greek theater, his work exhibits and employs a certain form of dramatic irony, demanding a critical reflection from its readers of which the characters on his historical stage were incapable and for whom the consequences of this incapacity were catastrophic.

"[T]he *History*," writes James Morrison, "is an *interactive* work in which Thucydides invites the reader to juxtapose one argument with another, compare speech and narrative, and test maxim against particular episode. There is what we might call a *dialogic* quality to his presentation."[127] Thus, like tragedy, writes Peter Euben, "it shows us and engenders in us a process of reflection and (self-)discovery through a persistent (re-)interpretation of particular incidents and patterns of language."[128] As with tragedy, it is a text that is to be *experienced* rather than simply read. Just as, perhaps, the text seeks to engender a hope that it also depicts, the book offers its readers the opportunity to do precisely that which Athens itself tries to do, "to reconstitute the world in words and to make sense of it." An attempt, writes White, "that will always in some sense fail. That is the condition of life that this book makes real and upon which it insists."[129] Such failure is, however, potentially instructive and productive. Stripping away the illusion of control that generates the more pernicious forms of hope that Thucydides identifies – the same hope or optimism that underpins the hubris of the "never again" – in favor of a more qualified hope of coping with and pushing back against the tragic condition, the text seeks to cultivate precisely those skills that are required for democratic resilience in the face of the catastrophic. "Thucydides' writing," as MacLeod observes, "both teaches and stirs its readers."[130]

Such claims about the pedagogical value of Thucydides' text as a tragic form of mourning – one that seeks to cultivate values appropriate to democratic resilience – would, nevertheless, seem to flounder on the seemingly solipsistic nature of private reading. Tragedy was a necessarily communal

---

[127] James V. Morrison, *Reading Thucydides* (Columbus: The Ohio State University Press, 2006), 3. See also Emily Greenwood, *Thucydides and the Shaping of History* (London: Duckworth, 2006), 109–129.

[128] Euben, *The Tragedy of Political Theory*, 191.

[129] White, *When Words Lose Their Meaning*, 88. See also Euben, *The Tragedy of Political Theory*, 197. "By construction of a text that replicates the difficulties for the reader that he faced as an historian describing and making sense of his real world, Thucydides presents for us the problem of trying reconstitute and comprehend a collective experience."

[130] MacLeod, "Thucydides and Tragedy," 146.

experience. Thus, the claim that private reading could be a form of public mourning seems hard to sustain. Nevertheless, there are two ways in which we might think of the *History* and the experience of reading as being productively collective. The first is in the relationship that it models between author and reader. In any given text, writes White, "the writer establishes a relation with his or her reader: a community of two that can be understood and judged in terms that are not bound by the language and culture in which the text is composed."¹³¹ In a text such as the *History*, which is deliberately designed to mimic the style, structure, language, and themes of tragedy, this community of two might be thought to model something like the communal experience of the theater. Writes John Zumbrunnen, "we might think of the *History* as itself a fundamentally democratic text, enacting a dynamic relationship between an author trying to craft meaning from the complex world around him and readers alive to the ways in which that world always overwhelms any attempt at interpretive control."¹³² Zumbrunnen's pluralization of "reader" may, however, seem to beg the very question that it would answer: the extent to which private reading might be considered a democratic activity. In Antiquity reading was, of course, both public *and* private, "with Greek literature being destined on the whole for public reading."¹³³ As such, the distinction there was much less pressing. Far from complicating the problem of democratic reading in modernity, however, the less finely wrought distinction between public and private reading in the Ancient world might be thought to suggest the ways in which this distinction is also overdrawn in the contemporary one.

He who laughs alone, Henri Bergson once observed, imagines the company of others. While humor is most definitely not a part of Thucydides' rhetorical toolkit, it may be that mourning for a collectivity such as Athens, for the Americans killed by terrorism, or for the Iraqis or Afghanis killed by the American response to terror, is also to imagine the company of others. In the case of *The New York Times*'s "Portraits in Grief" series, numerous readers testified to the ways in which they imagined themselves communing not only with the dead but also with the other members of their imagined community of grief.¹³⁴ If public mourning is, as has been

---

¹³¹ White, *When Words Lose their Meaning*, 13.

¹³² John Zumbrunnen, *Silence and Democracy: Athenian Politics in Thucydides' History* (University Park, PA: Penn State University Press, 2008), 191.

¹³³ Loraux, *The Invention of Athens*, 361.

¹³⁴ Simon Stow, "*Portraits 9/11/01: The New York Times* and the Pornography of Grief" in *Literature After 9/11* edited by Jeanne Follansbee Quinn and Ann Keniston (New York: Routledge, 2008), 224–241.

suggested, one of the few moments in which the nation comes together – at least in the sense of having a shared focus – it may be that there are entirely nonritualistic ways of engaging in public mourning, of reaching out to others as writers or readers or as speakers or listeners, that might serve to cultivate the values of democratic resilience in the face of loss. Thus, the notion of the isolated reader is something of a fallacy. For to read is to be in a relationship with the author, and with the imagined – and often, actual – audience for that text in ways that suggest the public possibilities of an apparently private experience of loss.[135]

Such mourning requires, of course, democratic poets capable of producing texts that generate such responses in their readers. Originally this book was to have ended with discussions of W.E.B. Du Bois's *The Souls of Black Folk* and Bruce Springsteen's 2002 album *The Rising*. Both were to be offered as examples of the way in which an artist or author might seek to generate tragic responses to different kinds of losses in their audiences through different textual strategies. Ultimately, however, these discussions undermined the book's broader argument, for they seemed to suggest that such responses were only available to the artist or the intellectual rather than to the citizen-reader armed with an awareness of our tragic condition and a desire to live well in the face of loss. Political theory, it was suggested at the outset of the book, is concerned with those things that might be different if *we* chose to change them. It is to this "we" that the book is addressed, both as individual citizens and as part of a democratic polity. The central claim of the book is that the stories a polity tells itself about its dead serve to shape the lives of the living. Nationalistic, romantic, antihumanist, and nostalgic narratives of loss, it has argued, serve to undermine democratic politics by cultivating revenge of responsibility, unthinking commitments to consensus over political agonism, the heroization of our security forces, and the counterproductive demonization of our enemies. Nevertheless, as this final discussion has suggested, the responsibility for more productive responses to loss lies not just with our storytellers but also in our own role as readers, as listeners, and, above all, as democratic citizens.

---

[135] See, for example, Simon Stow, "Reading Our Way to Democracy? Literature and Public Ethics," *Philosophy & Literature*, 30, 2006: 392–405. This is especially true, perhaps, in an age of the e-reader, when it is possible to see which passages are most frequently highlighted by other readers even as one reads the same text. For a discussion of literature as resource for democratic dialogue, see also Simon Stow, "The Way We Read Now: Oprah Winfrey, Intellectuals, and Democracy" in *The Oprah Affect: Critical Essays on Oprah's Book Club* edited by Cecilia Konchar Farr and Jaime Harker (Albany: State University of New York University Press, 2008), 277–293.

Index